101
One-Weekend
Toy Projects

101
One-Weekend
Toy Projects

Percy W. Blandford

TAB BOOKS Inc.
Blue Ridge Summit, PA

FIRST EDITION

FIRST PRINTING

Copyright © 1989 by TAB BOOKS Inc.

Printed in the United States of America

Library of Congress Cataloging in Publication Data

Blandford, Percy W.
   101 one-weekend toy projects / by Percy W. Blandford.
      p.   cm.
   ISBN 0-8306-9064-6   ISBN 0-8306-3264-6 (pbk.)
   1. Wooden toy making.   I. Title.   II. Title: One hundred one one
-weekend toy projects.   III. Title: one hundred and one one-weekend
toy projects.
TT174.5.W6B17   1989
745.592--dc20   89-37591
                                                            CIP

TAB BOOKS Inc. offers software for sale. For information and a catalog, please contact TAB Software Department, Blue Ridge Summit, PA 17294-0850.

Questions regarding the content of this book should be addressed to:

   Reader Inquiry Branch
   TAB BOOKS Inc.
   Blue Ridge Summit, PA 17294-0214

Acquisitions Editor: Kimberly Tabor
Technical Editor: Stephen Moro
Production: Katherine Brown

Contents

Introduction

The usual reason for making toys is because there are children who will enjoy them, either connected with you or whose parents are potential customers, if you want to make a business of it. In both cases there is double satisfaction. You will enjoy the work of making the toys, then enjoy seeing the appreciation of the children using them.

There is an ongoing demand for toys. Children are always being born and growing, with toy needs from the basic to the more sophisticated. The treatment that toys get means they often finish unsuitable to pass on—at least, most proud parents want new toys for a new child. This means there is an industry geared to providing toys. Advertising and promotion are geared to adult purchasers, so appearance and packaging, which must be paid for, are aimed at getting the best price for what a parent is led to believe is what the child needs.

These are mass-produced toys, to designs based on parent demand and what are believed to be average children. Of course, the child probably does get a lot of enjoyment and education out of bought toys, but there are alternatives. You can make toys to suit your individual child that will be appreciated just as much and will cost very much less.

In general, manufactured toys include many complicated designs. Ingenious mechanisms appeal to adults, but they might not mean much to a young child. If we consider the children of our forefathers or even look back to our own child-hood, we realize that enjoyment came from playing with simple things. A child can be happy with something basic. His imagination fills in gaps.

That does not mean all toys should be simple. There is a place for compli-cated toys, but if you are to make toys, trying to copy elaborate manufactured toys is not always the way to go. There are traditional toy designs which have proved their worth over many generations. They might be a better guide to what a child wants, will understand, and will use, probably with more satisfaction than if presented with an expensive and ingenious device that caught the eye of the purchaser. Let these considerations play a part in your choice of toy to make.

Wood is the traditional material for toys. Today, plastics have taken over for many toys and might be better for some, but a great many toys are better made of wood. This book is full of examples.

Almost anyone should be able to make toys from wood. Not many of us have facilities for working plastics. What you make in wood is your individual product, or one of just a few. It is tailored to the needs of a particular child. It incorporates your ideas and workmanship.

Most wooden toys are simple to make. The skill needed is not in the same class as furniture making. If you are skilled in that type of woodworking, it is an advantage, but many toys can be made with just the ability to cut shapes and nail them together. This means that if you select the right design, you can get results with minimum skill and only a few hand tools. If you have a shop full of power tools, you will use them. Skill and equipment anywhere between these extremes can be employed. Toymaking is for all types of woodworkers. The satisfaction of saying "I made that" will only be exceeded by the child saying "My dad (or mom) made that."

Most toys are small, so materials are cheap and might even be free scraps or salvaged wood from old furniture or other sources. If you accumulate a stock of these small pieces, that would be no use for anything else. You can make many toys at little or no cost. Even if you have to buy wood, the amount needed for most toys is small. The total cost will be slight compared to buying toys that are not individually matched to a child and might not be as durable.

In addition to making wooden toys for your own or friends' children, you might find possibilities in toymaking as a business. You could make individual toys to order or produce short runs for sale through stores. After you have made a few attractive toys, you will almost certainly get requests from parents who want something similar for their child. This may soon develop into more than just obliging friends and you will have to get commercial, either as a spare-time or a full-time business. There is always a demand for well-made toys by an individual craftsman. The opinion of your craftsmanship by your customers should do something for your ego!

Do not try to imitate toys that are mass-produced—that can be bought in a store. That is not the way to go. Offer something individual that is well made.

Some things to think about when planning to make toys are outlined in chapter 1, which follows; then, toys to make are divided into broad groups for convenience in identification, but some toys could fall into several categories. Large things, like playhouses and ride-on toys, are easily defined, but many smaller toys could be in other groups than those shown, so check most of the book when selecting toys for your needs.

The construction of every toy is described fully and materials are specified, but you can alter sizes to suit your needs. If you make large alterations, however, make sure that you do not affect safety. The designs suggested have due regard for safety, but as every parent knows, a child's behavior can be unpredictable and we need to guard against every eventuality.

I have had a fourfold satisfaction out of preparing this book: making most of the toys for grandchildren, writing about the toys, giving you an opportunity to make the toys, and having the satisfaction of seeing children playing with them. May you get at least some of the double satisfaction as a result of reading this book.

1

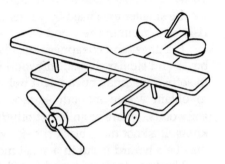

Preparations

This is a project book—a full 101 wooden toys to make. Except for a few special circumstances, the book does not tell you what tools to use and what methods to adopt. This is not a book on tool handling or woodworking techniques. It is assumed that the reader has some knowledge of basic woodworking practices, as well as the necessary tools and the ability to handle them.

Fortunately, most wooden toys can be made without using advanced techniques. Some toys are extremely simple to make. Some toys of basic form depend largely on decoration with paint for the greatest effect, so if you are artistic there is a scope for your talents. However, it may only be adults who are impressed by your art—the young user may get as much out of a plain toy as from a highly decorated one.

You should take into account the ages of the intended users. In general, the toys described in this book are for children aged from the youngest to about twelve, although some toys—particularly the games—will appeal to teenagers. Some woods and methods of construction that would be satisfactory for use by an older child might be dangerous for a toddler, with a risk of finger trapping, scratching, or problems if put in the mouth.

Your knowledge of woodworking, even if it is basic, and your tool kit, whether minimal or comprehensive, will guide you in choosing toys to make, but there are a few points to note, as detailed in this section.

WOOD

There is an enormous range of species of wood available in the world. Hundreds are native to North America, so it is difficult to be specific about the choice of wood for any particular purpose. The broad division between hardwoods and softwoods provides a guide, but within these categories there are wide variations.

Softwoods, from the needle-leafed trees, include the many firs, pines, and spruces. Most of them are lightweight and knotty. Most tend to splinter easily. Some are very resinous. Although they may have uses for toys for older children, particularly boxes and structures for use outdoors, they are mostly poor choices for the smaller toys used by young children. Splinters and cracks are too great a risk; also, resin in the wood would be risky if chewed.

Lightness and cheapness are advantages. For large parts, such as shelves, big boxes and similar things, softwood boards should be satisfactory. Look at knots in softwood. Small ones might not matter, although they might make it difficult to obtain a safe smooth surface. Large knots weaken the wood. In some softwoods, where resin is not otherwise apparent, it will ooze to the surface in knots. If a knot has a black rim, it may fall out, leaving a hole, and the knot itself may be a hazard if put in a small mouth or opening.

Hardwoods, from broad-leafed trees, come in a much wider variety. Some, such as oaks, have a rather coarse open grain, which may splinter and crack; they should not be chosen for a toy for a young child. Other hardwoods, such as beech and sycamore, have a much more compact grain, where it is not always easy to distinguish markings. These woods have a more even character, making them easier to work. Finer details are less likely to break away; they are the best woods for turning. Hardwoods vary in density and weight. A few are as light as softwoods. Because the close-grained hardwoods are unlikely to splinter and knots are few, these are the woods to use for toys with small parts.

The only snag with a few hardwoods is their oiliness. Teak suffers in this way and should not be used for toys for small children. A few hardwoods have a disagreeable smell, which makes them unsuitable for toys.

Many toy parts are small and it will not be necessary to buy wood specially. You can use scraps from larger jobs, or you may be able to salvage material from old furniture or other unwanted woodwork. Wood of suitable type that has already had a use will be well-seasoned and stable. Some wood, direct from a lumberyard, may still contain too much moisture. As this dries out, after the toy has been made, the wood may, shrink, warp, or crack. Reused wood should not have this problem.

Old wood may have had an applied finish, such as paint or polish. Some older finishes might be hazardous if sucked. When you use old wood, remove any existing finish, so you start again with bare wood.

If you make climbing frames and similar structures for outdoor use from natural poles, remove the bark. In softwood trees, in particular, a large number of insects live between the bark and the wood. Leaving on bark may encourage rot, as moisture becomes trapped. The smoothed poles will be safer for young hands and knees. If you use preservative that would be ineffective if applied over bark.

PLYWOOD

There are many uses for plywood in toys, but care is needed in its choice. The commonly-used Douglas fir makes a good plywood for a great many purposes, but the thick coarse-grained plies are soft and tend to splinter. This is not really the plywood to use for toys for small children. If it is used, edges and corners should be rounded and sanded smooth. Its total thickness may also be a problem, as the usual ½ inch or more is too big for many toys.

Many hardwoods are made into plywood. These are nearly all made from close-grained woods, as they better suit the manufacturing process. The resulting plywood has a smoother surface and the risk of splintering is less. Another advantage is in the range of thinner sheets available. Much of the plywood has metric thicknesses, even down to an aircraft plywood 1 mm thick (¹⁄₂₅ inch). Common thicknesses are 3 mm (⅛ inch), 6 mm (¼ inch), 9 mm (⅜ inch), and 12 mm (½ inch).

As well as being available in thinner pieces, many hardwood plywoods are made of thinner veneers, which makes for stiffness. The more plies in a given thickness, the stiffer is the sheet. Where softwood plywood might have three thick veneers (FIG. 1-1A), there could be five veneers (FIG. 1-1B) or seven veneers (FIG. 1-1C), resulting in rigidity and more permanent flatness. If what you are making uses plywood mostly unsupported, this stiffness is important.

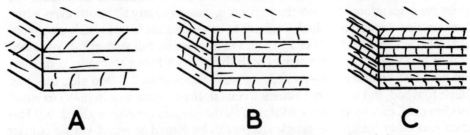

Fig. 1-1. Plywood of the same thickness may have different number of plies.

Plywood can be obtained with special surface veneers to match solid wood. That might not be important for toys, although you might have uses for plastic veneers, either as manufactured or as applied by you with contact adhesive.

Edges of hardboard do not stand up very well to a child pulling or biting, but surfaces are durable. If possible, in the few places where hardboard may be preferable to plywood, use tempered hardboard, which is tougher. Veneered particleboard has a few uses in toy making, but some wood or plastic veneer, whether applied in manufacture or by you, particularly on edges, is not very secure and small hands may pull it away.

JOINTS

If you have the skill and equipment for cutting special joints, such as mortise-and-tenon and dovetails, there are places in the making of toys where you can use them and will probably get a lot of satisfaction out of these methods. However, for many toys parts there need only be nailed or screwed joints, usually with the added strength of glue. Of course, these metal fastenings should be used so skin cannot be scratched. Be careful that points do not go through. Do not let a screwdriver slip so it roughens a screw head. Do not allow nail or screw heads to project above the wood surface.

For most toy construction, casing or finishing nails with their smaller heads, can be punched below the surface with a set, then the hole can be filled with stopping (FIG. 1-2A), so no metal is visible. Driving nails at slight opposite angles, in dovetail fashion, increases strength in a joint (FIG. 1-2B). An open corner gets most load and you could use more or longer nails there (FIG. 1-2C). At any place where there might be a risk of splitting, drill undersize holes for nails. A screw is stronger than a nail and has the advantage of being able to pull a joint close. For most toys, use flathead screws. Always drill a clearance hole in the top piece of wood, then an undersize hole in the lower piece (FIG. 1-2D). The top part will be pulled closed by the squeezing between the screw head and the thread gripping below.

On a long overlap with an open end you could use nails for most of the length and a screw, instead of extra or longer nails, at the open end.

Modern glues are much stronger than traditional types. It is best to buy one described as waterproof or water-resistant. Besides the qualities described, the glues are extra strong. It is worthwhile using glue in nearly all joints, even when they are also screwed or nailed. Surfaces to be glued should be in fairly close contact. Glue will not fill much of a gap and contribute its full strength. If you need to fill a gap with glue, mix sawdust with the glue for better strength. Glue does not hold well on end grain—it needs nails or screws as well. Wood glue may join fabric to wood, but it will not adhere to metal. If you want to join metal to wood by glue only, choose an epoxy adhesive. Some plastics cannot be glued, but Formica and other melamime plastic sheets can be joined to wood with a contact adhesive. Check the maker's recommendations.

If parts which meet are thick in relation to their depth, nailing or screwing a simple overlap may not be enough. A simple alternative is a bridle or open mortise-and-tenon joint, with a nail or screw through it (FIG. 1-2E). Make the center tongue slightly more than one-third the total depth. Glue alone might be sufficient, but a metal fastening the other way increases security.

A simple nailed overlap is stronger one way than the other. You can increase overall strength by nailing both ways. Cut a rabbet in one piece to take the other. Going to two-thirds the thickness should allow for both lots of nails and should suit most wood sizes (FIG. 1-2F).

Joints must withstand a child's efforts to pull them apart. Do not trust screws to plywood only. They should go through into solid wood for strength. If you have to attach something, such as a hinge, to plywood, there should be a strip of wood behind the screw ends (FIG. 1-3A), if possible. In some places you might not be able to include a solid wood backing. In that case it is better to use rivets. Have

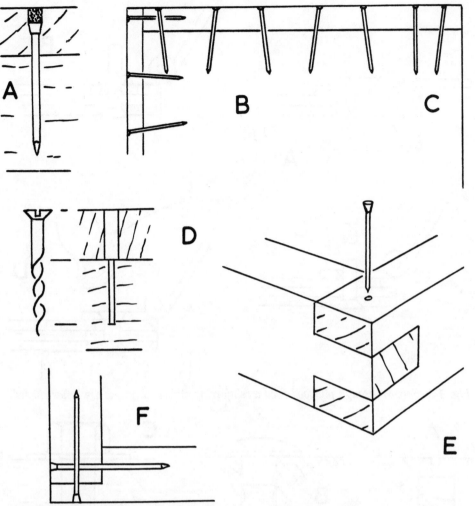

Fig. 1-2. *A nail may be set below the surface (A), but dovetail nailing is stronger (B, C). Drill for screws (D). A nail will strengthen a joint (E). A rabbeted corner may be nailed both ways (F).*

the prepared rivet head under the plywood (FIG. 1-3B). Cut off the rivet end (FIG. 1-3C) to leave enough to spread into the countersunk hole of the hinge (FIG. 1-3D), hammering while the head in the plywood is supported on an iron block. It is easiest to use soft metal rivets. You may be able to use the head ends of copper or aluminum nails.

Some toy parts have to be bolted. The countersunk head of a stove bolt (FIG. 1-4A) or the shallow curved head of a carriage bolt (FIG. 1-4B) avoid the possible hazard of the projecting full bolt head (FIG. 1-4C) on one side of a joint. At the other side there is less of an obstruction if you use a thin nut and cut off the bolt end and file it level (FIG. 1-4D).

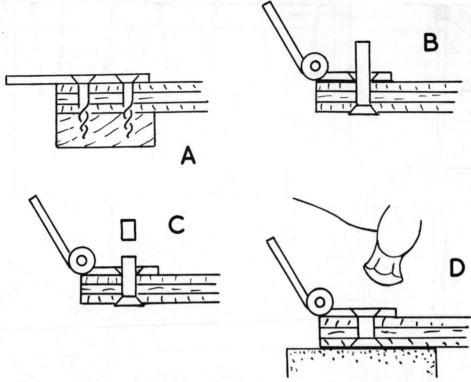

Fig. 1-3. Screws through plywood need a reinforcing strip and hinges are better riveted.

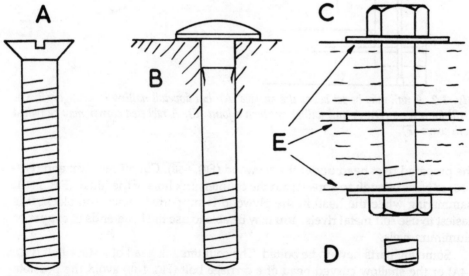

Fig. 1-4. The head of a stove bolt (A) or carriage bolt (B) is less of a hazard than a normal bolt head (C). Cut off a bolt end (D) and use washers (E).

If the nut has to be locked, a second nut may cause too much projection. You may be able to use a friction nut, such as a nylon lock nut. An ordinary nut could be secured to the bolt end with epoxy locking compound.

Use washers, under bolt heads and nuts, as well as between some moving wood parts, without them, there will soon be wear. Wide washers spread the load (FIG. 1-4E) and produce a smoother action.

FINISHES

Current thought has been directed to the safety of paints and other finishes. Some older paints, which looked good and had been used for a long time, contained lead, which is poisonous and could be very dangerous if it entered a child's mouth. If you are reusing wood, do not be tempted to keep an old finish, even if it looks good. It is better to clean off and start finishing from bare wood.

There are paints and other finishes sold as nontoxic or described in some way to show they are safe to use with children. Check that you buy and use the right type.

There is nothing wrong with bare wood for some purposes, but it should not be resinous or naturally oily. Rubbing with something as simple as vegetable cooking oil works if all you want is to give a satin finish that resists the entry of dirt.

TOOLS AND TECHNIQUES

It is difficult to estimate what can be done in one weekend because so much depends on your ability and the extent of your tool kit. All of the toys described in this book can be made entirely with hand tools and not necessarily with many of them, but if you have power tools the work will be quicker and accuracy easier to obtain. Some toys would take more than one weekend with just a very few basic hand tools, while someone with a well-equipped shop of power tools might make several toys in a weekend.

Today, most of us use power tools to varying degrees, but if you get your wood from the lumberyard already prepared to size, a surprising amount of good work can be done with a few hand tools. Power tools have advantages when you want to cut wood to new sections or convert salvaged wood.

What you will get done in a given time depends largely on planning and preparation. When you have decided on a project, study the design details closely. Make sure you understand what has to be done and that you have the tools to do it. Try to visualize all the steps. Do you have the skill, or would it be better to modify some details?

Check on materials. Get everything together before you start work. Delays become disproportionate if you find you need a bigger piece of plywood or have to go to the hardware store because you do not have enough of the right size screws.

In many toys the suggested sizes need not be rigidly adhered to, but check what would happen if you change a wood section or the size of a panel. An alteration in one place will probably affect a size in another place, that may not matter, but you should look at all aspects of the job. Obviously, if you have some lumber of a slightly different size to that specified it would be silly to put it aside and buy something different, if what you have would do the job just as well.

Satisfaction in making toys depends largely on understanding what you have to do, having all the materials ready and knowing the sequence all the way through to the finish. You will then discover it more convenient drilling holes or preparing some other step ahead of when it is needed, then in the overall concept you will do a better and speedier job.

As aids to planning, most descriptions and drawings take you step by step and a materials list tells you what you need. Unless stated otherwise, all sizes are in inches. In most cases widths and thicknesses are finished sizes, but lengths are full to allow for trimming during assembly. Very small pieces that can be cut from scrap lumber are not listed.

2

Puzzles and Indoor Games

TRIANGULAR CHECKERS

Triangular checkers is a game for one person to play. The triangular board has a pattern of fifteen holes. You start with fourteen pegs, leaving one vacant hole. Jump a peg over another, as in normal checkers, into the vacant hole and remove the peg you jumped over. Continue doing this until all but the last peg has been removed. This sounds simple and is possible, but choosing the correct moves is puzzling and you can spend a long time trying to find a solution. Of course, the sequence of moves will vary according to which hole you leave vacant at the start.

Start by choosing what you will use as pegs. They should be 1 inch to 1½ inches long to provide something to grip. Pegs intended to be used with a cribbage board would be suitable. You could use kitchen matches or other small pieces of wood. It would be possible to use nails, but they would be inadvisable for children. Pieces of plastic knitting pins would do. Plastic golf tees would be comfortable to handle. The choice of pegs will settle the size of holes to drill and might require an increase in the size of the board if they are very big. The board shown (FIG. 2-1A) suits pegs not more than 1½ inches long and needing ³⁄₁₆-inch holes.

Almost any wood can be used for the board. Thick plywood is suitable, but polished hardwood ⅝ or ¾ inch thick would make a game to keep. The board is shown with a groove for removed pegs (FIG. 2-1B), or you can provide a row of close holes for them (FIG. 2-1C). Arrange the grain of solid wood in the direction of the groove.

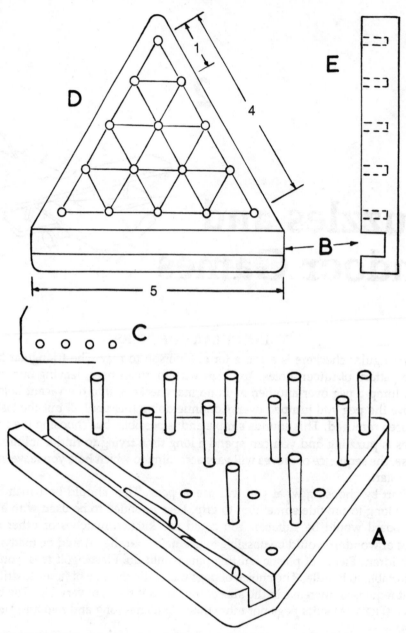

Fig. 2-1. *A triangular checkers board uses pegs in holes.*

Although you can mark out directly on the wood, avoid marks which have to be removed later as well as cut more economically, if you first draw the pattern on paper and mark through onto the wood when you are satisfied.

Start by setting out the holes pattern. On a 4-inch baseline draw the other sides of the triangle at 60 degrees to its ends. Either use a 60-degree drafting triangle or set a compass to the line length and swing it from opposite ends of the line so the arcs cross. Join the crossing to the ends of the lines. Divide each edge into four and join the marks (FIG. 2-1D). Holes will come at each crossing. You might scratch these lines into the wood as decoration. Mark the wood outline outside the pattern, with a margin at the bottom for the groove or line of storage holes.

It will be easier to plow the groove before doing other shaping. Drill all the holes to a controlled depth (FIG. 2-1E). Lightly countersink their tops. Shape the outline; then, well round all edges. Apply your chosen finish.

You will probably take longer to find the right jump sequences to remove all the pegs than you do to make the game. Get your son or daughter to show you!

BAGATELLE BOARD

Pinball games are always popular, but many of them depend on luck, so interest soon palls. If you or a child can exercise some skill to influence results, interest is maintained and you can use the game competitively. Two or more players of almost any age can play and try to get the highest scores. Even a child playing alone can have some fun improving skill and trying for particular results.

This bagatelle board (FIGS. 2-2 and 2-3) uses a cue to send steel balls round the board, so they bounce off a pin and drop into various scoring positions. The amount of thrust given to the ball determines where it goes, and that is where the skill comes in. There could be any number of balls, such as steel ball bearings

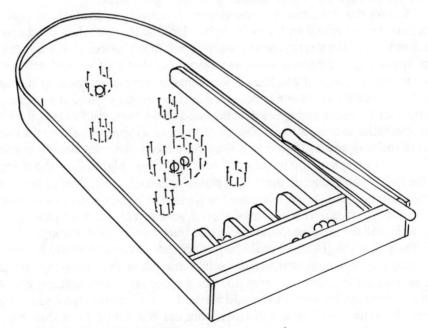

Fig. 2-2. A bagatelle or pinball board is popular.

at least ½ inch in diameter—twenty would be fine. Glass or other marbles might be used, but the weight of steel is an advantage.

The base of the board should be ¾- or 1-inch plywood. If it can have a face veneer of an attractive hardwood, that will improve appearance. Otherwise you can paint it.

The only unusual constructional problem is in making the outside piece. It is nearly 5 feet long and 3 inches wide. If you can get aircraft-quality thin plywood, that will bend to shape easily. You may get ⅛-inch hardwood plywood that will bend. The alternative is to use two or three thicknesses of veneer, bent and glued. Whatever method is used, the rim should be up to 3/16 inch thick. Suggestions for making it follow.

Cut the base (FIG. 2-3A) to shape. Be careful to have all edges square.

Make the bottom strip across the end (FIG. 2-3B), glued and screwed to the edge of the base. The other pieces go on to the surface. Round exposed ends and edges (FIG. 2-3C). Mark their positions and drill through the base for fine screws or nails upwards. Assemble these parts.

If you have one length of thin plywood that will go round the whole edge, glue and pin it on. You may need a few screws on the curve to hold it close.

If you have plywood long enough for the curve, but not one or both straight edges, you can splice on another piece of plywood or solid wood. Cut both meeting ends to matching long tapers (FIG. 2-3D). On a thickness of 3/16 inch, the taper should be about 1½ inches. Make this joint in position on a straight edge, then use screws and a small clamp to hold the parts until the glue has set. If you try to splice on the curve, it will be difficult to make a good joint.

To make the rim from veneers, you might be able to laminate in position. Bend one veneer round with glue and pins. Let that glue set, then bend another piece outside it. Have small clamps ready to pull in any places on the upper edge that open—paper clips may serve as clamps. Let that glue set and add a third layer in the same way. If you have to join veneers to make up the length, stagger the joints, but try to have a continuous surface inside around the curve. Use veneers for the curve and splice to solid wood of the same thickness at the sides. The alternative to laminating in position is to make a former similar to the curved part of the base and bend to that, so you have a complete rim already in shape.

Make the traps on the board from nails that stand higher than the diameter of the balls when driven in. Brassed or plated nails look good. Domed heads look better than flat ones. You can arrange the pattern to preference, but a suggestion is offered (FIG. 2-3E). The openings should give a reasonable chance of a ball entering, and the spacing round the curves must not let a ball through.

The striker pin (FIG. 2-3F) could be just another nail, but it would be better to use tempered steel, giving the ball a better rebound, with a satisfying "ping." A hardened steel masonry nail may do. Cut a piece off a steel knitting pin. Any piece of stout spring steel wire would serve. The pin should stand about 1 inch above the surface and be at a distance from the rim a little more than half the diameter of the balls.

Make the cue of hardwood a little shorter than the trough across the bottom, so it can be stored with the balls there. A simple cue is square with rounded corners and a slight taper (FIG. 2-3G). If you have the use of a lathe, you could make the cue round with a knob end hollowed to push the ball (FIG. 2-3H).

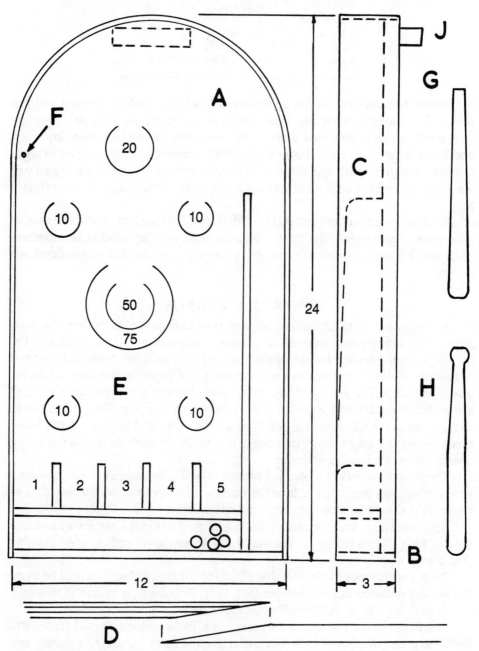

Fig. 2-3. *Sizes and details of the bagatelle board.*

Materials List for Bagatelle Board

1 base	12 ×	24 ×	¾ or 1 plywood	
1 end	½ ×	3 ×	13	
1 guide	½ ×	2¼ ×	18	
1 division	½ ×	2¼ ×	11	
4 divisions	½ ×	2¼ ×	4	
1 block	1 ×	1 ×	8	
1 cue	1 ×	1 ×	10	
1 rim	3⁄16 ×	3 ×	60 laminated	

When the bagatelle board is on a table, it has to be tilted so the balls will run down. Try the game with temporary support under the far end, to determine how much packing is needed there. With too much tilt the balls run down fast and there is not much control over them. With a moderate tilt it is easier to regulate the strength of push and direct the ball where you hope it will go. When you are satisfied with the amount of tilt, put a strip permanently across the end (FIG. 2-3J).

What scoring numbers you put on will depend on the layout and the ease or otherwise of getting into the traps. You may wish to delay settling on numbers until you have experimented with the game for a while, but suggestions are shown.

TOWER RING CHANGE

The story is that in an eastern country they built one of their tapering temples in the wrong place. Because of religious superstitions, they could not dismantle it completely and build it again in the right place. They could only move it in sections. While doing so, they must never put a larger section over a smaller one. The puzzle (FIG. 2-4) uses rings to represent the sections of the temple. They are in different sizes and you start with them on an end peg. The problem is to move them to the same relative positions on the other end peg, using the intermediate peg and only moving one peg at a time. At no stage must you put a ring over another of a smaller diameter.

The lowest number of moves is believed to be 31. To simplify the puzzle for a very young child you could reduce the number of rings to three, but an adult or older child should be able to manage with five rings.

Suggested sizes are given and these use rings made in the same way as those for the Ring Clown (FIG. 8-5). The stand has three dowel rods spaced suitably (FIG. 2-4A).

Turn a set of rings in the way described for the clown, but they will be more convenient rounded top and bottom (FIG. 2-4B). Drill them ⅞ inch in diameter.

Round the tops of the ¾-inch dowel rods (FIG. 2-4C).

The base could have square corners, but it looks better rounded (FIG. 2-4D). Drill and glue in the dowel rods. Be careful that the holes are drilled squarely and the rods stand upright.

Paint the rings five different bright colors. You could also paint the stand, but it would look better varnished if it is made of hardwood.

Materials List for Tower Ring Change

1 base	1 × 5 × 15
3 rods	8 × ¾ diameter
rings from	1 × 3½ × 12

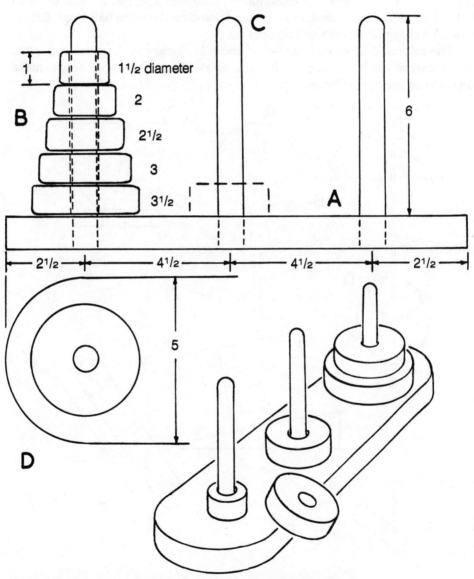

Fig. 2-4. A tower ring change puzzle that requires some thought.

STOP-GO BALL

Stop-go ball is a trick which even a young child can operate to mystify his friends and impress adults. A length of cord with handles at the ends has a ball sliding on it. When held vertically the ball will slide down, but you can make it stop and go on instruction from the operator or his audience. The important thing is a bent hole through the ball (FIG. 2-5A), made by drilling diagonally from opposite sides. When the cord is held taut there is enough friction to stop the ball sliding. When you relax the tension, the ball will slide. A braided synthetic fiber cord is advisable. The size and smoothness of the bent hold has to be adjusted so only slight difference in tension is needed to stop or allow the ball to go. Otherwise, the change in stretch will be obvious.

The ball could be turned hardwood about 1½ inches in diameter (FIG. 2-5B). An alternative would be a cube of the same size with its corners cut away to make octagons on each face (FIG. 2-5C, D).

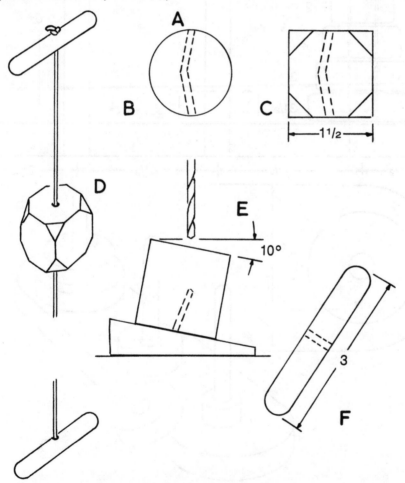

Fig. 2-5. *The stop-go ball can be made to slide or stop to order.*

For cord ⅛ inch in diameter start with a hole ⁵⁄₃₂ inch, if this gives too much friction, open it out with slightly larger drills until you get the effect you want.

The angle of the hole chosen is not critical, but somewhere between 5 and 10 degrees from vertical should be satisfactory (FIG. 2-5E). Enter centrally at each side.

Make the handles from ½-inch dowel rod (FIG. 2-5F) with holes to suit the cord. Round the ends if you wish.

The length of cord depends on how much the young operator can stretch, but 24 inches would probably be suitable.

CANNON MARBLE BOARD

Rolling marbles at a board with holes in it is always popular. Children and adults compete against each other to see who can get the highest score. The interest in a simple board with just a few holes may pall after a short time. This is a marble board with a difference (FIG. 2-6). There are two sections to take direct rolling, then another section can be hinged at various angles and the marbles rolled so as to "cannon off" a board hinged to it. You have to judge the place and angle to aim the marble at the board to get a rebound toward a hole. Varying the angle allows for different degrees of skill.

Although the game could be played with traditional clay or glass marbles, it may be better to use steel balls. The game is designed to suit ½-inch steel balls. They could be rolled freehand, but some players may prefer to use a chute. Most parts are ½-×2½-inch wood. Softwood would be satisfactory and the joints could be nailed or screwed.

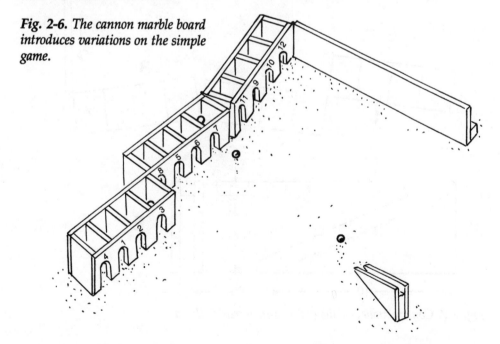

Fig. 2-6. The cannon marble board introduces variations on the simple game.

The sizes allow for playing on a table (FIG. 2-7A). For floor use the game could be made larger. The cannon board folds on the two sections, so the game closes to about 27 inches long × 2½ inches wide × 5 inches high.

The three sections are laid out the same way, but the back of section 1 continues as the front of section 2. Mark out the fronts first (FIG. 2-7B).

Drill 1-inch holes for the tops of the openings. Cut into the holes and smooth the edges. This size of holes gives the players a reasonable chance of scoring with ½-inch or smaller balls. If you use other size balls, make the holes about twice their diameter.

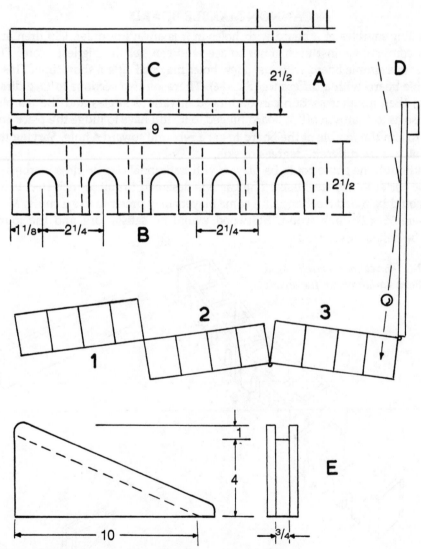

Fig. 2-7. *Constructional details of the cannon marble board.*

Materials List for Cannon Marble Board

1 piece	½ × 2½ × 20
4 pieces	½ × 2½ × 10
15 pieces	½ × 2½ × 3
1 piece	½ × 2½ × 17
1 block	1 × 1 × 6
1 chute	¾ × 4 × 12
2 chute sides	5 × 12 × ½ plywood

Make the back for sections 2 and 3, and make fifteen spacers (FIG. 2-7C) to go between them.

Assemble the parts with nails or screws. Work squarely and keep the bottom edges level.

Use one long or two short hinges to join the backs of sections 2 and 3 together.

The cannon board should be of a length that will fold onto the fronts of sections 2 and 3 with a little end clearance (FIG. 2-7D). Put a block at the end to rest on the table and provide friction to stop the board moving in use. Cloth glued under the block will provide more friction, if needed.

Hinge the board to the end of section 3 in the same way that is hinged to section 2.

Finish by painting. Paint or use decals to put numbers over the holes, so scoring is proportional to the relative difficulty in aiming.

If a chute is wanted, a suggested size is shown (FIG. 2-7E). The center part is solid wood and the two cheeks may be plywood. Steepness depends on the weights of the balls and the distance they have to travel. The chute shown should suit average table top use. If you can hollow edges, with a router or other means, the sloping edge of the center part could have a hollow to direct the ball more accurately.

FIRST JIGSAW PUZZLE

Jigsaw puzzles appeal to all ages, right up to adults who may enjoy those with 1000 parts. If you are introducing a child to jigsaw puzzles he needs something simple enough for him to assemble, yet which offers a challenge. You have to make something estimated to be within his capabilities; he will be dissatisfied if it falls into place too easily.

Such a puzzle may have about twelve pieces. A much larger number could be too difficult to sort out. No part should be much less than 2 inches square. Very small pieces would be difficult to handle and sort out. They might also be chewed or swallowed. The parts should interlock—it is frustrating for a child to find what he has painstakingly put together falls apart.

The picture should be of a subject with which the child can identify. It may be from a familiar story, a place he has seen, or maybe a collection of colored building bricks. Colors should be bright and different, so sections of the picture are easy to identify. If there is a border to the picture, that could be included in the puzzle as a help in finding pieces. Cut a suitable picture from a magazine or draw it yourself. The child will not be looking for art. He might be pleased to be able to say, "My mom or dad drew that."

Use a plywood that is unlikely to splinter. This will probably mean a hardwood type, which may be anything up to ½ inch thick. Glue the drawing on securely. It would be a nuisance if cut edges peeled back. Leave the drawing under pressure until the glue is really hard. Plane the edges straight. Sand them and take any sharpness off the edges.

Cutting should be with a fine fretsaw blade. If that is used at a fairly fast stroke and little pressure, the shaped edges should need no further treatment. A powered scroll saw is the ideal tool. Despite the name of the puzzle, a modern portable jigsaw is not the tool to use. It will not take a fine narrow saw and its cut on the up stroke would leave a poor surface. A hand fretsaw frame can be used.

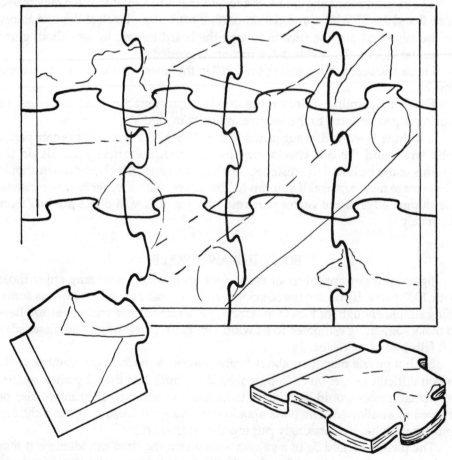

Fig. 2-8. *A first jigsaw puzzle has to be simple and with big pieces.*

You might manage with a coping saw frame with the finest blade you can get, but that would only do for very bold lines.

In this puzzle (FIG. 2-8) the size would be about 6 inches × 8 inches, depending on the picture. To keep the parts about the same size, mark on the edges at 2-inch intervals. You could lightly pencil across the front, but that will probably not be necessary. Your cuts across should go from one edge mark to the other. Between every two pieces include a rounded dovetail link. Do not make the curves too tight, or the wood may crumble in use; do this freehand. If each joint is a slightly different shape from all others, that helps in selecting parts during assembly.

If you are using any form of power fretsaw there will be no difficulty in keeping the cuts upright. If you are cutting by hand try to keep the blade upright—it will not go round the smaller curves properly if it is sloped forward. However, slight slopes of edges do not matter, as the parts will still match.

You might consider making a shallow box for the puzzle to be assembled in, but most young users should be happy with just the loose parts on a table. The simplest puzzle may not last very long for its user, who will demand something more elaborate as he gets more skillful. The first puzzle may then be passed to someone younger.

SHOVE HA'PENNY BOARD

The name, shove ha'penny (pronounced hay-penny) comes from the British origin where this game was played with the old-time English half-penny. Any coins could be used or even metal washers or plastic discs. The original coins were just under 1 inch diameter. Five was the usual number for the game.

The board hooks over the edge of a table. It has lines across it spaced somewhat wider apart than the diameter of the coins or discs, with seven lines making six "beds." A coin is put so it overhangs the edge of the board; then it is shoved (knocked) with the flat of the palm of one hand. The object is to get the coin *between* lines, but not overhanging one. Each player uses the five coins in turn without removing any from the board. One can be knocked into place by another if you are skillful. After five coins have been shoved, you score a point for each one between lines and a chalk mark is made on your edge of the board (FIG. 2-9A). Then, your opponent has his five shoves, and so on in turn. The aim is to score three points in each bed, until there are three marks in each of the spaces on your edge of the board. To complicate play, you could deduct points for any coins finishing in a bed where you have already fully scored. It is not as easy as it sounds and quite a lot of skill can be used.

This board can be marked double-sided. The strip that is put against the side of the table acts as a stop for the coins when the board is the other way up (FIG. 2-9B). Plywood ½ inch thick is suitable, but smooth surfaces are needed. Suitable markings are shown for discs 1 inch diameter (FIG. 2-9C). Cut the lines in with a sharp knife and fill with contrasting paint. Alternatively, paint the lines on the surface, but to stop paint creeping along the grain give the board several coats of varnish or lacquer first. Lightly sand off the gloss before painting.

For the scoring edges you need a surface that will take chalk and be easily wiped clean. That might be grey or black nongloss paint. One side of the board could be marked with the lines spaced wider for easier play by young children.

Materials List for Shove Ha'penny Board

1 piece	14 × 22 × ½ plywood
2 strips	1 × 1 × 15

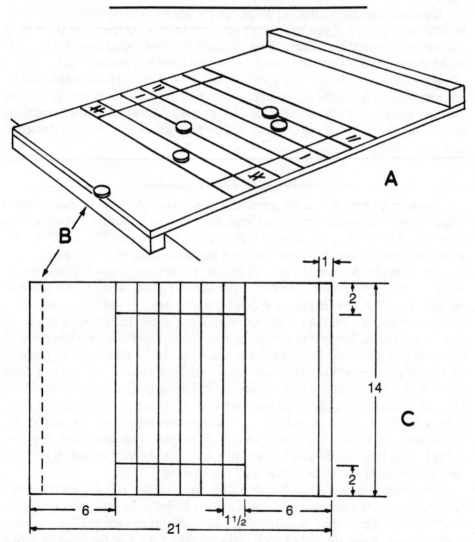

Fig. 2-9. Shove ha-penny is played with coins.

BEAD PUZZLE

It may not take a weekend to make one of these puzzles, but it could take you most of the weekend solving it, if you do not read the instructions. However, it is the type of project that lends itself to quantity production. You could make a series of puzzles almost as quickly as one, so you could produce a number to mystify your child's friends or they should sell well. The puzzle (FIG. 2-10A) consists of a piece of wood with cord knotted through two holes and passed through a central hole too small for beads on the loops to pass through. The object is to move one bead across so there are two on one loop (FIG. 2-10B), then move it back again.

The beads could be bought wood or plastic ones ¾ inch in diameter (FIG. 2-10C), they could be drilled pieces of dowel rod (FIG. 2-10D), or you could cut square stock and take the corners off (FIG. 2-10E). The wood strip (FIG. 2-10F) may be ¼ inch thick. Make the central hole too small to pass the beads through and the other holes to suit the cord, which can be almost any type under ⅛ inch diameter. Loop it as shown and knot the ends behind the small holes. The central knot is called a *lark's head*.

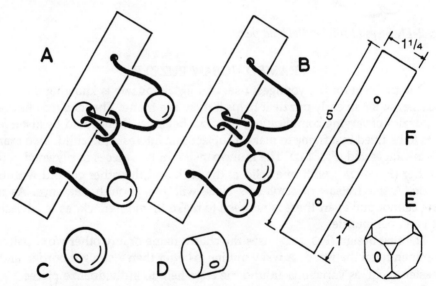

Fig. 2-10. In this bead puzzle, one bead has to be moved to join the other.

If you want to solve the puzzle yourself, stop here. If not, read on:

Slacken the *lark's head* enough to pull through the bead to be moved with part of the loop it is on (FIG. 2-11A). Push all the turns from the back through the center hole to the front, then pass the bead along the cord through the loops (FIG. 2-11B, C). Pull those loops back through the hole. Slacken the *lark's head* and pass the bead through the bottom of it (FIG. 2-11D) to join the other bead. To return the bead, perform the same actions in the opposite direction.

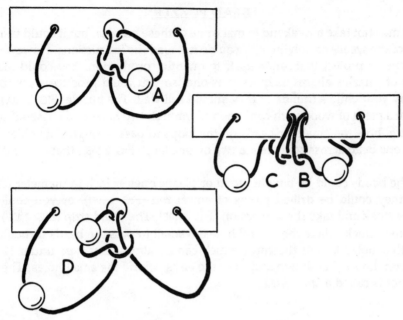

Fig. 2-11. Steps in solving the bead puzzle.

FRAMED JIGSAW PUZZLE

One problem for the youngest user of a jigsaw puzzle is knowing the limits and size, so for an early puzzle it helps if there is a frame. The idea may be used for puzzles of varying complication, but for a beginner there could be just a few parts to be fitted in a frame to make a subject that interests the child. Two examples are suggested (FIG. 2-12). The frame consists of two pieces of plywood glued together (FIG. 2-12A), with one solid at the back and the other cut out with the puzzle. A fine fretsaw or scroll saw blade will give enough clearance. As the parts cannot pull apart there is no need to make them interlock, as is advisable with an open puzzle.

The first design (FIG. 2-12B) uses the child's name or any other word painted prominently on the wood. A wavy outline is better than a straight border, and it is easier to cut, as variations around the edge help to individualize pieces.

So far as possible, make the cuts so they include part of a letter as well as the background. Keep the pieces fairly large for a first puzzle. The overall size will depend on the number of letters, but if you start with an outside width of at least 3 inches, that will be suitable.

The second design (FIG. 2-12C) has the parts of the caterpillar painted brightly in different colors. The antennae above the head are painted directly on the border. Make the parts of the body sufficiently different from each other, so there will be no risk of them being too closely interchangeable; this might cause a beginner frustrating difficulties.

If the puzzles are intended to teach spelling, there could be several puzzles with different words, such as family names and friend's names. Besides the caterpillar, many other animals or birds could be made, but avoid fine outlines. Anything too fine for cutting out could be painted on the border, like the caterpillar antennae.

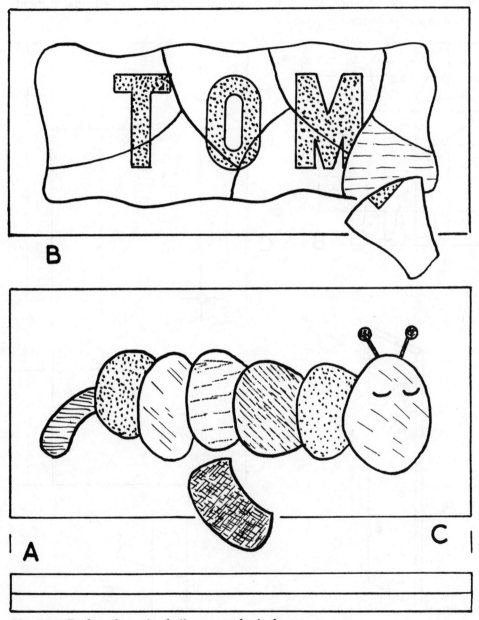

Fig. 2-12. Enclose these simple jigsaw puzzles in frames.

FALLING CLOWN

In this toy, a cutout figure is hooked over the top peg on a tall board and he proceeds to fall with a swinging action (FIG. 2-13A) from peg to peg until he lands on a pair of bottom pegs. The simple lively action will provide plenty of amusement for children and adults. The board could be any length from around 18 inches to 5 feet or more. It may be hung on a wall or propped near upright against a wall or fence.

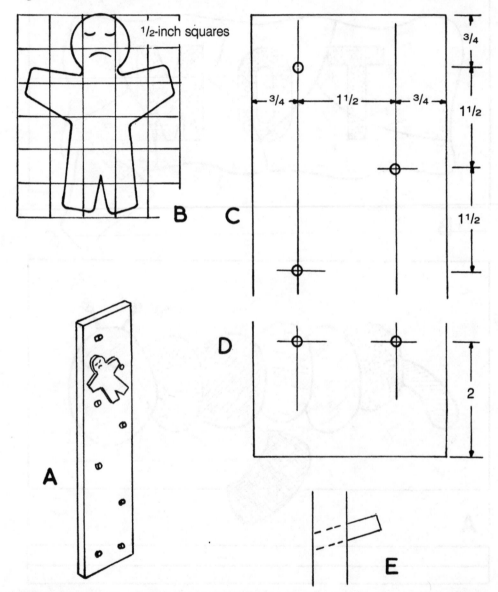

Fig. 2-13. When the clown is dropped onto the top peg, he will swing from side to side to the bottom.

Materials List for Falling Clown

1 figure	4 × 3 × ⅜	plywood
1 board	½ × 3 × 18 or more	
pegs from	20 × ¼ diameter	

The suggested sizes are for a clown 2½ inches wide and 3 inches high. The board is then 3 inches wide and a minimum of 12 inches high. You could make everything 1½ times as large or double the sizes if you wish.

The figure (FIG. 2-13B) may get rough treatment, so cut it from hardwood plywood, if possible, ⅜ inch thick. Round all edges. Leave painting it until you have checked the action. You could make two or more clowns, so one could follow the other down the board.

Make the ½-inch-×-3-inch board any length, but arrange the pegs on lines 1½ inches apart and at 1½-inch intervals (FIG. 2-13C), with two at the same level at the bottom (FIG. 2-13D). Drill for ¼-inch dowel pegs at a slight angle (FIG. 2-13E) to reduce the risk of the clown falling off. Glue in the pegs.

If the action is satisfactory, paint the clown brightly, with some face details. The other side could be painted to a different design to add to interest.

SPINNING BIRD

This bird on a perch (FIG. 2-14) can be made to continue to turn over and over in opposite directions for quite a long time after setting in motion. The cutout bird is attached to the dowel rod perch. The strings at the ends go through holes in the perch. When the bird is turned over, the strings wind round the dowel rod. When the bird is released, the strings unwind and the bird acts like a flywheel. This causes the strings to wind up the other way, and so on backwards and forwards for some time until the energy is exhausted, and you can wind it up again. The outline needs a large lower part to achieve balance. The head can be any type of bird you wish. Cut the bird from any plywood up to ½ inch thick (FIG. 2-15A). Round all edges and drill for the perch (FIG. 2-15B).

The length of the ½-inch dowel rod perch is not important, but it could be 8 inches and the rod above 6 inches. Drill both for the strings. The extra length on the perch allows for the string winding without slipping off the end.

Glue the bird to the center of the perch. Arrange the strings for hanging. Keep the top rod high enough to allow the bird and perch to wind up the strings below it many times without touching it. Locate both bars with knots.

Try the action. If it is satisfactory, paint the bird in appropriate bright colors.

Materials List for Spinning Bird

1 bird	8 × 9 × ⅜	plywood
1 perch	9 × ½ diameter	
1 rod	7 × ½ diameter	

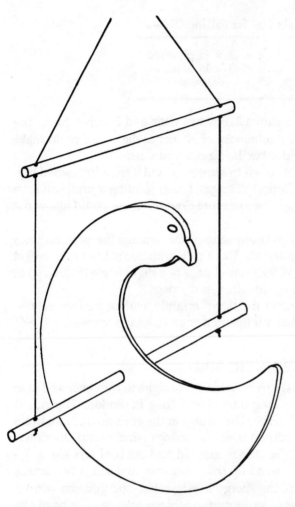

Fig. 2-14. This bird on a perch can spin forwards and backwards for some time.

TABLE TENNIS TOP

If young people want to play table tennis, or Ping-Pong, they need space. A standard table tennis table is 5 feet × 9 feet, and you need further space to move around it. For younger players you could reduce the size, but even for the youngest children the game ceases to be interesting if the table is too small. One way of arranging the game in a more reasonable space is to make a top 4 feet × 8 feet to fit over your dining table. It can be made from a standard sheet of plywood and divided across the middle for easy storage. One bonus is being able to also cover it with a cloth and use it for a meal when you have an extra large party to dinner.

The top can be ½-inch plywood and its stiffening is mainly 1-×-2-inch strips (FIG. 2-16). Arrangements are made underneath to secure the tennis top to the dining top and to lock the two parts together. The existing dining table is likely to be much smaller than what is going over it.

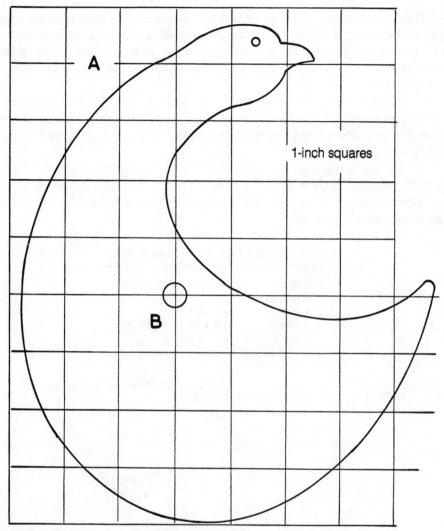

Fig. 2-15. *The shape to cut for the spinning bird.*

Cut a sheet of plywood across the center and stiffen underneath each piece on three edges (FIG. 2-17A). Glue and plenty of fine nails can be used, possibly with screws near the corners.

The plywood will rest directly on the existing tabletop. Mark its shape underneath the two parts.

Put locating pieces against these lines towards the ends of the undertable. If the table is suitable to take it, arrange a lip on each end piece to slip underneath and keep the new top flat (FIG. 2-17B).

Near the center, where the two parts meet, there have to be blocks for joining bolts (FIG. 2-17C). Make them thick enough to take ¼-inch carriage bolts with washers and wing nuts.

There will have to be clamps near the joint to keep the table tennis top tight against the dining tabletop. Make four like broad turnbuttons on blocks (FIG. 2-17D). Undercut slightly, so the turnbutton is pulled in against the dining tabletop when you tighten the wing nut. Screw the bolts into undersize holes in the blocks, so they will not loosen.

When assembling, put the top in place, with the turnbuttons turned out of the way, then pull the parts together with the bolts through the blocks. Finally, move the turnbuttons into place and tighten them. The top should then be stable and ready for play.

A table tennis top is usually painted green with a 1-inch white border. Use a matte finish paint as there must not be any gloss on the playing surface.

If the net clamps will not open enough to grip the stiffened edge, cut it down just at the clamping places.

Materials List for Table Tennis Top

2 tops	48 × 48 × ½ plywood
6 frames	1 × 2 × 50
6 guides	1 × 2 × 18
2 guides	3 × 18 × ½ plywood
joints from	1 × 2 × 40

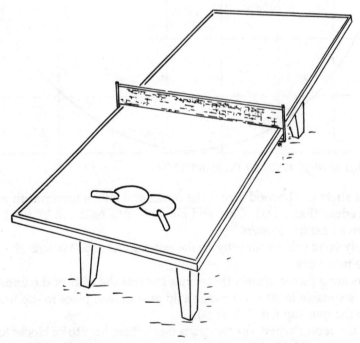

Fig. 2-16. This table tennis top is designed to fit over a dining table.

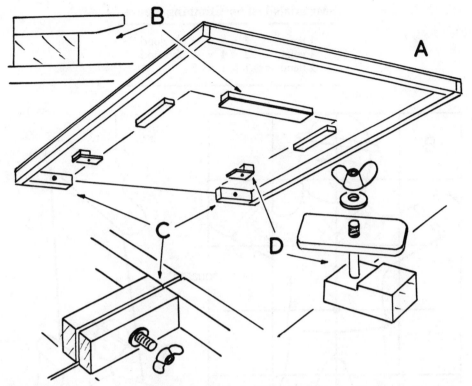

Fig. 2-17. How to arrange attachments for holding the table tennis top on the dining table.

CLIMBING FIGURE

A cutout man or animal that can be made to climb two strings by pulling them alternately is a traditional toy. This version (FIG. 2-18A) is drawn as a man, but you could make it an animal. The important parts are the arms or paws and the holes through them. Sizes are not crucial, but a figure 5 inches high on strings up to 48 inches long will be reasonable for most children.

Common string may do, but braided cotton or synthetic fine cord will be better. Its choice affects the hole sizes, so get it first. The figure is any wood ½ inch or thicker. The yoke could be plywood. At the bottom of the cords, you could put two large beads, but some weight there keeps the loose cords taut, therefore, turned handles are suggested.

Mark out and cut the outline of the figure (FIG. 2-18B). Round the edges.

Drill the arms. The holes should be about 45 degrees to vertical (FIG. 2-18C) and a size that will slide on the cord. Err on the small side at first; then, enlarge it if necessary after trials.

The yoke (FIG. 2-18D) could have string holes drilled across, but it is slightly better with them vertical. The top holes is for a hanging cord and may be any size.

Materials List for Climbing Figure

1 figure	4 × 5 × ½ plywood
1 yoke	2 × 4 × ½ plywood
2 handles	1 × 1 × 3

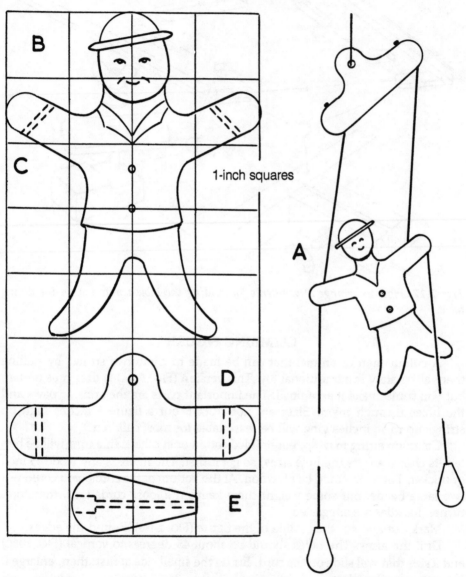

1-inch squares

Fig. 2-18. *When this suspended toy has its cords pulled in turn, the figure climbs.*

Make turned handles (FIG. 2-18E) with the hole enlarged at the end to hide the knot. If you prefer wooden beads, choose fairly heavy ones.

Knot the cords through the yoke. Slide them through the holes in the figure and knot them through the handles. Use another string in the top hole of the yoke to hang the toy high enough for action. If all is well, when you pull each handle in turn, the man will climb to the top a little at a time. When you relax, he will slide down again ready for the next time. You may have to enlarge the arm holes and countersink their ends slightly to get the best results, but first uses should soon have the man climbing and sliding smoothly.

JUNIOR TABLE SOCCER GAME

Junior table soccer, a game where miniature footballers on rods are manipulated to kick a ball towards the opponent's goal, intrigues young people, but the four bars to operate eleven kickers each way may be too complicated for them, even when there are two operators on each side. In this game (FIG. 2-19) the kickers are reduced to seven each side with six operating rods. The box-shaped game could be used on a table, but it will be better on its own legs. All parts are wood, except the ball, which should be dense plastic or rubber, with little bounce and about 1 inch in diameter.

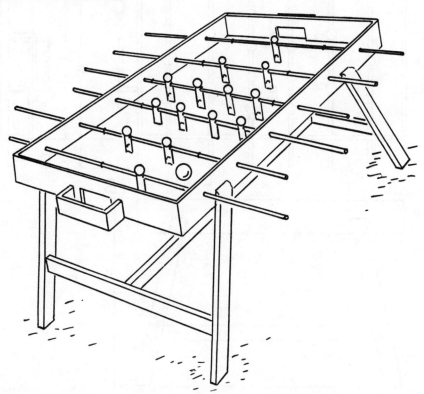

Fig. 2-19. This junior soccer game has been simplified to suit children.

The rods are dowels. The kickers could be turned or made from dowel rods. The bottom should be plywood with a smooth surface. Other parts are solid hard- or softwood.

Make the main parts as a simple box. Reinforcing blocks (FIG. 2-21A) in the corners will strengthen the assembly and deflect the ball back into play if it bounces into a corner.

Cut goal holes in the ends, 5 inches wide × 2 inches high (FIG. 2-21B).

In the sides drill holes for the ½-inch dowel rods to slide in easily (FIG. 2-20A), spaced symmetrically (FIG. 2-20B) 1¼ inches down from the top edge. At the center, drill a hole in both sides large enough to pass the ball. A game is started or play resumed after a goal is scored, by pushing the ball through a hole.

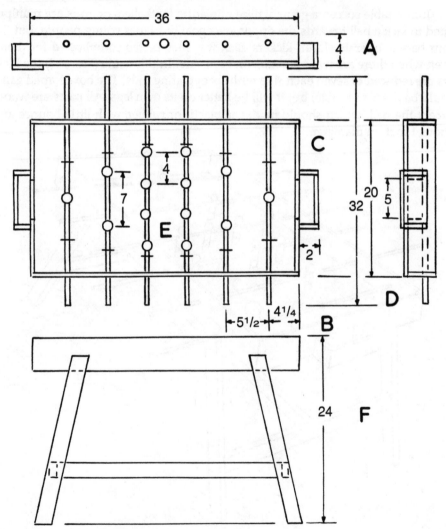

Fig. 2-20. Suggested sizes for the junior soccer game.

Put the box parts together. At each end there has to be something to catch the ball when it passes through a goal. Make a tray (FIGS. 2-20C and 2-21C) with a bottom to go under the box; then, the ball drops as it goes through and is unlikely to bounce back, which may cause a dispute.

The control rods are all the same length (FIG. 2-20D). Two have four men, two have two men, and two have single men, spaced as shown (FIG. 2-20E).

Make the 14 men identical and 1 inch in diameter (FIG. 2-21D). The foot end should just clear the bottom of the box. Flatten that end both sides, for kicking either way. Drill across to glue and screw on the rod and shape the top as a head, which can be painted with a face.

To resist sideways movement of the rods you need two spring washers and two cotter pins for each rod. Drill for the cotter pins in the positions shown (FIG. 2-21E), according to the number of men on the rod. Have these parts ready, but do not fit them until final assembly after painting.

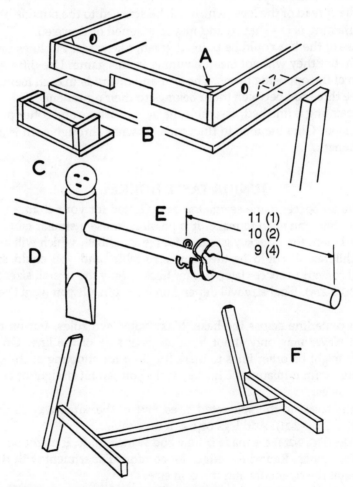

11 (1)
10 (2)
9 (4)

Fig. 2-21. Details of parts of the junior soccer game.

Materials List for Junior Table Soccer Game

1 base	20 × 36 × ½ plywood
2 sides	½ × 4 × 38
2 ends	½ × 4 × 21
2 goals	½ × 2 × 8
4 goals	½ × 2 × 3
2 goals	½ × 3 × 8
4 legs	1 × 2 × 24
2 rails	1 × 2 × 22
1 rail	1 × 2 × 36
14 men	1 × 1 × 6
6 rods	33 × ½ diameter

If the game is to have its own legs (FIGS. 2-20F and 2-21F), they can be made from 1-inch-×-2-inch strips.

Mark the spread of the legs, which will be screwed to the outside of the box. The lower framing is H–shaped and maybe tenoned or doweled.

The base of the box could be painted green, like grass. Put lines on it like a soccer pitch, but they will not mean anything in this game. Use different colors for the men of the opposing teams. The four and one rods in each team play one way, but the three rod between them belongs to their opponent.

When painting is finished, assemble the men, washers and cotter pins on the rods in position. Glue the men to their rods; a screw through each is advisable for extra strength.

JUNIOR TABLE HOCKEY

If the junior soccer game seems too complicated for your children, or more complicated than you wish to make, it is possible to use a similar table, without the rods and men, for a hockey game or for blow football, which will amuse the youngest children. It could be the same size table, and you could start with hockey and convert to soccer later, but for hockey only the overall sizes could be reduced (FIG. 2-22A). Goal size will depend on how difficult you want the game to be.

Mark a centerline across the base. Make your own rules, but on a smaller board each player may only shoot from his own side of the line. On a bigger board there might be other lines to mark the limit for shooting at the goal. The puck is a coin. With miniature ice hockey sticks you can hit straight or bounce the coin off the sides.

Make the board to the suggested sizes, but in the same way as the soccer board (FIGS. 2-20 and 2-21). Add legs or use it on a table.

The sticks (FIG. 2-22B) are made from wood ¼ inch thick. It might be advisable to have a few spares. Round the edges for comfort. Experiment with the size of the end to suit the operators and the coin size.

Paint the board with a base color in contrast to the coin.

Materials List for Junior Table Hockey

1 base	14 × 28 × ½ plywood
2 sides	½ × 2 × 30
2 ends	½ × 2 × 15
2 goals	½ × 2 × 8
4 goals	½ × 2 × 3
2 goals	½ × 3 × 8
2 sticks	¼ × 2 × 11

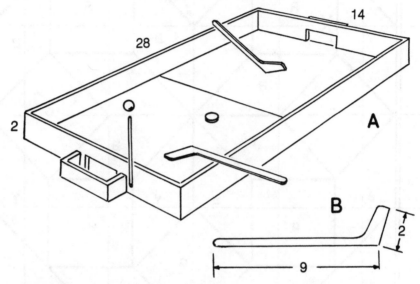

Fig. 2-22. Details of a junior table hockey game.

For the alternative game of blow football you need a table tennis ball or another almost as light, plus a blow pipe for each player. At its simplest this could be a drinking straw, but for something more durable you might find sections of cane or plastic or metal tubes about ⅛-inch bore. A length of 12 inches would be satisfactory.

MOSAIC PUZZLE

Putting together a mosaic pattern is more difficult than doing a jigsaw puzzle. It should be within the scope of a child aged about 8 years and this could keep him or her busy for a long time. The object is to get a number of pieces together in a pattern, with colors as well as shapes symmetrical and with no two pieces of the same color adjoining. This puzzle (FIG. 2-23) is assembled in a frame, arranged with two stages of difficulty. The pattern is outlined on one side, without the colors indicated. This gives a beginner a starting formation and he only has to get the colors correct. The other side is blank, so the design has to be worked out and the colors arranged.

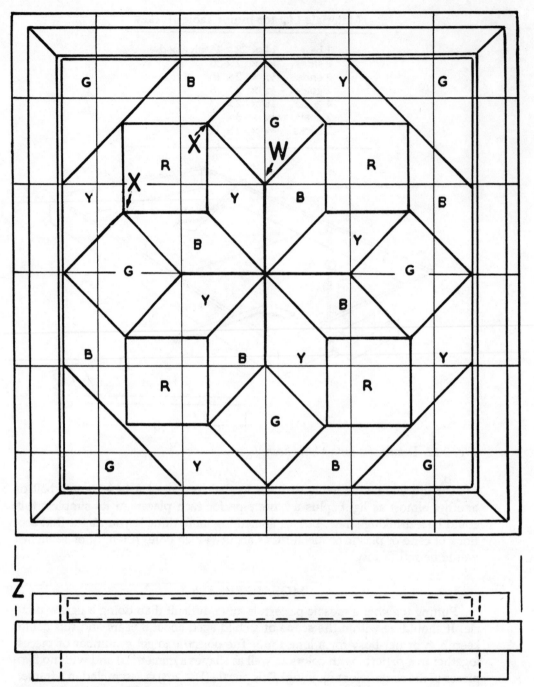

Fig. 2-23. *Layout and colors of a mosaic puzzle.*

Materials List for Mosaic Puzzle

1 base	9 × 9 × ⅜	plywood
8 frames	⅜ × ⅜ × 9	
squares from	¼ × 1½ × 14	
diamonds from	¼ × 1½ × 36	
triangles from	¼ × 1½ × 12	

There are eight square pieces, sixteen diamond shaped, and three triangles. The key size is the length of the side of a square. If this is 1½ inches, the overall size of the frame will be 9 inches. With 1-inch squares it will be 6 inches. Each side of a diamond must be the same length as the side of a square. The long side of each triangle should be twice this.

If you set out a background pattern of six squares of the chosen size each way on a piece of plywood, start by marking four diagonal squares where they meet the grid (FIG. 2-23W). The extremities of these diagonal squares are the outsides of the puzzle. Draw in those lines. Four more squares touch the first four (FIG. 2-23X). With these positioned, draw in the diamonds. The triangles complete the layout.

You can cut the shapes by hand, although a table saw will allow you to make them uniform. Sand the edges and lightly round them. Suggested colors are indicated (R = red, G = green, B = blue, Y = yellow).

The frame base (FIG. 2-23Z) is a square of plywood with frame strips slightly thicker than the wood used for the mosaic. Allow enough clearance for easy handling of the pieces. Draw the pattern on one side. The frame could be white or varnished.

3

Outdoor Games

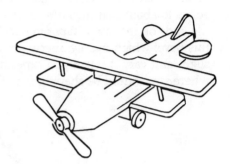

BOOMERANG

Australian aborigines devised boomerangs from any wood they could find, so sizes and shapes varied, but a principle of design became established. Heavy boomerangs were throwing sticks intended to kill animals and did not return, but a lighter version makes a sporting type that can be thrown to varying distances, so it will curve in flight and return near you. Without knowing anything about airplane wings, the aborigine shaped the arms of his boomerang to very similar sections to produce airfoil shapes. Any boomerang you make has to be worked to the correct sections if it is to fly properly. This is most easily done with a file or rasp; a Surform tool is very suitable for most shaping.

Original boomerangs were made of solid wood, but because of the shape, a boomerang made from a single piece of wood, unless it had a very twisted grain, would have a point of weakness due to short grain lines. There could be a joint between the arms, but in the thin section this would be very difficult to arrange strongly and successfully. It is better, particularly for a boomerang to be used by young people, to use plywood. This should be hardwood plywood ¼ inch (6mm) thick. If you can get five-ply that should be stronger than three-ply. Have the lines of grain of the outer ply across the V, if possible. Start with a flat piece of plywood.

Exact sizes and angles of the outline are less important than getting the two arms to match and their sections correctly formed. The sizes suggested (FIG. 3-1A) will produce a boomerang that can be thrown by a child, but it will also provide fun for an adult. The two arms are parallel in their length, but there is an increase in the width, for strength, around the root curve. The angle between the arms may be between 95 and 105 degrees.

Cut to shape and true the edges so the whole thing is balanced in outline. You must now decide if the boomerang is to be righthanded or lefthanded. The instructions and drawings are for a righthanded one. To make a lefthanded boomerang do the section shaping the other way round.

In flight, the two arms have leading and trailing edges. The outer edge leads on one and the inner edge leads on the other. Bevel the undersides of the leading edges to about half thickness at the tip of the section, with most bevel towards the ends on the arms. Taper to nothing towards the root curve (FIG. 3-1B, C). It is this bevel which mainly affects performance and you may wish to start with it slight and vary it when you experiment to get the best flight. This is the point where you should be shaping the other way for lefthanded use.

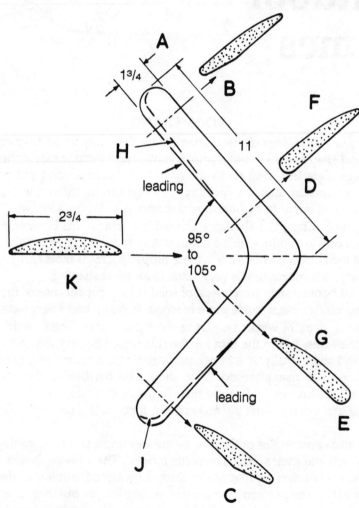

Fig. 3-1. *Sizes and sections of a boomerang.*

Except for these bevels, the underside of the plywood remains flat. Round the leading edges from the root curve to right around the tips to a semicircular or elliptical section (FIG. 3-1D, E). The lines of plies exposed will serve as a guide to even shaping.

For most of the length of each arm you have to get an airfoil shape to the top surface (FIG. 3-1F, G). Pencil lines on top and bottom surfaces, about ½ inch at the tips (FIG. 3-1H and J) will serve as guides to shaping. Do not bevel the trailing edges too thinly, or they will become damaged—leave one whole ply. Take these sections almost to the root curve, where they blend into a more symmetrically curved section (FIG. 3-1K). Watch the ply lines you expose, they will soon show you if you are leaving high spots or making hollows.

Bring the wood to as smooth a surface as possible all over, by working through progressively finer grades of sandpaper. This should leave your boomerang comfortable to hold and without sharp or rough edges. You could use it at this stage, but even if you may want to do some adjusting to sections later, it is advisable to seal the wood to prevent absorption of dirt, with one or two coats of lacquer or varnish. For the final finish, use any color and decorate it with pictures or the wavy lines favored by aborigines.

Throwing is best learned on a calm day or with the lightest of breezes. If there is any air movement, throw into it. Hold the boomerang in one hand upwards and with one of its arms facing forward and the curved side towards you (FIG. 3-2). Aim as you throw at an imaginary point in the air, maybe 50 feet away and 10 feet off the ground. Keep trying. Each boomerang has its own peculiarities. Try having it slightly off upright, one way or the other, as it leaves your hand. Give it a slight flick as you throw. When thrown correctly, the boomerang will go away on a fairly straight path, then bank round and come back.

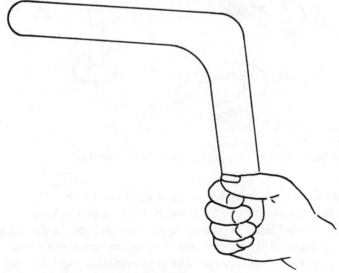

Fig. 3-2. How to hold a boomerang for throwing.

YARD RING GAME

There are many games where rings have to be thrown over pegs. For outdoor use it is convenient to have the pegs to press into the ground. Then they can be arranged how you wish, but for a traditional game of quoits or yard rings, they should be arranged in a diamond pattern, with the highest scoring peg in the middle (FIG. 3-3). How you space the pegs depends on the degree of skill and standing distance. Contestants throw three or six rings at a time and the scores are totalled. Whoever gets the highest score or reaches an exact total first, is the winner. A variation is to work through the numbers in turn—aiming at #1 first and not moving to #2 until #1 has been ringed.

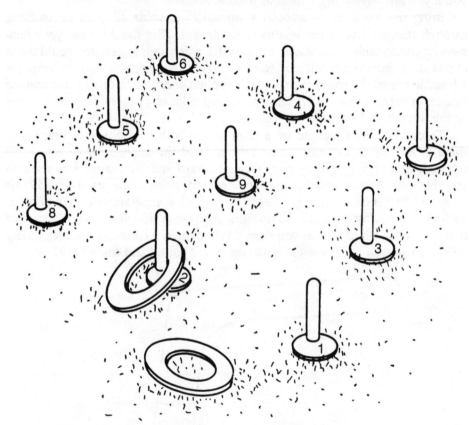

Fig. 3-3. This yard ring game has pegs to press in the ground.

The pegs shown are intended to be turned on a lathe (FIG. 3-4A), but you could make very similar ones with dowel rod. Use a close-grained hardwood, if possible. The reduced lower ends have to fit through holes in the discs, so drill a hole in a scrap piece of plywood to test the pegs as you make them.

Cut the discs from exterior or marine plywood (FIG. 3-4B). You could use hexagonal or other outlines. Drill a hole towards one side, so there is space for the number at the front. Glue each disc to its peg. Finish with a bright color paint to contrast with the green grass. The numbers 1 to 9 can be applied with decals or painted freehand.

Rings may be cut from plywood (FIG. 3-4C). A reasonable weight is an advantage and ½-inch plywood is suitable. True the edges after sawing and well round them for a comfortable grip. Paint or varnish the wood. Hardboard, or composition board, could be used, but it lacks weight and would not be very durable.

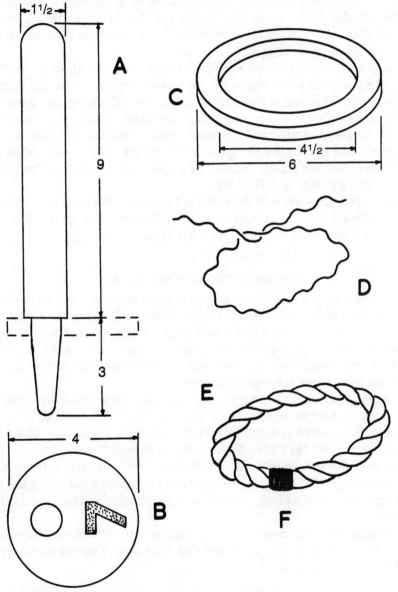

Fig. 3-4. Sizes and construction of parts of the yard ring game.

Materials List for Yard Ring Game

9 pegs	1½ × 1½ × 13
9 discs	4 × 4 × ½ plywood
3 or 6 quoits	6 × 6 × ½ plywood (or use rope)

Traditional quoits are made of rope. You do not have to be an expert rope worker to make them. Choose a three-strand rope about ¾ inch diameter. One piece will make three quoits. The length cut should be about 3½ times the intended diameter of the quoit. For quoits 5 to 6 inches in diameter, the rope length should be about 22 inches.

Unlay the three strands without disturbing the natural kinks or "lay" of the rope. Take one piece and form a ring; then, twist opposite parts into each other (FIG. 3-4D), so the hollows fit together. What you are doing is laying up the rope in its original form, but in a continuous ring. Continue twisting together until you have the three-strand effect fitting snugly together (FIG. 3-4E) and the ends overlap. Stretch and manipulate the quoit so the strands fit into each other evenly and closely; then, cut off the ends so they come tightly together. Bind over the end with fine string or cord (FIG. 3-4F).

Most rope quoits will hold their shape, but if you have used very soft rope, it can be stiffened with lacquer or varnish. Although three quoits or rings are enough for a game, you should make a few spares.

FRAMED YARD RING GAME

The ring game just described has pegs to push in the ground, so obviously it cannot be used on a hard surface or indoors. For use on a deck, a patio or the floor indoors you can make a frame with pegs mounted on it (FIG. 3-5). Size will depend on how you plan to play the game. As shown (FIG. 3-6A), the frame is intended to suit quoits about 6 inches in diameter thrown from about 8 feet away. For regular indoor use, it could be made smaller.

To resist movement, it is helpful to make the frame heavy by using hardwood, but, softwood should also be satisfactory. Friction on the underside can be provided with rubber feet at the corners or pads of leather or cloth glued on.

Cut the parts for the frame. Mark them together (FIG. 3-6B).

Cut the halving joints (FIG. 3-6C) to fit closely with the level surfaces.

Turn the pegs (FIG. 3-6D) with reduced ends to fit into holes in the top half of each frame joint. Alternatively, use dowel rod and drill the frame to take the full diameter.

The frame holes are only drilled into half of each joint to avoid weakening. When you assemble, glue all parts, but also drive screws upwards into the pegs (FIG. 3-6E).

There could be blocks to serve as feet under the frame ends at the corners (FIG. 3-6F), they will help the frame to stand without wobbling if the surface below is uneven. Rubber, leather or cloth could be glued below to provide friction.

If the frame will sometimes be used on soft ground, holes towards the ends of parts of the frame will allow you to push spikes through into the ground.

Round all exposed ends. Paint the wood brightly and either paint on the numbers or use decals.

Make plywood or rope quoits as described in the last project.

Materials List for Framed Yard Ring Game

6 frames	1 × 2 × 32
9 pegs	1¼ × 1¼ × 8

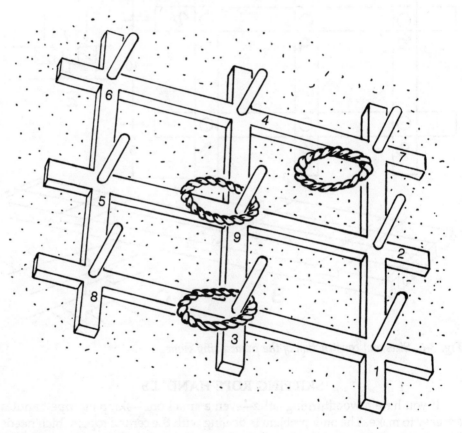

Fig. 3-5. The framed ring game can be used indoors or outdoors.

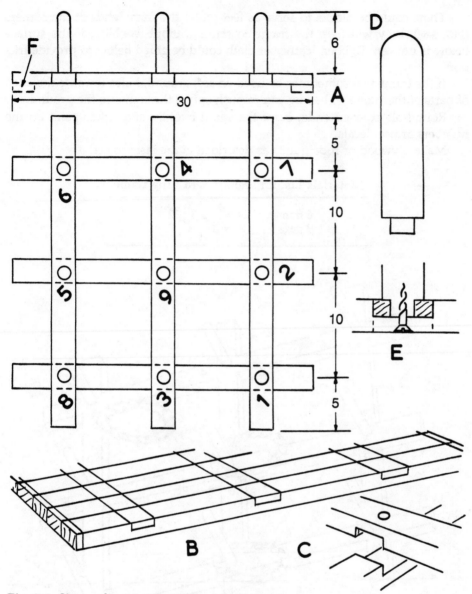

Fig. 3-6. Sizes and construction of the framed ring game.

SKIPPING ROPE HANDLES

If you have a woodturning lathe—even a small one—skipping rope handles are easy to make. The only problem is dealing with the central rope, which needs its end enlarged to allow for the knotted rope. Several outlines are possible and two are suggested (FIG. 3-7). Almost any wood could be used, but turning is easier with a close-grained hardwood, and the resulting handles should stand up better to rough use.

Have the wood up to 1 inch longer than the handle.

Center it and turn the outside cylindrically. The diameter depends on the chosen pattern, but the final grip should be about 1 inch, or less depending on the child. For the ball end handle you could turn the cylinder to about 1¼ inches in diameter.

Holes sizes depend on the rope, which will probably be ¼ inch or ⅜ inch. The enlargement for the knot should be about twice this measurement. If you can mount a drill in the tailstock, drill from there; otherwise, drill on a press if possible, or drill by eye, with an assistant watching that you keep the drill straight.

Drill the small hole for the length the handle will be, but leave some solid wood at the driving end (FIG. 3-7A). Enlarge the end of the hole (FIG. 3-7B); this need not be very deep, so long as the knot will pull inside. You may prefer to drill the large hole first and follow with the smaller one, particularly if you are using spur center drills.

Turn a plug to fit in the hole, with a dot for the tailstock center (FIG. 3-7C).

Turn the outside to any design you wish and finish its surface by sanding; then, part off into the end of the hole. If the first hole is not deep enough, you can drill back into it. In any case, working a drill by hand through the hole will smooth it, for easy entry of the rope.

In a weekend you should be able to make a large variety of pairs of handles.

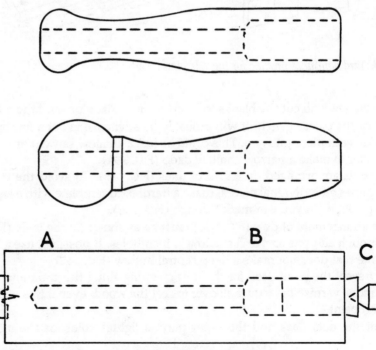

Fig. 3-7. *Shapes and construction of skipping rope handles.*

YARD DOMINOES

The small pieces used for a game of dominoes on a table may be difficult for a child to handle and he may not want to understand the game then, but if you make a set of large ones to lay out on the lawn or patio, he will find it easier to understand and will be intrigued by the patterns built up. The different arrangements of dots will also help him with counting, as he needs to match them.

A full set of dominoes total 28 pieces. You have to consider your available space and how the layout will spread. It does not have to go all the way in a straight line, but can be taken squarely (FIG. 3-8) more than once, although you do not want the game to be too restricted. There is also the need for a child to handle the pieces, so they should not be too big or heavy. In the example the dominoes are each 4 inches × 8 inches and cut from ¾-inch plywood. For older children and ample space you could make them bigger.

Fig. 3-8. Yard dominoes provide for outside play.

A table saw will cut the blanks to uniform size. Plane or sand the edges and check that the pieces match. It will probably be advisable to cut a few spares.

Divide each piece into two. This could be just a shallow saw cut or you might use a router to make a narrow shallow dado (FIG. 3-9A).

The dots are arranged on a grid of lines (FIG. 3-9B). To avoid the trouble of marking lines on individual pieces, make a hardboard template with a small hole at each position, so you can mark through (FIG. 3-9C).

The arrangement of dots (FIG. 3-9D) must be as shown in the table (FIG. 3-10). Mark through all parts and drill shallow ½-inch holes. If possible, use a Forstner bit, or one that does not make a deep central hollow (FIG. 3-9E).

To prevent the paint used for the dots creeping along the grain and spoiling appearances, varnish or lacquer all over to seal the wood, even if this will be covered with paint.

Paint the dots dark and the other parts a lighter color, or the other way round.

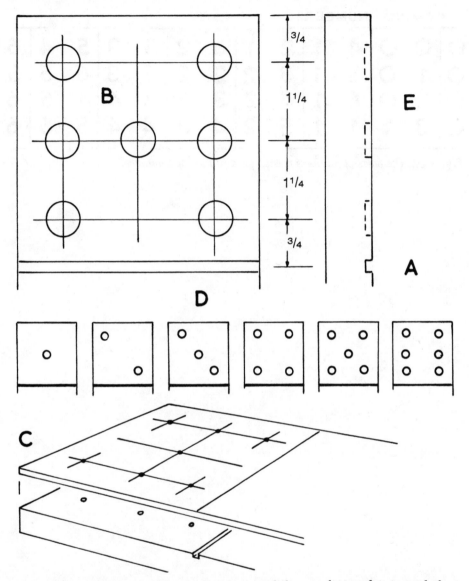

Fig. 3-9. *The arrangement of dots on dominoes and the use of a template to mark them.*

For a simple game, shuffle the dominoes face down and divide them between players. Whoever has *double-six* starts and has another chance to put a six against it. The opponent puts a number against the one exposed or against the six, and so on. Anyone putting down a double gets an extra chance. Anyone not having a matching number to put down misses. The winner is the first one to use all his dominoes. A straight line with these dominoes occupies about 9 feet, so direction can be changed to fit into a space. Dominoes may be added at either end, if the numbers match.

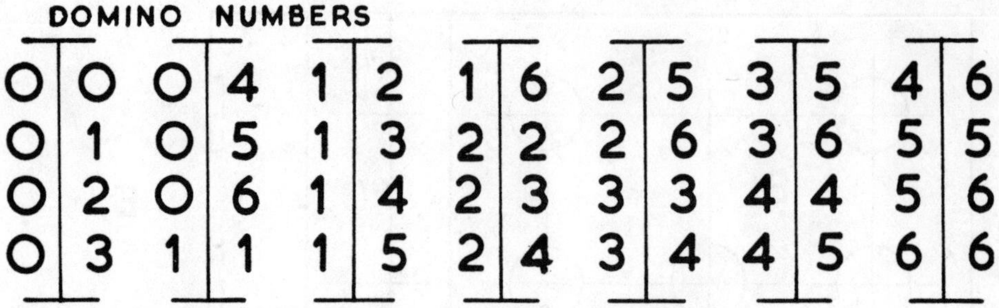

DOMINO NUMBERS

O	O	O	4	1	2	1	6	2	5	3	5	4	6
O	1	O	5	1	3	2	2	2	6	3	6	5	5
O	2	O	6	1	4	2	3	3	3	4	4	5	6
O	3	1	1	1	5	2	4	3	4	4	5	6	6

Fig. 3-10. The pairs of numbers needed for a full set of dominoes.

4

Activity Equipment & Play Furniture

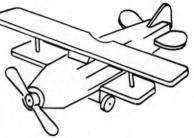

STEP STOOL

A step stool allows a child to take two moderate steps up; it permits a toddler to see what mother is doing, or reach a table or worktop without assistance. Moreover, it can be sat on with different heights to suit leg lengths. It also has play possibilities; a child can set out items on the shelves in his play store or the shelves can be somewhere to put books or ornaments when playing house. The whole thing turned on its face may be a broad stool or a small table. This step stool (FIG. 4-1) should be stable in use and allow its young user to climb 10 inches in two steps.

The step stool is designed to be made from softwood bought as 1-inch-×-12-inch section, which in its planed condition will be nearer ¾ inch × 11½ inches. Sizes may be adapted to suit your needs.

Start by marking out the pair of ends, with the outlines and positions of steps and back (FIG. 4-2A). There are several possible ways of arranging construction, depending on your skill and equipment. It would be possible, but unwise, to merely nail or screw through the ends into the steps. Loads on the steps, particularly if used by adults, would soon break or split the joints. Plenty of dowels through the ends may be satisfactory (FIG. 4-2B).

Put cleats across under the steps, glued and screwed to the ends (FIG. 4-2C). For added strength, cut dadoes in the ends (FIG. 4-2D). This is easy with a suitable cutter in a router, but otherwise it means careful work with a saw and chisel. The steps could have rounded fronts with a matching end on each upper dado, avoiding the need for work with a chisel after using a router. Screws through the ends supplement the dadoes, or for maximum strength use cleats underneath (FIG. 4-2E).

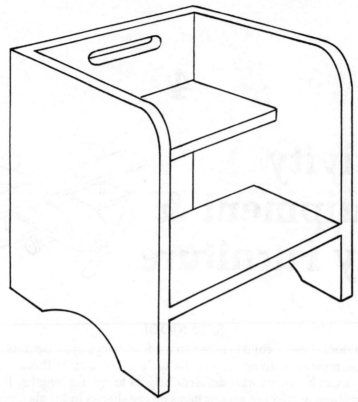

Fig. 4-1. *The step stool can be used by a toddler to climb or sit.*

The back could be put between the ends and screwed through, or it would be neater and stronger to cut rabbets in the ends (FIG. 4-2F). The top dadoes would then blend into the rabbets.

Make the back with its grain upright. Cut the hand hole (about 4 inches × 1 inch) by drilling two end holes and sawing away the waste (FIG. 4-2G). Well round the edges of the hand hole. Round what will be exposed edges in the finished assembly.

It is important that the step stool should stand without wobbling on most surfaces. With straight bottom edges it will only stand firm on an absolutely flat floor. There will be less risk of rocking if you cut curves to leave feet at the corners (FIG. 4-2H).

Smooth all surfaces and drill most of the screw holes while the wood is flat; then, assemble with glue and screws. The back and steps should pull the assembly square, but check overall squareness before the glue sets. Test on a level surface. You will be able to correct stability by planing bottom edges, if necessary.

Seal the wood with lacquer or varnish to prevent it from absorbing dirt, but a young user might prefer to have the wood painted brightly, possible with fairy tale or other decals on the ends and back.

2 ends	¾ × 11 × 16
1 back	¾ × 11 × 16
2 steps	¾ × 5½ × 12

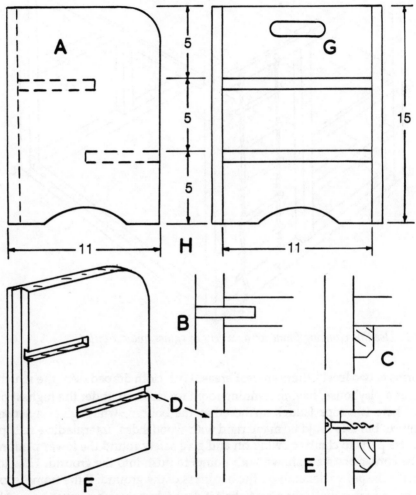

Fig. 4-2. Suggested sizes and construction for the step stool.

CLIMBING FRAME

All children want to climb. They may not always be aware of dangers, so we have to limit their activities. A strong climbing frame within their range allows them the exercise with minimum risk.

This frame (FIG. 4-3) is based on a 42-inch cube and is intended for toddlers up to about age 5. You can complete the frame in many ways, but as shown with

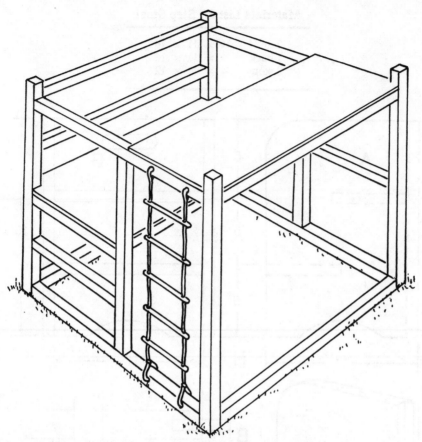

Fig. 4-3. *Use this climbing frame for a variety of games and activities.*

platforms at two levels, there are rest areas. With cloth draped over, the structure becomes a playhouse, having standing room for children under the highest platform. There is a rope ladder, anchored at the bottom, which gives a sense of adventure, but this could be made rigid with wood sides. Intermediate rails provide extra parts to climb or swing on and give safety round the lower platform.

The corner posts are shown with points to push into the ground. How long you make the points depends on the hardness of the ground. If the frame is to go on a hard surface you might have to bolt it down, but grass is a better base. Also, you can move a spiked frame around.

The structure could be 1½-inch-square hardwood or 2-inch-square softwood. Although the wood might be protected by paint and preservative, a durable hardwood is advisable if the frame is to be left outdoors.

It would be possible to dowel the parts together, but it is better to cut mortise-and-tenon joints at most meeting places. When possible, arrange rails to posts at different levels, so you do not cut away too much at one place and weaken the posts; this is particularly important at the tops of posts. Let the posts project upwards with rounded tops and arrange the top of one rail to come level with the underside of the other rail (FIG. 4-4A). If a rail is to cross a post, you can use a halving joint, but a rail in the other direction should come to one side (FIG. 4-4B). Rails at the lower level could meet, with tenon ends mitered to give them maximum length and glue area.

The climbing frame does not have to be the same size in all directions, but that is assumed in these instructions (FIG. 4-4C). Allow for the posts projecting at the top and with sufficient length at the bottom for the points.

Decide on the intended layout and prepare ample wood, all of the same section. Check straightness. It is difficult to pull a warped strip very much during assembly. You may be able to cut it for shorter parts.

Mark out the four corner posts and any intermediate uprights that have to match them (FIG. 4-5A).

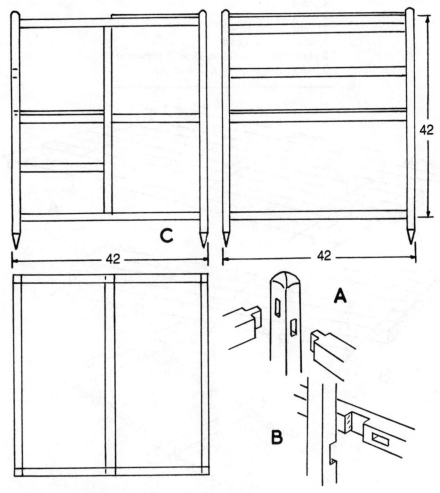

Fig. 4-4. Sizes and suggested joints for the climbing frame.

Mark out all horizontal rails, with intermediate positions of other parts, where appropriate (FIG. 4-5B). Mark and cut the joints between these parts.

Round the tops of the corner posts and point their bottoms. Do not cut these to fine points. Leave about ½ inch square, so the end does not shatter or split.

Make short intermediate rails where needed. They can come in sections between the floor and the first platform or between that and the top, giving a spacing about 10 inches—enough to allow climbing and to prevent the user from falling off.

Assemble two opposite sides first. Check squareness; compare diagonals and see that the outline of one frame is a pair to the other.

Materials List for Climbing Frame

(1½ × 1½ or 2 × 2 softwood)	
4 posts	52
2 uprights	42
11 rails	42
4 rails	24
2 platforms	24 × 44 × ½ plywood
5 ladder rungs	14 × 1 diameter

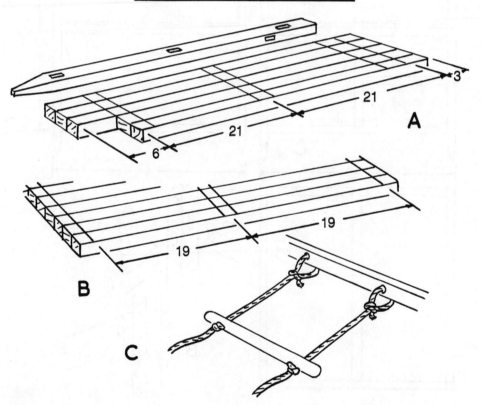

Fig. 4-5. *Mark out the climbing frame parts (A, B) and details of the rope ladder (C).*

Join the rails the other way. If you have the plywood for the platforms ready, it can be glued and nailed or screwed on to hold the assembly square.

The rungs of a rope ladder can be hardwood dowel rod 1 inch in diameter. Use synthetic rope, such as polypropylene about 5/16 inch in diameter. Drill top and bottom frame rails so you can knot the rope ends (FIG. 4-5C). Seal the rope ends with heat. Hold the end in a flame from a match or a cigarette lighter. Moisten your finger and thumb and roll the softened end into a tight mass.

If you use waterproof glue and treat the wood with preservative, the climbing frame should last indefinitely. A canvas or plastic sheet could be put over to keep the wood clean and protect it while out of use.

STILTS

The idea of walking tall appeals to all children. Stilts are the traditional toys to give extra height. The circus performer might use stilts of considerable height attached to his legs only, but a child needs to use his arms and hands as well as his legs. Also, he should be able to dismount rapidly and safely in an emergency. Stilts with long shafts are often seen being used held in front of the body, but most children will have more success with shafts that come nearly to head height and are held to the sides with their tops projecting behind the shoulders.

Stilts could be made any height. A beginner will not want to be more than a few inches above the ground, but anyone aged 8 to 10 should soon be skillful with their feet up to 18 inches from the ground. These stilts are designed for a child in that age range, but their sizes can be varied. You could make them for an older child and cut them down for a younger brother or sister. As shown (FIGS. 4-6 and 4-7A) the footrests have projections to prevent feet sliding off.

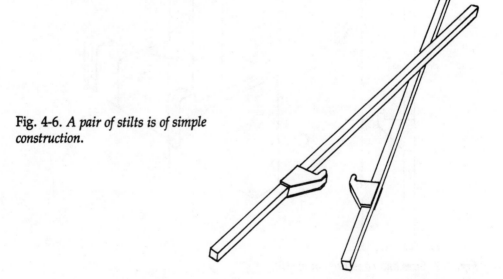

Fig. 4-6. *A pair of stilts is of simple construction.*

The shafts should be fairly light, but they need to be strong, so choose straight-grained softwood. The slightly resinous types, such as Oregon and Columbian pine, are suitable. The footrests are any wood as a filler and plywood for cheeks or sides.

Materials List for Stilts

2 shafts	1½ × 1½ × 74
2 footrests	1½ × 3 × 6
4 cheeks	6 × 6 × ½ plywood

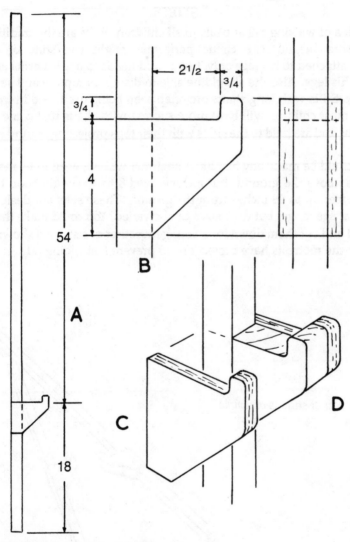

Fig. 4-7. *Sizes and construction of stilts.*

Prepare two matching shafts and mark on the positions of the footrests. Leave the wood square to about 6 inches above and below the footrest positions, then plane off the sharp angles and well round the edges. There is no need to completely round the wood, but aim to finish with sections that are square with well-rounded corners. Round the tops of the shafts.

Cut one plywood cheek (FIG. 4-7B, C) and use it as a template to mark the shapes of the other cheeks and the filler pieces (FIG. 4-7D).

Check that the thicknesses of the filler pieces exactly match the shafts. Glue and screw the cheeks to the filler pieces. Well round all edges, except where the cheeks are against the shafts. Round where a foot will bear, to fit comfortably under a shoe instep.

Glue and screw the footrests to the shaft. For extra strength put a thin bolt right through, near the top. It should not be more than ¼ inch in diameter (³/₁₆ inch may be enough). A thicker bolt would weaken the shaft wood at a point where there is the most stress.

If the stilts are to be used on a hard or slippery surface, it is helpful to nail on rubber or leather pieces to reduce the risk of slipping.

Finish the stilts with paint, but the young user will probably be happy with them untreated.

YARD SWING

A swing provides activity and enjoyment for children of many ages. For a family it needs to be durable so it can be used for many years. It also needs to be safe. Children should be able to play with it without supervision, so it needs to be rigid, it must not move and there should be no fear of collapse or breakages. Besides the need for strength in the structure, the moving parts must be strong enough to resist chafe and be able to stand up to constant use with the need for only occasional inspection.

This swing (FIG. 4-8) is of a basic type, which may be fastened to the ground and is braced so there should be no fear of the structure weakening and flexing in use. Vigorous use of the swing, which must be expected, can put considerable loads on the parts and joints. The best way of making the rope swinging parts is described.

The entire structure can be made of 2-×-4-inch section wood. Softwood treated with preservative should be sufficiently durable for many years of use. Hardwood could be expected to last even longer. Assembly is with ½-inch bolts. Galvanized carriage bolts would be ideal. The seat could be solid wood or exterior grade plywood. The choice of rope is discussed later.

You need to know certain angles and you can get this by setting out the side view (FIG. 4-9A). The main lines are all you need. This should be full-size on the floor, if possible, but you could draw it to scale. The angles will be the same, but you will have to carefully scale lengths. Note the *actual* sizes of your wood. Planed wood will be about ¼ inch *under* the nominal measurements. Allow for this discrepancy in your drawing.

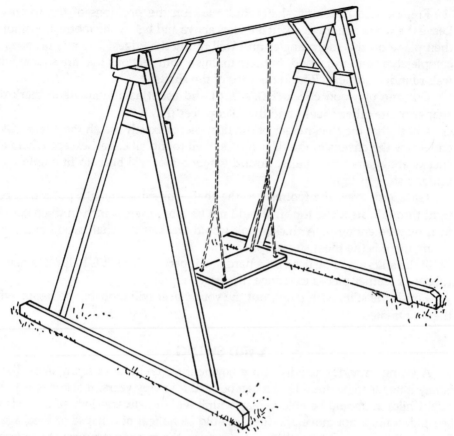

Fig. 4-8. This yard swing has strong supports.

With the aid of your drawing, mark out the four legs (FIG. 4-9B). At the top they form a notch to fit under the beam (FIG. 4-9C).

Make the two feet, (FIG. 4-9D) and mark where the legs will come.

Put a side on the floor with the legs and foot in position. Put pieces across for the braces (FIG. 4-9E, F). They can be too long, to be trimmed after bolting on.

Drill for bolts at each crossing. Two in each place should be arranged diagonally in the direction of the longer way of the overlap.

If the wood has not already been treated with preservative, apply plenty of preservative on the meeting surfaces; then, bolt all the joints. With carriage bolts, let the head pull in and put a washer under the nut. If you use bolts with square or hexagonal heads, put a washer under each head as well as under the nut. Final tightening can be left until later. Assemble both sides; check that they match as a pair.

The length of the top beam (FIG. 4-9G) determines the width of the assembly. You might want to modify this to suit your individual needs.

Materials List for Yard Swing

4 legs	2	×	4	× 96
2 feet	2	×	4	× 76
1 beam	2	×	4	× 86
2 braces	2	×	4	× 14
2 braces	2	×	4	× 22
2 struts	2	×	4	× 30
1 seat	1	×	10	× 24

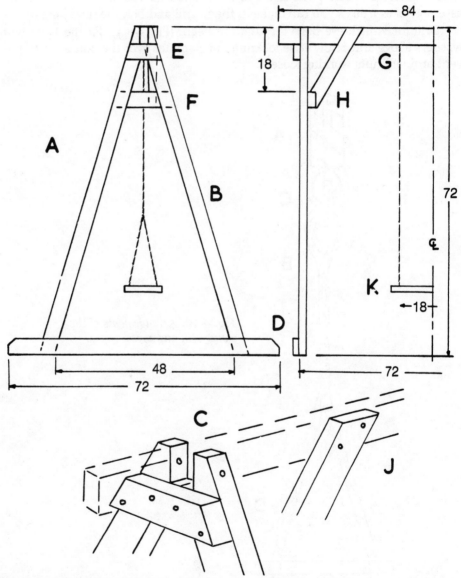

Fig. 4-9. *Sizes and details of the yard swing supports.*

Fit the beam across the sides and use the assembly to obtain the size and angle of the pair of struts (FIG. 4-9H). The lower end of a strut notches over its brace in a similar way to the top of a leg on the beam. At the top it bolts to the beam (FIG. 4-9J). The arrangement of struts keeps the assembly square, so be careful to make the struts and their angles matching. Before you drill for bolts through the struts, check squareness by comparing diagonal measurements over the whole structure. Alternatively, have the whole assembly ready to erect, except for drilling bolt holes through the struts and beam. Erect the swing and check squareness. Clamp the struts to the beam until you are satisfied that the assembly is as true as you can make it; then, drill and bolt the final joints.

Drill for ⅜-inch eye bolts through the beam (FIG. 4-10A). Fit the bolts with washers above and below. Use locknuts, or hammer over the bolt ends to prevent ordinary nuts working loose.

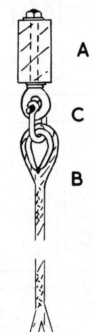

A

C

B

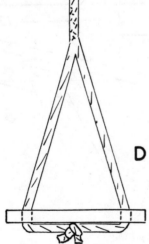

D

Fig. 4-10. Arrangements of the swing seat and ropes.

Use synthetic fiber rope, which does not absorb water or rot. Natural fiber rope cannot be trusted for more than a season, because of the risk of rot.

Use rope ½ inch or slightly thicker, to provide enough grip. You could knot the ropes, but they would be better spliced. Splicing three-strand rope is easy, but if you cannot do it yourself, anyone used to working with boats should be able to do it for you.

The main risk of chafe or friction, comes at the top. Splice or tie the rope around a metal thimble, which is grooved and heart-shaped (FIG. 4-10B). Use shackles (from a boat shop) to link the thimbles to the eye bolts (FIG. 4-10C).

The seat (FIGS. 4-9K and 4-10D) is a plain board with its edges rounded. Drill it near the ends for the rope.

Join in a piece to each rope about 18 inches above the seat, by splicing or knotting. Take the ends through the holes in the seat and splice or knot them together. This is better than putting single knots below each hole, as the rope across relieves the wood of some possible splitting strain. Use knots underneath and allow some spare length of rope; this give you an adjustment if you need to level or adjust the height of the seat. (Instructions on rope splicing can be found in Tab Book #3004, *50 Practical and Decorative Knots You Should Know*).

COVERED SANDBOX

Digging in sand is always popular with children, but sand in a pile can soon become an untidy mess, with leaves and dirt mixed in, so it could become a hazard to health as well. If sand is kept within bounds it needs a lid as well to keep it clean. This box to contain sand is about 48 inches square, which is probably enough for the amount of sand you want to provide and for one or two young children to enjoy being busy with bucket and spade.

The box is designed so the top and bottom can be cut from one standard sheet of 48- × -96-inch plywood (FIG. 4-11A). The lid is intended to lift off. Its slope will allow rain water to run away. At the lower edge there is a seat or step. Besides this obvious use, it also does something to prevent sand being thrown outside the box when a child is digging.

The plywood should be exterior grade. Other parts are fir or a similar softwood. Construction is by screwing or nailing. When viewed from above, the box is square.

Mark out one side (FIG. 4-11B). Measure the slope and compare this with the plywood and edging strips for the lid. It should fit over with an easy clearance; up to ½ inch all round would be satisfactory.

Cut the pair of sides.

Make the pieces for the other two edges to fit between the sides so the overall sizes will be the same both ways. Bevel the top of the high piece; the low piece remains square.

Nail these parts together. Include a strengthening piece at the higher corners (FIG. 4-11C).

Materials List for Covered Sandbox

3 sides	1 × 12 × 48
1 side	1 × 6 × 48
1 seat	1 × 6 × 48
2 cleats	1 × 2 × 8
2 corners	1½ × 1½ × 14
4 lid sides	1 × 2 × 50
1 bottom	46 × 46 × ½ plywood
1 lid	48 × 48 × ½ plywood

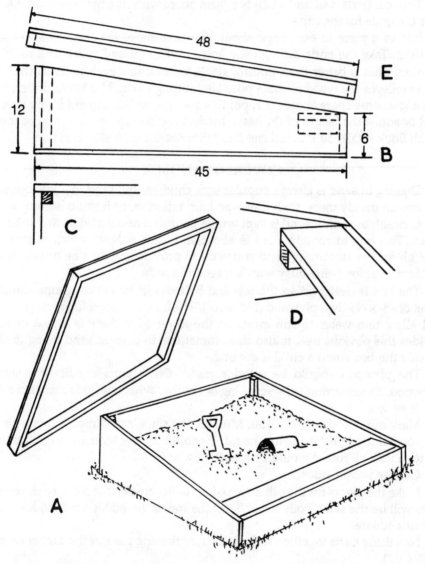

Fig. 4-11. A sandbox with a protective cover.

Nail on the bottom, checking squareness; otherwise, the lid may not fit. Trim all outer edges level and remove any sharpness.

At the lower edge, fit the seat inside, to rest on two cleats (FIG. 4-11D). Nail through securely, as this will brace the assembly and strengthen the lower corners.

Make the lid (FIG. 4-11E) as a shallow box. If your sizes are correct, it will be 48 inches square.

If the sandbox is to stay in one place on bare soil or turf, but battens around at the edge to raise most of the bottom and reduce the risk of the wood becoming saturated with moisture. In any case, the wood should be treated with preservative. It could be painted, but be prepared to repaint whenever bare wood is exposed.

SANDBOX TOOLS

If you make your children a sandbox, the next request will be for tools to use in it. They want to move the sand around and build castles and many other things. The sand has to be made into piles to represent the needs of the moment, then dispersed and made into something else. The need is for tools to do this efficiently and in the hands of less-skilled workers.

All of the tools needed can be made of wood, which will be stronger than most plastic things and less hazardous than metal ones. You can use up scrap lumbers, but as far as possible use close-grained hardwood, rather than splintery softwood.

The tools suggested are a spade for digging and stirring up the sand, rather than transporting large amounts. The tools for moving quantities of sand is a scoop. There are two molds; one like a bucket for turning out conical piles or transporting more sand, and another for producing brick shapes. To help pack sand into a mold there is a trowel.

The spade (FIG. 4-12A) is a piece of hardwood not more than ½ inch thick. After cutting the outline, thin the edges of the blade and well round all other parts, particularly inside the handle hole.

The bucket-shaped mold (FIG. 4-12B) has two solid sides (FIG. 4-12C) with plywood nailed on. You could use ½-inch solid wood and ¼-inch plywood.

Cut the two pieces of solid wood to the outline (FIG. 4-12D). Mark the two pieces of plywood from this outline so their insides will be the same as that and there is enough left for overlap. Nail the plywood on, then put ½-inch-square strips across the edges (FIG. 4-12E) to take the bottom (FIG. 4-12F).

Remove sharp edges all round. Paint the outside if you wish, but anything put on the inside will soon wear away.

A mold to produce a brick shape (FIG. 4-12G) is made in the same way. Give it a slight taper so the compacted sand can be turned out without damage. A taper of ¼ inch at each edge in the 3-inch depth should be enough.

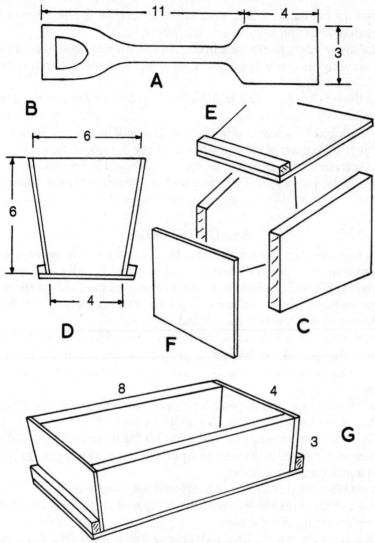

Fig. 4-12. *A spade and molds are used when playing with sand.*

The scoop (FIG. 4-13A) is a tapered box with a handle. Make the two sides from ½-inch solid wood. The top and bottom are parallel pieces of ¼-inch plywood nailed on (FIG. 4-13B).

To thicken for the bottom, put ½-inch-square strips across the inside (FIG. 4-13C), so there are no external projections to interfere with smooth scooping.

Screw the handle to the top before nailing it to the sides. It is the same as that for the trowel, (FIG. 4-13D) but tapered a little on its underside.

Finish the scoop by rounding its edges and painting outside.

The trowel has a ¼-inch plywood or thicker solid wood blade (FIG. 4-13E). If you use solid wood, thin the edges to about ¼ inch.

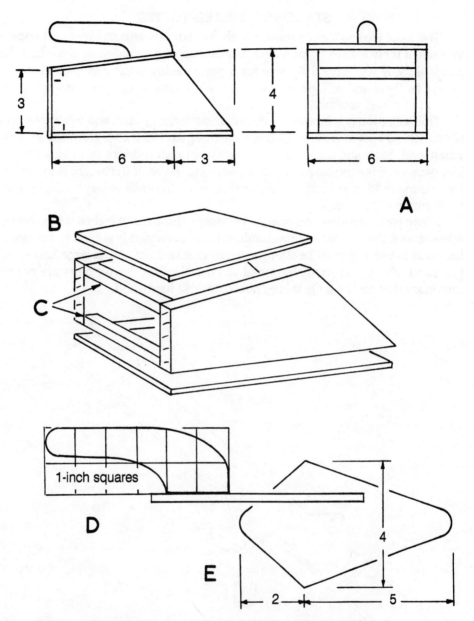

Fig. 4-13. *A scoop will move sand and a trowel will work it into shape.*

Make the handle from wood between ¾ inch and 1 inch thick. Cut to the outline; then, form the grip into a circular section and well round all other parts except where the joint comes. Screw it on. Paint all over.

So the tools can be seen when partly buried in sand or scattered around the yard, paint them brightly. Red is the color most easily seen against grass, but any vivid color other than green could be used.

STANDARD TEETER-TOTTER

The basic teeter-totter or seesaw is always popular and children will improvise one if there is nothing provided, sometimes with unlucky results when the plank slips. If you have the space for a permanently setup teeter-totter it will always be there and will get frequent use, with none of the risks that might go with a temporary assembly.

This teeter-totter is intended to be attached to the ground and left in position (FIG. 4-14). As shown (FIG. 4-15A) it is 8 feet long and 15 inches from the ground when level. You could make it longer. Anything much shorter would be inadvisable, because of the increase in relative steepness in use. If the height is too much for a young child, you could put something under the ends as steps until his legs have grown long enough.

Many parts are based on boards 1½ inches thick and 9 inches wide. Adopt other sizes if they are more convenient, but the main part is subject to considerble loads in use and must be strong enough to take them. Avoid large knots and get wood which is as straight-grained as possible. The shorter parts are not so important, but for the longest life choose durable hardwood.

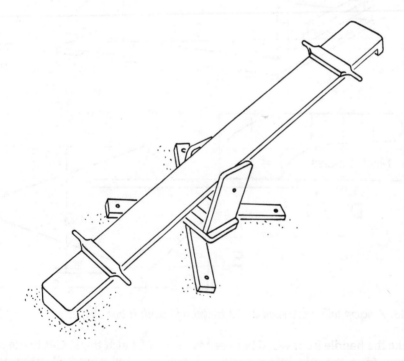

Fig. 4-14. *This teeter-totter is designed to be safe for young children.*

The center structure has to take loads in all directions without flexing or moving. It is shown over a crossed base, which may be pegged to the ground. If you want to spread wear on a lawn, the pegs could be withdrawn and the whole assembly moved. Otherwise, it may be worthwhile laying concrete and bolting the base to it.

Select the plank. Plane it and round the edges. Further treatment may be left until later, but it is needed at this stage to control the sizes of other parts.

Cut the pieces for the sides of the pivot assembly (FIGS. 4-15 and 4-16A).

Make the pivot base (FIGS. 4-15C and 4-16B). Mark the positions for the side up to ½ inch more than the width of the plank, to give clearance. You could attach the sides with long screws driven from below, or use dowels. The best joints would be mortise-and-tenon, with the tenons wedged underneath (FIG. 4-16C).

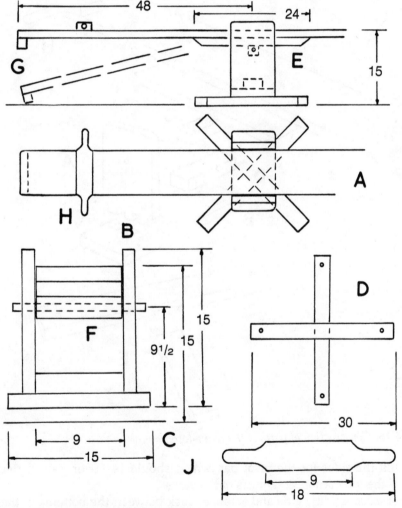

Fig. 4-15. Sizes and layout of the teeter-totter.

Materials List for Standard Teeter-Totter

1 plank	1½ × 9 ×	100
2 sides	1½ × 9 ×	18
1 base	1½ × 9 ×	18
1 stiffener	1½ × 9 ×	26
2 bases	1½ × 3 ×	32
1 crosspiece	2 × 4 ×	12
3 crosspieces	2 × 2 ×	11
2 handles	1 × 3 ×	20

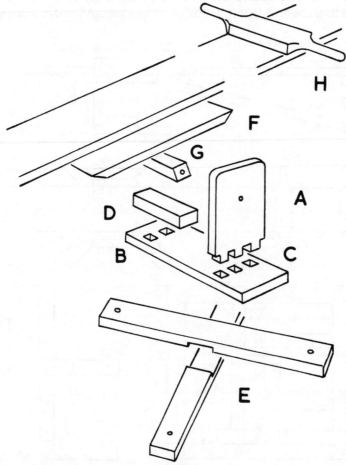

Fig. 4-16. Construction of parts of the teeter-totter.

Drill the sides for the pivot bar, which should be ⅝- or ¾-inch steel rod. Round the top corners and edges of the sides.

For extra rigidity, glue and screw a block between the bottoms of the pivot sides (FIG. 4-16D).

For the crossed base (FIG. 4-15D) halve the two pieces together (FIG. 4-16E). Drill the ends for pegs or bolts to the ground. Screw or bolt the crossed parts under the pivot base. Most loads will come near the corners of the overlap, so make the extreme fastenings there.

Put a stiffening piece under the center of the plank (FIGS. 4-15E and 4-16F). Bevel its ends. This piece is important to spread the bending load at the center when in use. If you make the plank longer, add a few inches to the stiffening piece.

Drill a square piece to take the pivot rod (FIGS. 4-15F and 4-16G). This can be a drive fit at first, as it will soon wear loose. Attach this under the center of the stiffening piece.

Put square pieces across under the ends of the plank (FIG. 4-15G), and round the ends. If the teeter-totter is used on stone or concrete, the pads under the ends may wear, so screw them so you can replace them when necessary.

Young children may be glad to have handles (FIGS. 4-15H and 4-16H). Make them with the wood full width across the plank, but reduce the ends to round (FIG. 4-15J)—not more than 1⅛ inches in diameter for small hands. Screw on without glue, as they may not be wanted when the children are older.

Drive the pivot rod through to complete the assembly.

Treatment with preservative may be advisable before assembly. Finish with bright colored paint. There could be padding for seats.

RUSTIC CLIMBING FRAME

If you have the space, a permanent climbing frame made from natural poles will prove attractive and inspire more of a spirit of adventure than a frame made of squared and planed wood. The surfaces have to be smooth enough to reduce risk of damage to the users, but the wood can still retain its natural shape. If parts are not absolutely straight, that does not matter.

Fir, pine, and spruce poles are usually obtainable reasonably straight and with little difference in diameter between one end and the other. Hardwood poles might not be as easy to find in suitable form. You need poles with an average diameter of about 3 inches. For a small structure you could use 2-inch diameters. Some hardwoods may have to be used with at least some of the bark attached, as it will not come away easily. Softwood poles should be stripped. You may have to pare with a drawknife or other tool, but when many softwood poles dry out, the bark almost falls off. Go over the poles with a coarse rasp or a Surform tool to remove the many little projections, so you are left with surfaces that can be handled without fear of harm.

Some joints could be nailed, screwed or bolted without any treatment of the wood, but it is better to notch the part nearest the upright (FIG. 4-17A). Do not cut too deeply, or the pole will be weakened. The hollow need not be an exact fit on the other pole, but it should be close enough to take some of the weight and prevent the nearest horizontal pole sliding down the other. Put a bolt through (FIG.

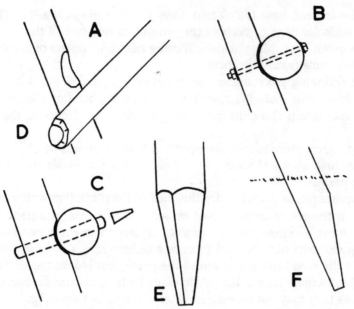

Fig. 4-17. Joints and shaping when using natural poles to make a climbing frame.

4-17B). With 3-inch softwood poles a ½-inch galvanized bolt would be suitable. Have washers under head and nut.

Use hardwood pegs. Oak, ¾ inch in diameter makes a good joint. Have the peg too long and taper its point. It should be a drive fit in the hole through both parts. Use waterproof glue in the hole, if you wish. Drive the peg through and cut off the tapered end. Leave both ends projected ½ inch, but take the sharpness off with your rasp (FIG. 4-17C).

When you cut a pole to length, bevel all round to remove roughness (FIG. 4-17D). If a pole is to go into the ground, do not shape to a fine point. Leave a flat end (FIG. 4-17E). If a pole into the ground is to slope, bevel most from the outer side, to ease driving (FIG. 4-17F).

Remember that a triangle cannot be pushed out of shape, so using poles sloping to join at a point will be stronger than just having upright poles in the ground or other joined with crossbars. The effect is four-sided and liable to move, unless braced with a diagonal to divide the shape into two triangles.

A basic frame has two pairs of poles driven into the ground and overlapped; then, horizontal poles are attached to them (FIG. 4-18A). You can arrange horizontal poles widely spaced at one side for older children and some closer ones at the other side for smaller children. There could be poles even closer across an end for use as a ladder (FIG. 4-18B).

An option is to take one horizontal pole out to another pair of legs (FIG. 4-18C). If you have space you could do the same at the other side at a different height.

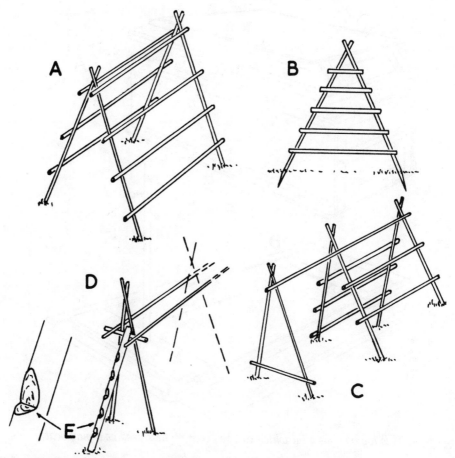

Fig. 4-18. Suggested forms of climbing frames using natural poles.

Another variation has two poles extended parallel to a support (FIG. 4-18D). Spread the legs for stiffness. There could be a single pole ladder, made by notching, to form steps (FIG. 4-18E). A high pole could be extended to support a swing. Incorporate structures already there, such as a tree or the side of a shed.

The parts which go into the ground should be soaked in preservative; in fact, the whole structure may be treated with preservative.

TOY BOX

There has to be something in which to put most of the accumulation of toys and a child is likely to put his things away if it is more than just a box. This box (FIG. 4-19A) may be mounted on casters, so it is easy to move about. The lift-off lid can be used on the floor as a play boat.

The parts of the box are built up with ½-inch plywood panels framed outside with 1-inch-square strips. Pieces across the ends form handles for the child to wheel the box or for an adult to pick it up.

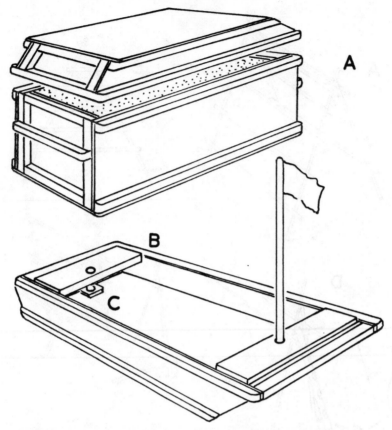

Fig. 4-19. This toy box has a lid which can be taken off and used as a play boat.

Cut the plywood for the two sides (FIG. 4-20A) and the ends which fit between them (FIG. 4-20B).

Frame the outsides of the ends (FIG. 4-20C), using glue and nails or screws. Put similar strips along the top and bottom edges of the sides (FIG. 4-20D).

Join the sides to the ends and fit the bottom. For strength at the top corners, use long screws from the side framing strips into the end ones.

This completes the box, except if there are to be casters; provide square blocks for them under each corner.

The lid is made in a similar way to the box, except for the sloping ends. Set out the slope (FIG. 4-20E) to get the angles, then make the ends with framing outside beveled at top and bottom (FIG. 4-20F).

Make the two side panels, using the box as a guide to length. Join them to the ends and put on lengthwise strips and the top panel.

At each end of the lid put pieces across, which the child will regard as seats or decks on his boat. Let them stand up ⅜ inch and locate them so they fit into the corners of the box, then they can position the lid when the box is closed (FIG. 4-19B).

2 sides	12 × 30 × ½ plywood
2 ends	18 × 15 × ½ plywood
1 bottom	18 × 32 × ½ plywood
2 lid sides	6 × 32 × ½ plywood
2 lid ends	9 × 15 × ½ plywood
1 lid top	16 × 26 × ½ plywood
14 framing	1 × 1 × 16
8 framing	1 × 1 × 32
2 decks	1 × 4 × 16
1 mast	24 × 1 diameter

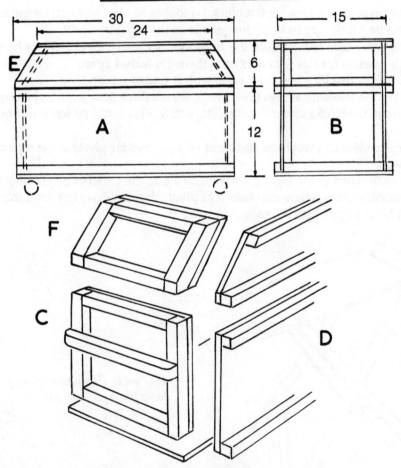

Fig. 4-20. Sizes and arrangement of external framing on a toy box.

Drill one piece to take a 1-inch dowel rod mast, which extends to a hole in a block below (FIG. 4-19C). Fly a flag or even add a sail, if that is what the children want. Many paint schemes are possible, and there can be waves on the side of the boat, as well as decals on the box.

JUNIOR IRONING BOARD

One pretend activity will be ironing like mother does. This folding ironing board (FIG. 4-21) is big enough for use with a toy iron, but shown 24 inches high (FIG. 4-22A), although it can easily be made lower by shortening the legs. It folds flat for storage, but in the erected position there is little fear of unintentional folding, if the turnbutton is used.

The top is ½-inch plywood. The other parts are solid wood. It will be helpful to draw the side view full-size (FIG. 4-22B) so you can check angles and sizes, but you can cut angles approximately and trim them during assembly.

Cut the top to shape (FIG. 4-22C) and mark on it the positions of the other parts.

The pivot for the long leg is a block 1½ inches square. Make its length so the legs will be a little way in from the outside of the top (FIG. 4-22D).

The other legs come inside the long legs, so their blocks have to be short enough to allow for this (FIG. 4-22E). Fit them 1½ inches apart.

Make the two long legs (FIG. 4-22F) with rounded top ends.

Make the two shorter legs (FIG. 4-22G), with a piece across the upper ends to fit between the blocks under the top (FIG. 4-22H). This could be screwed or dovetailed.

Drill for ¼-inch pivot bolts and stout woodscrews for pivots at the tops of the long legs.

Try the action of the legs. They should fold so the crossbar on the short legs fits inside the block where the other legs pivot. You may have to round the edge of that block to provide clearance.

Fig. 4-21. This junior ironing board looks like a full-size one.

Materials List for Junior Ironing Board

1 top	7 × 28 × ½	plywood
2 legs	¾ × 1½ × 37	
2 legs	¾ × 1½ × 30	
1 block	1½ × 1½ × 8	
3 blocks	¾ × 1½ × 8	
2 rails	¾ × 1½ × 11	
1 diagonal	¾ × 1½ × 20	

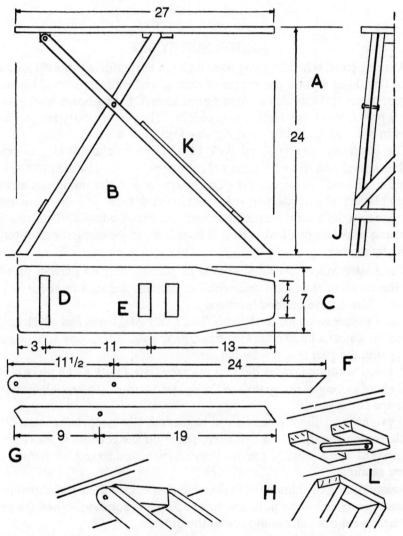

Fig. 4-22. Sizes and the arrangement of parts of the junior ironing board.

Assemble the legs to the top. Spread their lower ends to 2-inches wider than the top, and fit crossbars to hold this position (FIG. 4-22J). Put a diagonal brace on the outer legs to provide rigidity (FIG. 4-22K).

Fit a turnbutton to grip the top of the short legs and hold the assembled ironing board rigid (FIG. 4-22L).

Check that the ends of the legs stand level on the floor and trim them if necessary.

The top might be covered with cloth and a piece of hardboard or plastic put at the wide end for standing the iron on. Paint or varnish all the exposed woodwork.

JUNIOR PASTRY SET

A young cook, whether going right through to producing cooked food or just pretending, likes to have the means of mixing and rolling pastry. This means a wooden spoon and spatula for cleaning out a bowl, then a board with a roller for what is probably the most interesting process. The junior pastry set has all these things in reduced scale, but in serviceable form (FIG. 4-23).

The suggested pastry board (FIG. 4-23A) is of butcher block construction, which is strong and has a professional cook appearance. Use strips of any light-colored hardwood. To ensure the parts matching and the minimum amount of surface planing afterwards, join strips first in pairs; then, join the pairs until you have made up the width. Smooth surfaces and round edges and corners. When the young cook has finished with this board, it can be using for chopping and cutting by mother.

The pastry roller (FIG. 4-23B) should be turned with its parallel part longer than the width of the board and with the handles reduced to about ¾ inch in diameter. Use a close-grained hardwood.

Use a similar wood for the spatula (FIG. 4-23C). Make it ¼ inch thick and taper the end to almost a knife edge for scraping. You could thin one side in a similar way. Round the part that will be handled.

A wooden spoon is more difficult to shape (FIG. 4-23D). Cut a piece of ½-inch wood about as long as the spatula to the squared outline (FIG. 4-23E), and draw on the shape of the bowl.

If you have a lathe the handle can be turned. Without a lathe, start with the handle section square (FIG. 4-23F); then, plane off the corners to make a regular octagon (FIG. 4-23G). Finally, remove those corners and round the handle (FIG. 4-23H) by sanding.

Before cutting the outside of the bowl to shape, grip the parallel part in a vise and use a gouge to hollow it. Follow by scraping and sanding. When the inside is satisfactory, cut the outline and round the outside.

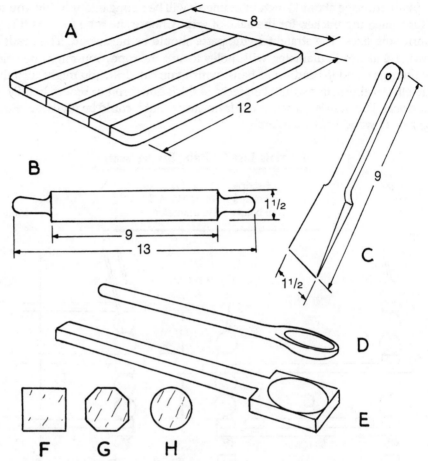

Fig. 4-23. This junior pastry set provides a child with a board, roller, a spatula, and a spoon.

BABY SWING SEAT

The smallest child wants to swing, particularly if he sees an older child swinging, but a simple straight seat would be unsafe for him and he should be secured in place. This seat (FIG. 4-24A) fits round the child and has a higher back, but the rails can all be lifted to put the baby in; then, it can be adjusted in height to suit his needs. The leg clearance can be anything from 3 inches upward; then the front rail will prevent falling forward.

The description here is for a seat only. It could hang from one of the climbing frames or swing structures already described, or be attached to a suitable bough or even a pole supported in some way. Such a young child does not need ropes as long as those of a bigger swing.

Synthetic rope about ¼ inch in diameter will be strong enough, but you may prefer something thicker, for the sake of grip. Choose the rope first, as this will govern hole sizes. The straight swing parts should be hardwood. The beads are shown 1½ inches in diameter, with holes to suit the rope. You might be able to buy them as wooden beads or as balls, which you can drill. You might turn them yourself. An alternative would be pieces of thick dowel rod or broom handle, left cylindrical. The base is shown made from strips, but it could be plywood. Round edges of all wood before assembly.

Materials List for Baby Swing Seat

5 strips	⅝ × 1¼ × 16	
9 strips	⅝ × 1¼ × 15	
16 beads	1½ diameter	

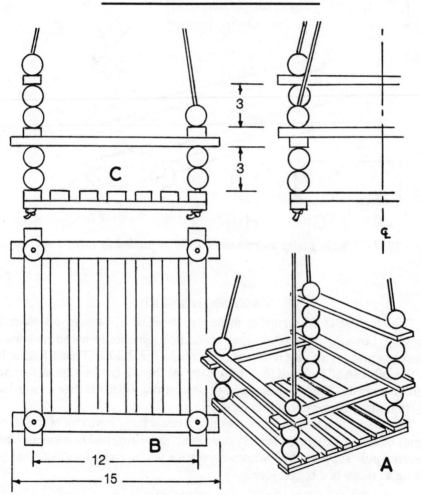

Fig. 4-24. *This baby swing seat can be adjusted and will hold a baby safely.*

The strips should be ⅝ inch × 1¼ inches, which is about the finished size of ¾ inch × 1½ inches. Cut five pieces 15 inches long, with holes 12 inches apart (FIG. 4-24B).

For the seat, cut nine pieces 13¼ inches long. Join them as seven pieces glued and nailed to the other two, to make a square. Drill the corners for rope at 12-inch centers (FIG. 4-24C).

Prepare sixteen beads or dowel spacers, with holes that will slide easily on the ropes.

Lightly countersink all holes above and below to reduce chafe on the rope and to allow easy sliding.

The beads could be painted a bright color to contrast with the colors of the other parts.

Although a rope could be taken down one hole and brought up another, this allows slipping and tilting; so it is better to knot under each seat hole.

NOAH'S ARK TOY BOX

A child may not be very inclined to put his toys away in an ordinary box, but if the box is disguised as something else, toy storage becomes more attractive. This box is in the form of a Noah's Ark and is on rollers, so it can be moved about (FIG. 4-25A). The roof opens in two parts to give access. The end decks can be used to put toys on, during play.

Box parts are stiffened plywood. The rollers and ends are solid wood. Plywood or hardwood provide that boat shape at the bottom.

Start with the box sides (FIG. 4-26A). They extend far enough to enclose the rollers and take the end blocks (FIG. 4-26B, C).

Make the bottom and ends to fit between the sides (FIG. 4-25B). Bevel the tops of the sides to match the slope of the roof. Assemble these parts with glue and fine nails, reinforced with strips inside (FIG. 4-26D).

The rollers are 2½ inches in diameter with a hole through to revolve on a ⅜-inch dowel rod. Turn them with rounded ends so they will not damage carpets. A roller should project ½ inch below the ark and have a ½-inch clearance between it, the box, and the end block. Mark and drill holes in the sides to allow for this (FIG. 4-25C and 26E).

Notch the end blocks (FIG. 4-26F, G) round the box side extensions.

Make a plywood top over each end (FIG. 4-26H). Fit the rollers on their waxed dowels, and assemble the ends.

Make plywood or hardboard boat sides (FIG. 4-26J) and ends (FIG. 4-26K), which may rise at the points to ½ inch above the deck.

The roof parts meet along the ridge and overhang ½ inch at the ends. The rear edge, which is hinged (FIG. 4-25D), should be level with the wall, but the front overhangs to provide a grip for lifting. Hinge the parts along the ridge and to the wall.

It would be unwise to cut windows and doors in the box, but you may improve appearance by painting them on when you paint all over.

Materials List for Noah's Ark Toy Box

2 sides	15 × 30 × ½	plywood
2 ends	12 × 16 × ½	plywood
1 bottom	12 × 21 × ½	plywood
2 roofs	7 × 23 × ½	plywood
2 end blocks	2½ × 8 × 13	
2 rollers	2½ × 2½ × 12	
2 axles	13 × ⅜	diameter
2 decks	10 × 13 × ½	plywood
2 sides	3 × 30 × ¼ or ⅛	plywood or hardboard
4 ends	4 × 9 × ¼ or ⅛	plywood or hardboard

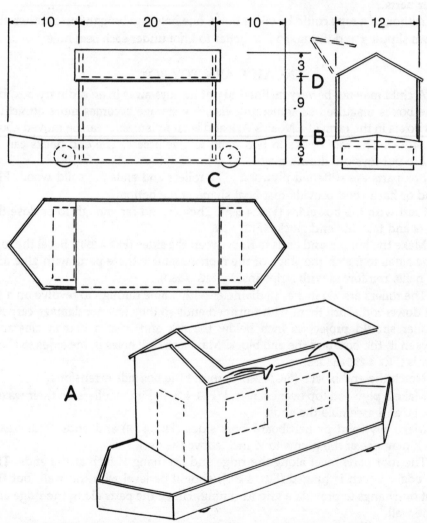

Fig. 4-25. *This is a toy box disguised as a Noah's Ark. The lid swings back, and the ark can be moved on rollers.*

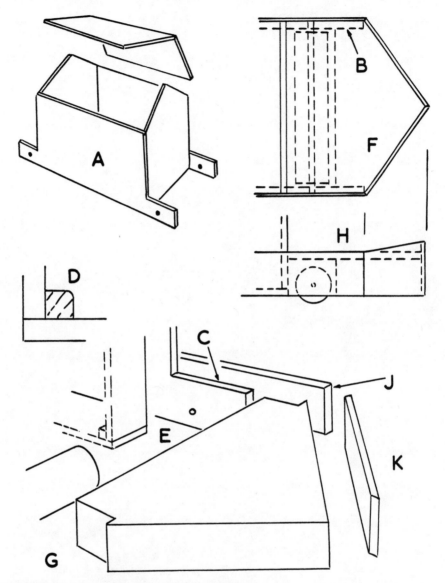

Fig. 4-26. *Construction of the Noah's Ark toy box.*

5

Moving Toys

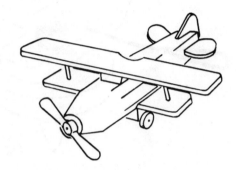

SPINNING TOP

A spinning top can provide a lot of enjoyment for a child—and probably his or her parents! Starting the top spinning can sometimes be a problem, but this top has a starting handle, which keeps it under control until it drops, to continue spinning freely for a long time.

The top and handle shown (FIGS. 5-1 and 5-2) are a size to be handled by a child aged about five years. It could be made larger for a more exciting spin for an older child.

All parts should be a close-grained hardwood. The top has a flywheel to maintain momentum and that could be a wooden toy wheel about 2½ inches in diameter. It might be cut from flat wood by careful work with a coping saw, but it would be better turned on a lathe, if you are unable to find a stock wheel. The spindle is a piece of ⅜-inch dowel rod. It fits into the lower part, made from ¾-inch dowel rod. This could also be trimmed to shape by hand, but would benefit from turning in a lathe.

Make the lower part of the top (FIG. 5-2A), tapered to about ⅛ inch and with a hole drilled centrally to take the dowel rod.

Drive a roundhead brad into the point. The top would work for some time without this, but if it is used on stone or concrete the brad will have less friction and will better resist wear (FIG. 5-2B).

Turn the flywheel or use a toy wheel (FIG. 5-2C) glued on the dowel rod spindle.

Make the handle (FIG. 5-2D). Mark it out and drill before shaping, with a 1-inch hole across for the end of the cutout. Drill through the other way, using a drill that will allow the dowel rod to turn easily and drop out when the cord

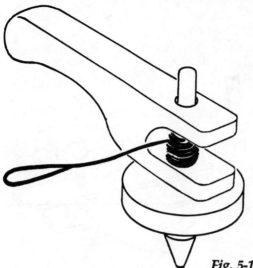

Fig. 5-1. *A spinning top with a starting handle.*

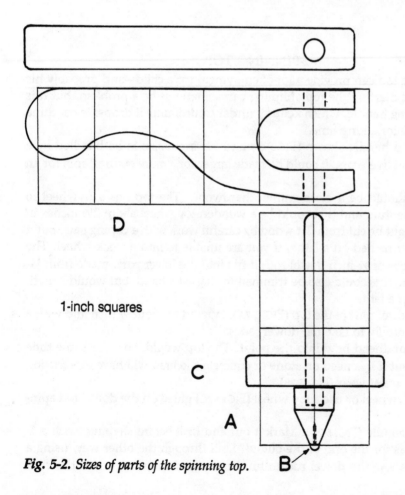

1-inch squares

D

C

A

B

Fig. 5-2. *Sizes of parts of the spinning top.*

releases and it is rotating. Cut away the opening and shape the outline. Note the small projection underneath around the spindle hole. That is to keep friction much less than there would be if the whole flat underside came against the flywheel. Either thoroughly round the part that will be gripped, or take the sharpness off the edges all round.

Try the parts together. Wax on the spindle and in the holes will serve as initial lubrication, but the parts will soon wear smoothly together.

To spin the top, use stout string or cord less than ⅛ inch diameter. A boot lace would also be suitable. A length of 24 inches is suggested for the first test. Tie a finger loop in one end. Put plenty of turns round the spindle in the gap in the handle. Hold firmly with one hand, having the top no more than 6-inches above the floor. Pull the cord hard with the other hand and you should be pleased with the result, as the top drops onto the floor while turning at high speed.

SAND WHEEL

Anything that can be made to move by a simple action will appeal to a young child. This sand wheel (FIG. 5-3) is intended to stand in a sand tray. Sand poured into the top will fall through onto the wheel and cause it to rotate, so the disc on the end spins and mixes the colors with which it is painted. The more sand that is scooped into the top, the faster the wheel will rotate. The toy could be used with water, if you can cope with the inevitable mess.

With the sizes shown (FIG. 5-4) the toy stands about 15 inches high and has a base about 10-inches square. Any wood can be used. Plywood should be exterior or marine grade and if you use particleboard, it should be the tempered type. In any case, protect everything with paint.

The blades of the wheel should be fairly thin, but they must be strong. Plywood ¼ inch thick would be rather clumsy. Aircraft plywood ⅛ inch thick could be used. Particleboard might not have a very long life. Rigid plastic, such as Plexiglas, would be suitable. Aluminum less than ⅛ inch thick would be satisfactory, if you well round all exposed edges.

The key part, which determines several other sizes is the wheel (FIG. 5-4A and 5-5A). The hub is a cylinder with a hole through it for the ⅜-inch dowel rod axle (FIG. 5-5B). If you have a lathe you can turn it, but otherwise you may use a section of tool handle, or something similar. Mark around it six equally spaced divisions.

Make the six blades (FIG. 5-5C). Make their lengths about ⅛ inch less than the length of the hub, so when the wheel turns they will not touch the uprights. Cut suitable slots, all to the same depths, in the hub, and glue the blades in. Glue in the dowel rod axle, with some excess at the ends, to trim to length later.

Make the top sand hopper (FIGS. 5-4B and 5-5D) with solid wood ends (FIG. 5-5E) and plywood back and front. A gap of ⅜ inch should allow sufficient flow of sand. Make the overall width about ⅛ inch more than the length of the wheel

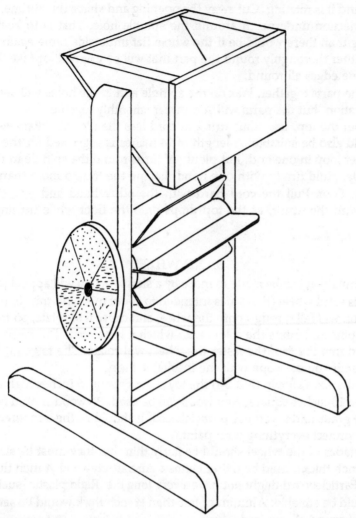

Fig. 5-3. *When sand is poured into the top of this toy, the wheel spins the colored disc rapidly.*

Materials List for Sand Wheel

1 wheel hub	7	×	1½ diameter	
6 wheel blades	⅛	×	2 × 7	
1 wheel axle	12	×	⅜ diameter	
2 hopper ends	½	×	4½ × 4½	
2 hopper sides	6	×	7 × ¼ plywood	
2 sides	¾	×	1½ × 15	
2 feet	¾	×	1½ × 11	
1 spacer	¾	×	1½ × 8	
1 disc	3	×	3 × ¼ plywood	

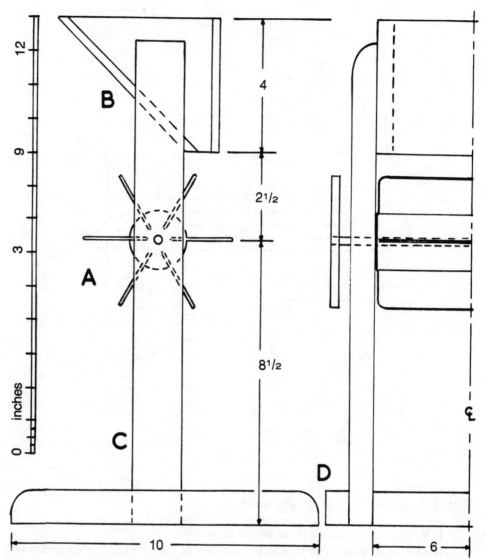

Fig. 5-4. *Sizes of the sand wheel toy.*

hub, so it will have ample clearance between the uprights. Well round all exposed edges of the hopper.

Make the pair of uprights (FIG. 5-4C), the feet (FIG. 5-4D), and the spacer between. It will probably be sufficient to glue and screw these parts together, but you could cut joints. Drill for the wheel axle, so it can rotate easily.

You could put a disc on each end of the axle, but one end will probably be enough. At the other end, cut the axle so it only projects a little way. At the disc end let it project about ½ inch and then through a ¼-inch, or thicker, plywood disc.

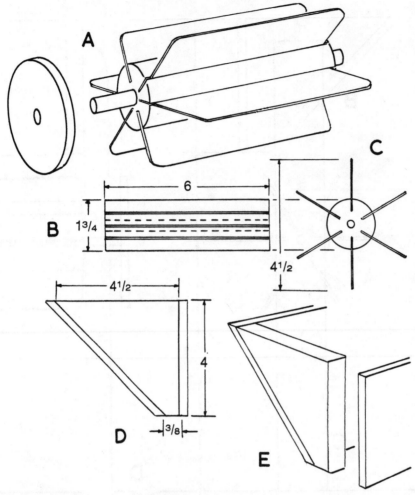

Fig. 5-5. Details of parts of the sand wheel toy.

It is simpler to paint all parts before assembly.

Assemble all parts. Put wax in the axle holes. Check that the assembly will stand upright and level.

Make a disc to glue on the end of the axle. Paint it in sections with contrasting colors.

VERTICAL SPINNING TOP

A method of starting a spinning top which some young users may find easier than the horizontal handle of the first one (FIGS. 5-1 and 5-2) has a vertical handle. Cord is wrapped round a spool on the top instead of round a piece of dowel rod; this gives more leverage for higher revolutions with fewer turns.

All of the parts are turned, but they can be formed on the smallest lathe. Hardwood is advisable. The more weight there is in the top, the better the flywheel effect to keep it spinning. It would be possible to turn the spindle of the top as part of the large part, but it is easier to use a piece of dowel rod in a hole.

Turn the body of the top with its upper end towards the tailstock (FIG. 5-6A).

Before reducing the bottom to size, drill for the dowel rod with a drill in the tailstock chuck (FIG. 5-6B). A 5/16-inch-diameter rod would be suitable.

Complete turning by reducing the end to little more than the diameter of the roundheaded nail that will be driven in (FIG. 5-6C).

Turn the dowel spindle with a tapered end (FIG. 5-6D).

Materials List for Vertical Spinning Top

1 body	3½ × 3½ × 5	
1 spindle	3 × 5/16 diameter	
1 handle	1 × 1 × 3	

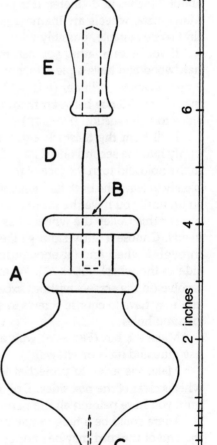

Fig. 5-6. This spinning top with a vertical handle is made completely on a lathe.

Make the handle (FIG. 5-6E) with a hole that is an easy fit, and which allows the dowel end to rest at its bottom; this will cause less friction than letting the end of the handle rest on the top.

Glue in the dowel rod and drive in the nail. Some wax or candle fat in the hole will lubricate the moving parts.

When you are satisfied with the performance of the top, paint it in bright colors, but leave the spindle untreated.

TROLLEY

A young child will get as much enjoyment out of a box on wheels as he or she will from a more elaborate pull-along toy, which may seem much more attractive to adult eyes. The box can be loaded with building bricks or sand and move about; this trolley (FIG. 5-7A) is just that. It is big enough to be used, but not so large that the child cannot pick it up. He may be happy turning it over and playing with the wheels.

General sizes are determined by the size of the wheels. They should be about 2 inches in diameter. It is possible to buy them, made of wood or plastic. Many metal wheels are inadvisable for a child's first wheeled toy, but you may find some suitable, possibly with rubber tires.

If you have a lathe, you can make a set of wheels. Choose a close-grained hardwood and have a piece longer than needed for the four wheels. Turn it to a 2-inch-diameter cylinder (FIG. 5-7B). Mark the thicknesses of the wheels and cut in a short distance between them with a parting tool (FIG. 5-7C). Shape the outsides to a tire section (FIG. 5-7D).

Drill from the tailstock end far enough to go through the first wheel and partly into the second one (FIG. 5-7E). Support the wood with the tailstock center in the hole and turn the face of the first wheel (FIG. 5-7F). Part off that wheel completely to leave the back flat. Repeat the operations to form the second wheel and so on until you have the set of four.

For this trolley the wheel axles can be strong screws, preferably with round heads. Choose a fairly stout gauge—#14 would be suitable—and a length to go through a wheel and far enough into the wood to be safe. Put washers on each side of the wheel (FIG. 5-7G). When you drill the wheels, make holes that will revolve on the screws without excessive slackness. With manufactured wheels, you may have to choose screws to suit the existing holes or open out the manufactured holes.

Make the box (FIG. 5-7H) with any joints that you wish. For a painted finish use glue and nails or screws.

Make the axles to project at least ⅛ inch each side (FIG. 5-7J) to keep the wheels clear of the box sides. Drill for the axle screws, but don't add the wheels until you have painted all the parts.

There could be a hole in one end to take a cord for pulling along. A loop in the end of the cord may be enough, or you could make a handle with a piece of dowel rod drilled across its center for the cord.

Materials List for Trolley

2 sides	½ × 2 × 13
2 ends	½ × 2 × 6
1 bottom	½ × 6 × 13
2 axles	1 × 1 × 7
wheels from	2 × 2 × 8

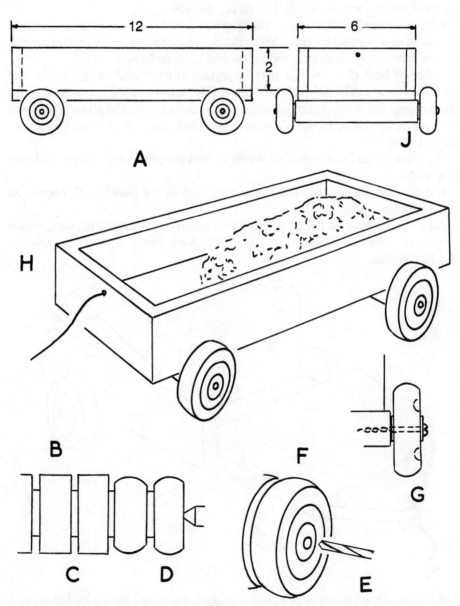

Fig. 5-7. Details of a pull-along trolley with turned wheels.

SIMPLE TRUCK

As with the trolley just described, a very young child will be happy with a very simple toy. If it only has a basic shape, it is less likely to be damaged and there will be no small parts to come off and possibly hurt the child.

A truck, which can be rolled about and has the general appearance of the real thing, will carry a load and be durable. This truck (FIG. 5-8) has a base similar to that of the trolley. The rear part takes the load and three pieces at the front will have a sufficiently authentic effect to satisfy the young user.

Wheels determine other sizes. You may buy 2-inch wood or plastic wheels or make them as described for the trolley (FIG. 5-7). Most parts could be ½-inch plywood or solid wood. Assemble with glue and nails or screws.

Make the base (FIG. 5-9A). It may be square at front and back, or you may extend it so there can be holes. A hole at the front allows a cord to be attached for pulling along (FIG. 5-9B). A similar extension at the back would allow a trailer to be tied on. Make the trolley with a similar extended base, which would become a suitable trailer.

The block at the front is the full width of the base (FIG. 5-9C). Shape it further if you wish.

The cab and the seat are also the same width as the base. Nail or screw all three pieces from below.

Put a piece across the back (FIG. 5-9D) and add the two sides (FIG. 5-9E), which may extend to form the sides to the seat (FIG. 5-9F), these sides go outside the edges of the base.

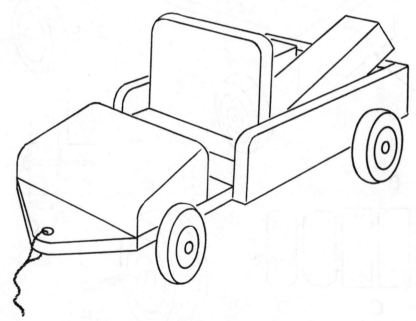

Fig. 5-8. This simple truck may be pulled or pushed, and it will carry a load of blocks.

Materials List for Simple Truck

1 base	½ ×	5	×	13
1 block	2 ×	3	×	6
2 sides	½ ×	2½	×	9
1 block	½ ×	2	×	6
1 cab	½ ×	5	×	6
1 seat	1 ×	1	×	6
wheels from	2 ×	2	×	8

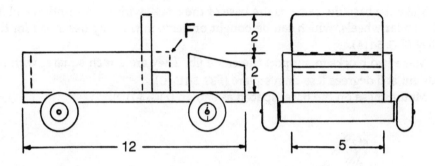

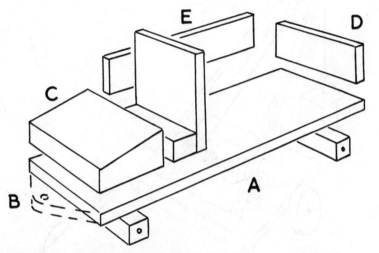

Fig. 5-9. Sizes and arrangement of the parts of the truck.

Put blocks across underneath. The rear one is longer than the front one, but let both extend about ⅛ inch each side to give the wheels clearance.

Fit the wheels on screws with washers in the same way as described for the trolley.

Paint the truck one color all over or paint a different inside color. Lamps and other features could be painted on. Decorations could go on the sides.

SMALL CRANE

If a child has a truck or trolley to carry things, he will be glad to also have a crane to lift things on and off. It does not have to be very elaborate. This crane (FIG. 5-10) is intended to be a matching toy to the trolley and truck just described. It is a similar size and can be moved about on wheels. It reaches high enough to lift most articles clear of the carrier sides.

The base is the same as for the truck, and it could be made mainly of ½-inch plywood or solid wood. The crane parts are a light section and may be better made of hardwood, but straight-grained softwood should be satisfactory.

Make the base the same as the base of the truck, with blocks underneath to take similar wheels, which can be bought or made in the way described for the trolley (FIG. 5-11A).

Make two blocks to support the crane jib. They are 1 inch square, with the ends cut at 5 degrees less than square (FIG. 5-11B, C).

Mount these on the base, spaced as shown (FIG. 5-11D).

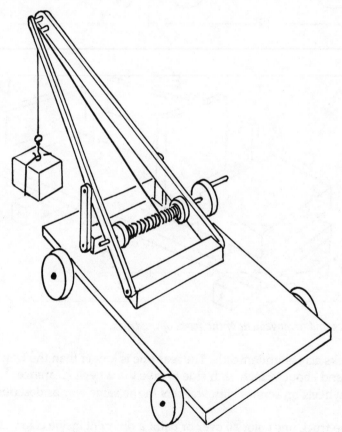

Fig. 5-10. A crane can be used to unload the trolley or truck.

Make the pair of jib arms (FIG. 5-11E) and the pair of supports (FIG. 5-11F). At the end of the jib are two holes for ¼-inch dowel rods (FIG. 5-11G). The hole, 3 inches from the other end, is for the ¼-inch dowel rod through the windlass. The other holes are for screws. The holes in the supports are also for screws.

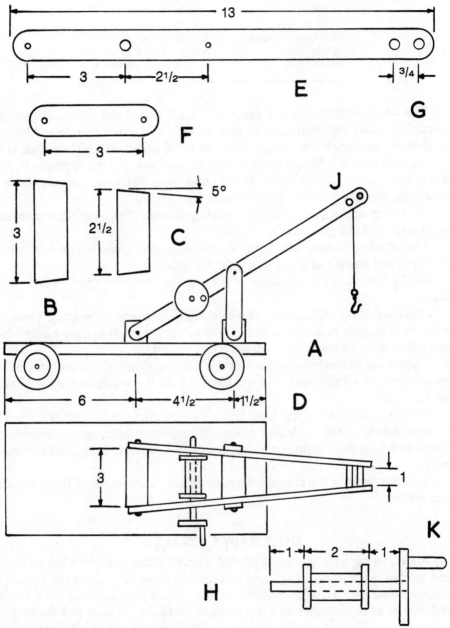

Fig. 5-11. The parts of the small crane.

1 base	½ × 5 × 13
2 blocks	1 × 1 × 6
2 crane blocks from	1 × 1 × 8
wheels from	2 × 2 × 8
2 jibs	¼ × ¾ × 15
2 jib supports	¼ × ¾ × 6
1 windlass drum	3 × ¾ diameter
parts from	10 × ¼ diameter
discs from	2 × 8 × ¼ plywood

The windlass (FIG. 5-11H) is made of ¾-inch dowel rod with a ¼-inch rod through it. Make plywood discs to glue on each end of the ¾-inch rod to keep cord on the winding drum. Allow the ¼-inch rod to extend 1 inch at each end.

Screw the ends of the jib to their block on the base and the supports to their block; then, screw to each other. At the same time, insert the windlass ends. If necessary, ease the holes so the axle rotates easily.

At the top of the jib glue in the two short dowels (FIG. 5-11J). Clamp there if necessary, until the glue has set.

The windlass handle (FIG. 5-11K) is a plywood disc glued to the axle, with a short piece of dowel rod glued in a hole, for winding.

Drill a hole in one of the discs of the winding drum to take the end of the cord.

The hook at the other end of the cord might be made by twisting a piece of wire about ¹⁄₁₆ inch in diameter. If this is not heavy enough to drop easily when unloaded, thread a heavy bead on the cord above it.

There is no ratchet provided to lock the winding drum up, as that may be too complicated for a young user. He will have to hold the windlass handle to keep the load up.

A hole in one end of the base will allow the crane to be pulled or tied to another vehicle. With truck and trolley the three vehicles can be linked and towed to where the young contractor wants to load or unload bricks or other items.

Paint the parts of the crane, preferably to match any other of these vehicles you make.

DOLL BABY CARRIAGE

A girl playing with a doll will wish to wheel it about in its own baby carriage and be able to adjust bedding, raise and lower a hood, and generally behave as mother would with a child. This baby carriage (FIG. 5-12) is intended for a toddler and may be suitable for her for a few years. It could also be used as a walking aid for a beginner. The body of the carriage is 12 inches × 24 inches. The handle is 27 inches above the floor, if 6-inch wheels are fitted. Try these sizes in relation to

Fig. 5-12. This doll baby carriage is all-wood construction.

your child. Allow for growing, but you might wish to modify some of the sizes.

Main parts, including the hood, are made from ½-inch plywood. The chassis sides fit between the body sides and under its base. The handles and hood come outside the body. The parts which are seen in side view are the important ones, and they should be made first.

The three views of the baby carriage show the general layout. The side view (FIG. 5-13A) should be used as a reference for sizes of the main parts. The plan view (FIG. 5-13B) is without the handle and hood. The end view is a section (FIG. 5-13C) and shows the chassis parts and base of the carriage between the sides. For the outline of the shaped parts, refer to FIG. 5-14. Except for the hood and handle, the carriage is symmetrical about the centerline.

Mark out and cut the two body sides (FIGS. 5-13D and 5-14A). Mark on them the positions of the other parts.

Make the two chassis sides (FIGS. 5-13E and 5-14B). Note that the top edges come against the body base and between the strips on the plywood ends.

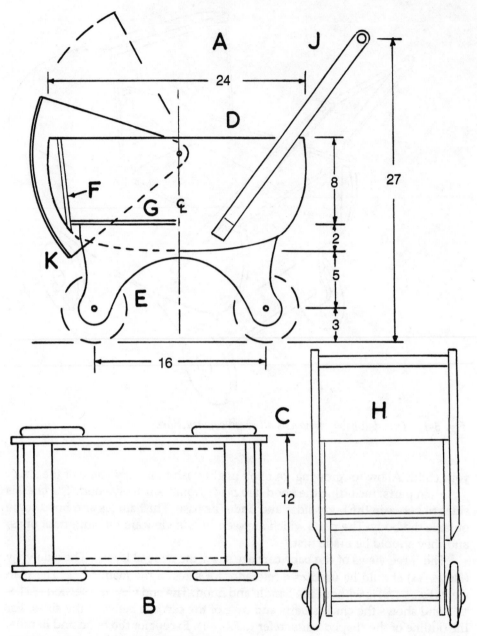

Fig. 5-13. Sizes of the doll baby carriage.

At the ends of the sides, add the pieces that will support the ends (FIG. 5-15A). Their inner edges follow the line of the plywood end, and the outer edges are shaped to match the side plywood.

Cut the plywood ends (FIGS. 5-13F and 5-14C) with their bottom edges shaped to match the curve of the body sides.

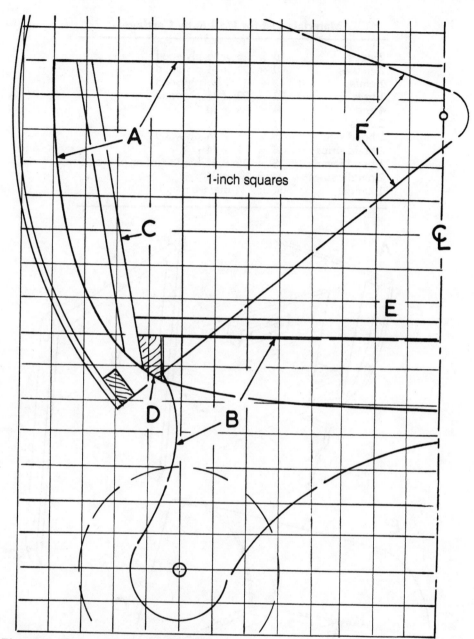

Fig. 5-14. *Shapes of parts of the doll baby carriage.*

Put pieces across to support the base (FIG. 5-14D), also shaped to the curve of the sides.

Fit the ends between the sides with glue and fine nails.

Fit the chassis sides by screwing from inside to the body sides. They should come up to the base line and fit between the strips across the ends.

Materials List for Doll Baby Carriage

2 sides	10	× 26 × ½	plywood
2 chassis	9	× 22 × ½	plywood
2 ends	10	× 12 × ½	plywood
1 base	12	× 22 × ½	plywood
4 ends	¾	× 1¼ × 10	
2 ends	1	× 1 × 10	
2 hood sides	15	× 15 × ½	plywood
2 hood strips	½	× 1 × 14	
1 hood cover	15	× 15 × ⅛	hardboard or plywood
2 handle sides	⅝	× 1¼ × 24	
1 handle	14	× ¾ diameter	

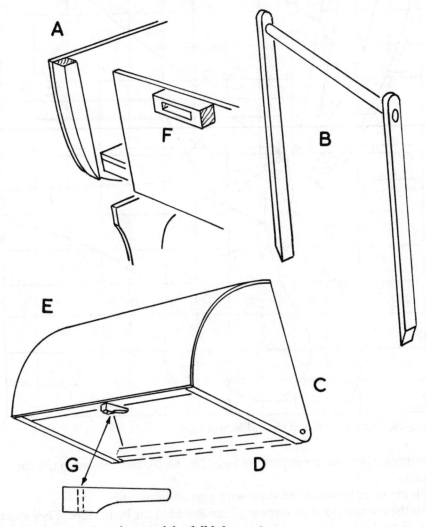

Fig. 5-15. *Construction of parts of the doll baby carriage.*

Make the base (FIGS. 5-13G and 5-14E) to fit closely. Glue and pin it in place. Make sure that the whole assembly is square, and check for twist by sighting across the top edges.

It should be satisfactory to leave the top edges of the body with the piles exposed, if you round and sand them well before painting. The alternative would be to put on solid wood lips before assembly. Round and smooth all edges and corners.

The handle is made with two flat sides and a piece of dowel rod across the top (FIGS. 5-13H, J and 5-15B). The exact location is not important and may be found by experimenting. It will be stronger to take the dowel rod right through the sides. Attach the handle sides to the body sides with glue and screws from the inside.

The hood sides (FIGS. 5-13K and 5-15C) are sections of a circle pivoted on screws on the centerline of the body sides. In the lowered position, the hood rests against the chassis sides with the top only a little way above the body edge. When raised, the hood edge is not quite upright, but it covers nearly half of the carriage.

Cut the two hood sides (FIG. 5-14F). Drill for pivot screws.

Make two pieces to go between the ends of the curve. Glue and nail them there. At the same time put a strip of scrap wood between the pivot corners with temporary screws to hold it (FIG. 5-15D).

Make a piece of hardboard or ⅛-inch plywood to bend round the curve (FIG. 5-15E). Plywood will bend easier if its outer grain is crosswise. Moistening will help bending if the material will not go round dry.

Use glue and screws into the strips and pins into the edges of the plywood sectors. Start at one end. Pull round gradually, preferably with help, to hold while you screw and nail. You might need clamps on the strips as well, until the glue has set.

To keep the hood in the up position there is a grooved block and a turnbutton. Make the block to go centrally on the carriage end (FIG. 5-15F). Remove the temporary piece from the hood and pivot it temporarily on two awls or screws. This will allow you to check the shape and length of a turnbutton to engage with the groove in the block. Make the turnbutton (FIG. 5-15G) and fit it with a screw and washer under the edge of the hood. Try the action of the hood in up and down positions; then, remove it for painting.

Wheels with tires will probably be intended for ⅜-inch-diameter steel axles, which you might buy at the same time. You might have to check on the method of fitting particular wheels. If there is no other arrangement, you will have to mount the wheels with washers inside and outside; then, drill across for a cotter pin to secure each wheel. Let the steel axles be tight in the wood chassis sides, as they do not have to rotate.

Paint all over, but you might use several colors. A light cream color inside is appropriate. The outside could be darker, with the hood a different shade from the rest of the carriage.

The hood could pivot on bolts taken right through or on stout wood screws. Put washers under the heads and between the wood parts.

LUMBER WAGON

Something that can be pulled about, which carries a load that can be used in various ways, will appeal to a toddler. This lumber wagon (FIG. 5-16) carries six boards which could be used alone or with building bricks to make houses and forts or bridges for other wheeled toys to cross. When the job is finished, the boards can be loaded up and towed elsewhere.

The wagon is shown with a handle which steers the front wheels. Alternatively, the extension could be made with a hole instead of a slot so it could be hooked onto another wheeled toy, such as a truck. The sizes drawn (FIG. 5-17A) are based on 2-inch wheels, which you may turn yourself or buy, but get the wheels first in case you have to make any adjustments to size to suit different wheels. It would be advisable to make the wagon of hardwood, but the boards could be softwood.

Make the base (FIGS. 5-17B and 5-18A) and drill it for ½-inch dowel rods.

The wheels have to clear the underside of the base by about ½ inch and their centers must be at the same height.

Make the bogey piece (FIGS. 5-17C and 5-18B) with a 1-inch slot for the handle.

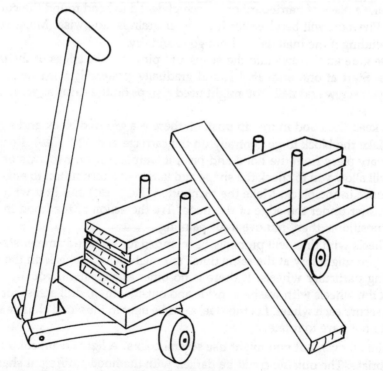

Fig. 5-16. *A pull-along and steerable child's lumber wagon.*

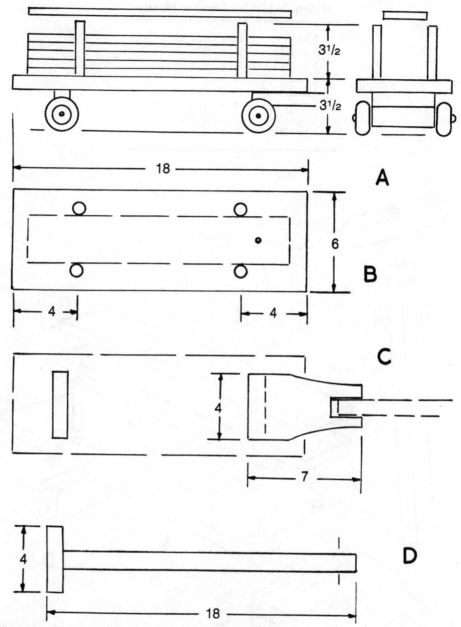

Fig. 5-17. *Suggested sizes for parts of the lumber wagon.*

Put a block underneath it (FIG. 5-18C) and another block at the other end of the base (FIG. 5-18D), with their wheel pivot centers at the same distance below the base.

Fit the rear block to the base, and drill for a bolt or screw to form the pivot for the bogey.

Materials List for Lumber Wagon

1 base	¾ × 6 × 20
6 boards	½ × 3 × 18
1 bogey	¾ × 4 × 9
1 axle	1 × 1 × 6
1 axle	1 × 2 × 6
4 supports	5 × ½ diameter
1 handle	1 × 1 × 20
1 handle	1 × 1 × 6

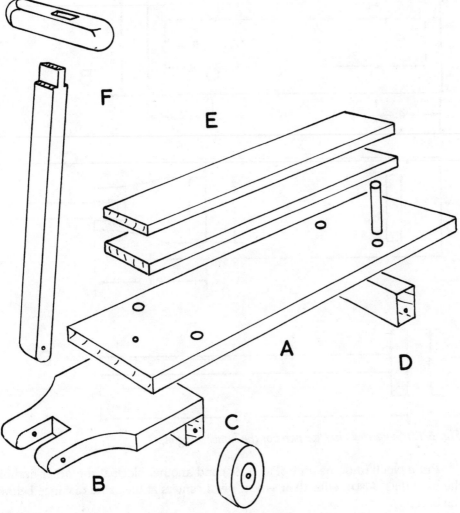

Fig. 5-18. Arrangement of the parts of the lumber wagon.

The dowel lumber supports should have their tops rounded, if possible, or sharpness should be taken off. Make the boards to fit reasonably tight between them (FIG. 5-18E), so they do not slip when being towed.

The handle (FIG. 5-17D) is a square strip with a T piece at the top. The best way of joining this is with a mortise-and-tenon joint (FIG. 5-18F). Join the handle with a bolt or screw through the bogey piece. Make sure it clears the corners of the base when pulled round.

Mount the wheels on screws with washers each side.

Paint all the wagon parts, but the load of boards may be left plain. Round their corners and edges, so there are no rough edges that might scratch small hands.

PULL-ALONG DUCKS

The youngest toddler enjoys something to pull along, preferably of a pattern which he can recognize, if only from a picture. These ducks on wheels (FIG. 5-19) can be painted brightly and pulled with a cord. There could be just one duck, or you could make mother duck and as many ducklings as you like to follow her.

The duck bodies maybe ½-inch or thicker plywood. The wings are ¼-inch plywood or solid wood. The bases are solid wood ½ inch or thicker, and the wheels are 2 inches in diameter.

Fig. 5-19. You can arrange a mother duck and her ducklings as a pull-along toy.

Decide on the size you want. If you treat the squares as 1 inch, the duck body is about 5 inches × 8 inches (FIG. 5-20). This is a suitable size for a single toy or for the mother duck, if there will be others. The ducklings could be the same shape, but based on ½-inch squares.

Jigsaw or fretsaw the bodies to shape. Cut out the wings and glue them on. Smooth all edges before assembly.

Make the bases. They should be wide enough for stability—3 inches would be satisfactory.

Attach the body to its base with two screws from below.

The wheels might be colored plastic, but plain wooden ones would be satisfactory. Emphasis should be on the bird, and plain wheels would not detract from it.

Mount the wheels on screws with washers on each side of a wheel.

Put a stout screw eye in the front to take the towing cord. If you want to link several ducks put screw eyes in each part. Then force one open to link with the other and squeeze it closed again, if you want the linkage to be permanent. If the young user will be able to hook and unhook them himself, use a screw hook instead of one eye at each joint.

Much of the appeal of bird toys is in the colors. The base may be blue for water, there should be a yellow beak and black eyes, with the rest of the bird white, grey, or brown.

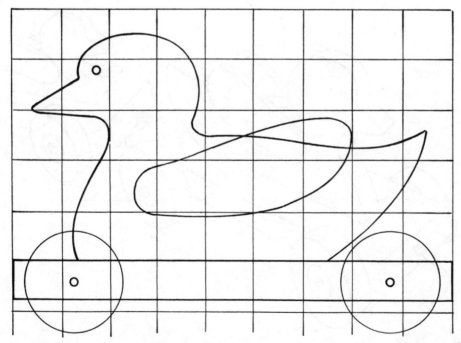

Fig. 5-20. *Outline of a duck and its trolley.*

TUG AND BARGE

Toys to push about the floor can be woven into many different games and adventures in a young mind. Boats can have voyages across the room and be brought into harbors made of anything available. This tug and barge (FIG. 5-21) are intended to slide on the floor, rather than float in water, although they would float. They are drawn 12 inches long, but you could make them any size to suit the children or available wood. There is a tug and one barge (FIG. 5-22A), but you could have any number of barges behind the tug. The barges are plain, but they could be made to hold cargoes.

Wood at least 1 inch thick should be used for the hulls. Softwood should be satisfactory, if it is a type that does not easily splinter when knocked.

Use the half drawing (FIG. 5-22B) to draw the outline of the tug hull. Cut the sides vertical, but the stern looks better sloped a little—10 to 15 degrees would be suitable (FIG. 5-22C).

The wheelhouse is a 1½-inch block cut to slope at about 10 degrees and with a thin piece as a roof (FIG. 5-22D) parallel with the deck.

Mount a parallel block as engine room behind it and drill it for a ¾-inch-diameter dowel funnel (FIG. 5-22E) at the same angle as the wheelhouse. Glue and a few fine nails should hold these parts together.

Use the other half drawing (FIG. 5-22F) to draw the shape of a barge. Cut this with the sides upright and the ends undercut in the same way as the stern of the tug.

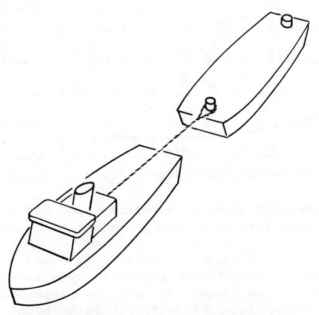

Fig. 5-21. *You can push a tug and one or more barges along the floor.*

Materials List for Tug and One Barge

2 hulls	1¼ × 5½ × 14
deck houses from	1½ × 2 × 6
1 funnel	4 × ¾ diameter
bollards from	4 × ⅜ diameter

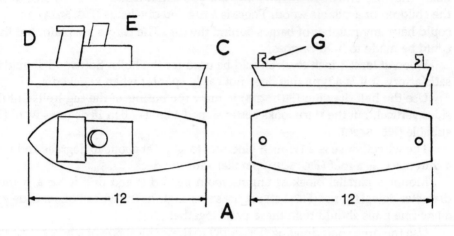

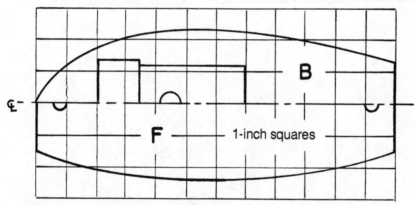

Fig. 5-22. Layout and sizes of tug and barge.

Drill for ⅜-inch dowel rods at the ends of the barge. They act as bollards to take a towing cord. To reduce the risk of the cord coming off, notch each bollard (FIG. 5-22G).

A tug tows from near its center. Put a screw eye in the back of the wheelhouse. Prepare a cord with a loop to drop over a barge bollard and tie the other end to the tug screw eye. If there are other barges, have looped lines to join them.

The funnel should be painted a bright color. The deck houses could be white or cream. The decks could be a light brown and the hull sides black. Keep the bottoms of the hulls smooth and free from paint.

WHEELBARROW

If a child sees an adult moving things about in the garden with a wheelbarrow, he will want to help and will appreciate a scaled-down wheelbarrow so he can move his own load. It will also be useful for taking other toys about the yard or even indoors. The suggested design (FIG. 5-23) is open towards the back, for easy loading. If he wants to move very much soil or sand, there could be a board across, either permanently or in slots.

Fig. 5-23. An all-wood toy wheelbarrow has a lift-out back.

The sides could be ½-inch plywood. The bottom and front could be ¾-inch solid wood or plywood. All other parts are solid wood. The 6-inch wheel might be bought, or you could cut a disc from 1-inch wood. If you can turn it on a lathe, that would be ideal, but a carefully sawn disc should be satisfactory for this barrow.

Start by making the bottom (FIG. 5-24A). Draw a centerline on its underside and use the strips that will form the handles to lay out their positions. At the forward ends they have to be beveled to fit each side of the wheel (FIG. 5-24B). Their other ends will be about 12 inches apart. Check that their position lines drawn on the bottom are symmetrical about the centerline.

Make the pair of handles (FIG. 5-24C). Reduce the handle ends to half depth and round them, blending into full depth so as to provide comfortable grips. Mark the positions of the legs and the bottom.

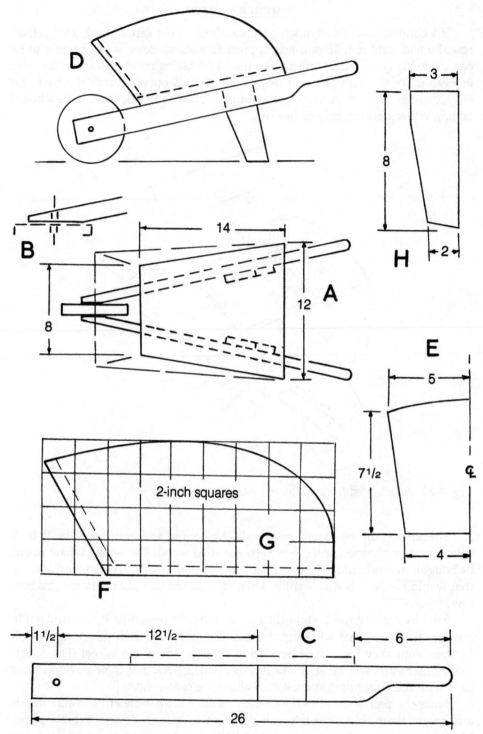

Fig. 5-24. *Sizes and details of the wheelbarrow.*

Materials List for Wheelbarrow

1 bottom	¾ × 12 × 16
2 handles	1 × 2 × 28
1 front	¾ × 8 × 12
2 legs	¾ × 3 × 10
2 sides	8 × 20 × ½ plywood
1 wheel	1 × 6 diameter

While in position on the bottom, mark the bevel on the ends to fit each side of the wheel and mark for drilling through. Use a piece of steel rod to suit the hole in the wheel or a bolt of a suitable size. You might even use a hardwood dowel as an axle.

Cut the front (FIG. 5-24D, E). Bevel its lower edge to fit against the bottom (FIG. 5-24F). There will have to be slight bevels at the sides, but they are best found by temporarily assembling with the barrow sides on the bottom.

Cut the two sides (FIG. 5-24G). Round their top edges and the top edge of the front.

Screw from below the bottom into the front and screw or nail the sides to the bottom and the front. Level the edges and take off the sharpness all round.

Make the two legs (FIG. 5-24H). Final cutting of the bottoms should be left until after assembly to see how the wheelbarrow stands. Then, bevel all round so the risk of splintering on rough ground is reduced.

Glue and screw the legs to the handles and those to the bottom and fit the wheel.

To fit a removable board at the back, put two guide strips each side to form grooves, and make a board to drop into them (FIG. 5-23).

If the wheelbarrow is to be left outside, treat it with preservative. Paint it all over, preferably in a bright color, but the young owner might want it to look functional rather than decorative if he is to imagine himself as a workman.

TIPPING BARROW

A young child may have difficulty in handling a normal wheelbarrow, with its single wheel, particularly when carrying what is a heavy load for him. Although the barrow can be tipped to shoot its load forward, he may not always manage to get everything out as he expects. It may be better for him to have a barrow on two wheels. It is more stable and can be tilted without risk of wobbling out of line. It cannot be used on narrow paths where the single wheel would go, but in the size needed by a child, the overall width is not great.

This tipping barrow (FIG. 5-25) is about 10 inches × 20 inches and has its handles about 14 inches above the floor when standing on its wheels and leg (FIG. 5-26). The wheels are 5 inches in diameter. If it would be better for your child to have handles higher or lower, you can alter the height at the sides or choose wheels of different sizes.

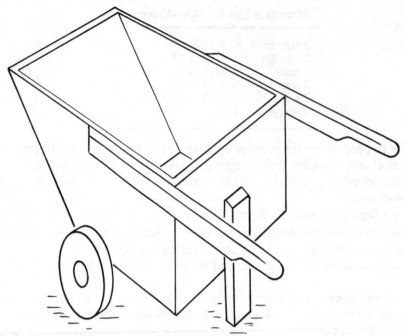

Fig. 5-25. This tipping barrow has two wheels.

The barrow could be made completely of solid wood, but plywood is suggested for the sides. The other parts could be any wood, but avoid heavy hardwoods which would make the barrow difficult to tip and push. A normal load comes behind the wheels, so there is no fear of it tipping accidentally, but when the user wants to shoot out the load, he can push up the handles so the front rests on the floor (FIG. 5-26A).

Most sizes are based on a 10-inch unit, but check your available wood and adjust sizes to suit, as minor variations do not matter. In the following instructions it is assumed that the wheels are 5 inches in diameter to fit on a ⅜-inch diameter steel rod axle. It would be advisable to get your wheels first, in case any modifications are needed.

Mark out the pair of sides first (FIG. 5-26B, C), allowing for overlaps on the other parts, but do not cut to size yet as you may have to allow for slight differences during assembly.

Make the bottom (FIG. 5-26D) and the back (FIG. 5-26E), which are plain rectangles.

Use your side setting out to get the size and angle of the front (FIG. 5-26F).

Assemble the body with glue and screws up through the bottom, and nails or small screws through the sides. It is advisable to use closer and extra long screws near the top corners, where most strain will come in use. Plane edges level and round all corners.

Put a strip across above where the axle will come (FIG. 5-26G), so its ends project ½ inch to keep the wheels clear of the sides.

Below this put two blocks drilled for the axle (FIG. 5-26H).

Make the handles to reach halfway along the sides. Reduce the ends to square and then round them (FIG. 5-26J, K). Screw the handles to the sides at the height you require.

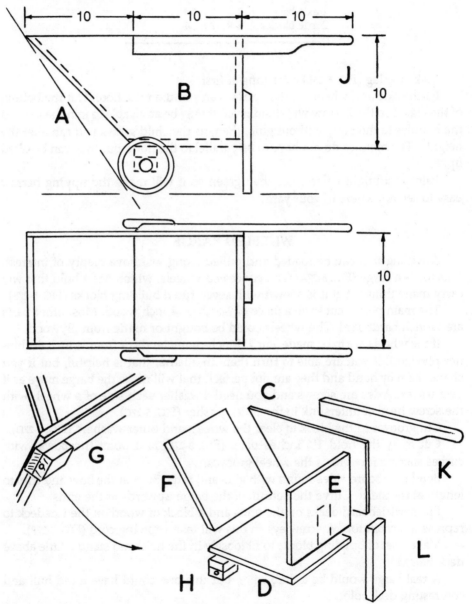

Fig. 5-26. Sizes and arrangement of the tipping barrow.

Materials List for Tipping Barrow

2 sides	10 × 20 × ½ plywood
1 bottom	10 × 12 × ¾
1 back	10 × 12 × ¾
1 front	10 × 15 × ¾
2 handles	1 × 2 × 22
1 leg	1 × 2 × 12
1 axle bar	1 × 2 × 13
2 axle blocks	1 × 2 × 4

Make the leg (FIG. 5-26L) extra long at first.

Fit the axle and wheels so the barrow can stand on the floor. Cut the bottom of the leg off so the barrow will stand level. It may be advisable to join the leg and the handles to the body without glue; then, as the child grows you can alter the heights. The handles do not have to be parallel to the floor, but they can be tilted up.

Paint in a bright color other than green so it will make the tipping barrow easy to see anywhere in your yard.

WHEELED BARGE

Anything that can be loaded and pulled along will have plenty of interest. This toy is a barge (FIG. 5-27A) with concealed wheels, which has a hold that will carry many things, but it is shown with seven fitted building blocks (FIG. 5-27B).

The main part is cut from a piece of 2-inch- × -4-inch wood. Most other parts are ⅛-inch hardboard. The wheels could be bought or made from plywood.

If the wheels are to be made, cut 1½-inch-diameter discs from ½ inch or thinner plywood. If you are able to turn them in a lathe, that is helpful, but if you shape them by hand and they are not perfect, that will make the barge move as if over waves. Axles are screws and you need a washer each side of a wheel, with the screw head countersunk in the outer washer (FIG. 5-27C).

Cut grooves in the block to clear the wheels and outer washers (FIG. 5-27D).

Cut away the hold 1¼ inches deep (FIG. 5-27E) and point the bows, with curves starting forward of the wheel grooves.

Bend hardboard sides round with glue and pins. Start at the bow and trim to length at the stern. Curve the bottom of the barge upwards at the ends.

Put particleboard decks on the ends and a block of wood on the foredeck to represent a cabin top. A screw eye in this will take a towing cord (FIG. 5-27F).

Make a set of building blocks to fit loosely in the hold and stand a little above deck height.

A real barge would be a drab color, but this one could have a red hull and contrasting deck color.

Materials List for Wheeled Barge

1 hull	$2 \times 4 \times 18$
2 sides	$2 \times 20 \times \frac{1}{8}$ hardboard
2 decks from	$5 \times 12 \times \frac{1}{8}$ hardboard
1 block	$\frac{1}{2} \times 2 \times 6$

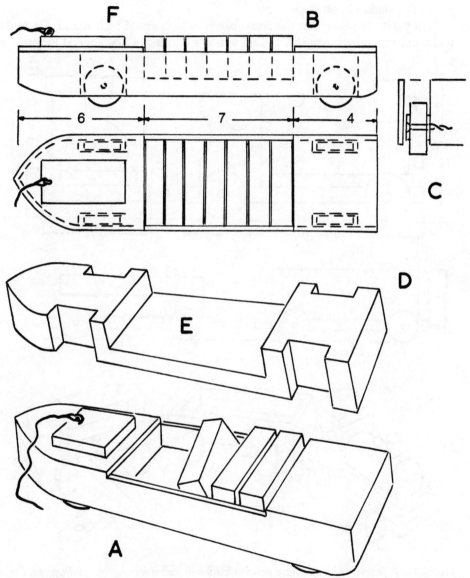

Fig. 5-27. This pull-along barge will carry a load of blocks.

FREIGHT TRAIN

Steam locomotives may be almost things of the past, but in the world of children's toys they live on as being of much more interest than their modern diesel or electric counterparts. The steam locomotive features in many children's stories, so a child knows what it is when he sees a steam engine toy. This freight train (FIG. 5-28A) is intended to pull along. The rolling stock can be hooked or unhooked easily. There could be any number of freight cars and you can use your imagination in other designs.

All parts are shown on the same bases, which are ½-inch wood, 3½ inches wide, cut into 8-inch lengths, unless you want to make any special longer cars.

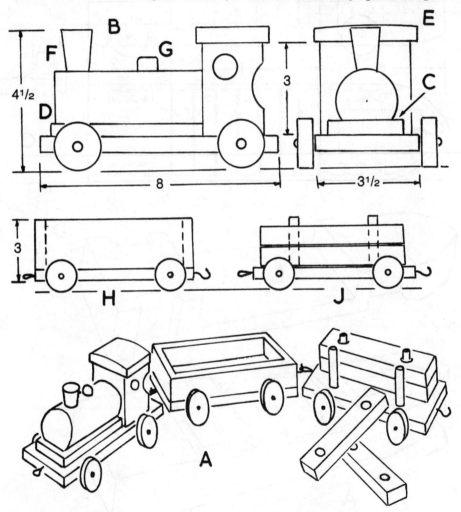

Fig. 5-28. *A freight train can have an old-fashioned steam locomotive and several cars of different types.*

Materials List for Freight Train

Locomotive

1 base	½ × 3½ × 8
1 block	½ × 3 × 6
1 block	2 × 3 × 4
1 roof	½ × 2¾ × 4
4 wheels	1½ diameter

Freight Car

1 base	½ × 3½ × 8
2 sides	½ × 2½ × 8
2 ends	½ × 2½ × 4
4 wheels	1½ diameter

Lumber Wagon

1 base	½ × 3½ × 8
4 blocks	¾ × 1¼ × 8
4 posts	3 × ½ diameter
4 wheels	1½ diameter

The wheels are 1½ inches in diameter and mounted on screws as axles, directly in the sides of the bases.

If you wish to turn your own wheels, prepare a cylinder 1½ inches in diameter and part off pieces ½ inch thick. Drill the centers to turn on #10 screws. Alternatively, you may obtain plastic wheels of about the same size.

For the locomotive (FIG. 5-28B), prepare a standard base and on it mount a block (FIG. 5-28C) under the boiler, which is a piece 2 inches in diameter, with a flat planed on it (FIG. 5-28D).

The cab is a block 2 inches × 3 inches, with a hollowed edge and a hole drilled through. Its appearance is improved with a curved overlapping roof (FIG. 5-28E).

The funnel could be a piece of ¾-inch dowel rod, but if you are able to turn it with a taper and an end plug in a hole (FIG. 5-28F), it will look better. The steam dome is a piece of ¾-inch dowel rod with a rounded top (FIG. 5-28G).

Add the wheels, preferably with washers on each side and roundhead screws.

An ordinary freight car is built as a box on the standard base (FIG. 5-25H). You will probably want to make more than one of these and there could be some building blocks to fit, as an added interest and an aid to learning.

The lumber wagon shown (FIG. 5-28J) has four ½-inch dowel posts to take four blocks which fit over them. Lay out the post positions carefully and have oversize holes in the blocks so they will fit in any place.

Use fairly large screw hooks and eyes for couplings, so they are easy to join and extend far enough for the units to turn corners without hitting each other.

The whole train will probably appeal most to the young owner if its parts are painted in many colors. Bases, wheels, wagon parts, and the locomotive could all be a different color.

TIP TRUCK

This pull-along tip truck will carry a load securely, but by moving a level at the side it will shoot its load of sand or anything else out of the back (FIG. 5-29A). It could be used in a sand pit or indoors with small blocks. The size allows a small doll to be the driver.

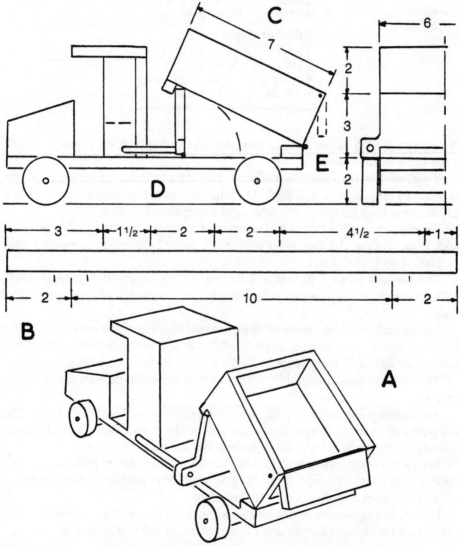

Fig. 5-29. You can tip this truck when a lever at the side is moved.

Most parts are ½ inch thick. They could be plywood, but are better made of solid wood. You can use up scraps of almost any wood. Construction is with glue and nails. There is no need for cut joints between any parts. Wheels are 2 inches in diameter and might be made or bought. If you buy wheels and they are bigger than 2 inches, alter the axle blocks so the tops of the wheels come level with the top of the base.

Make the base and mark the positions of the other parts on it; (FIG. 5-29B) that will set their sizes as well as positions.

Materials List for Tip Truck

1 base	½ ×	6	×	15
1 block	2 ×	3	×	7
1 cab back	½ ×	5	×	6
2 cab sides	½ × 1½	×	6
1 cab seat	1½ × 1½	×	6
1 cab roof	½ × 2½	×	7
1 box bottom	½ ×	6	×	8
2 box sides	½ × 2½	×	8
2 box ends	½ × 2½	×	6
1 hinge piece	½ ×	1	×	7
1 tilt piece	½ ×	3	×	8
1 lever	5 ×	¼ diameter
2 axles	1 ×	1	×	7

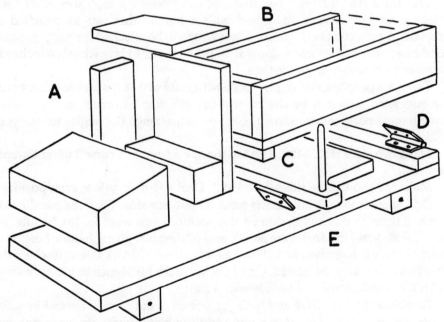

Fig. 5-30. *The arrangement of parts of the tipping truck.*

The front end is made up of simple pieces (FIG. 5-30A). Finished widths should be level with the edge of the base.

Make the tipping part as an open-ended box (FIGS. 5-29C and 5-30B).

Put a square strip under its front end (FIG. 5-30C) and a piece the same thickness across the end of the base (FIG. 5-30D).

The tilting piece should have its grain across and a 1-inch extension to take the ¼-inch dowel rod lever (FIGS. 5-29D and 5-30E).

The box could be left open, or there may be a back fitted in and pivoted on two nails at the top (FIG. 5-29E). Make it loose enough to swing open when the load is tilted.

Put axle pieces across and mount the wheels with washers on roundhead screws.

Hinges about 1 inch are suitable. Position the tilting piece so the operating lever is nearly horizontal when the piece bears against the stop block on the box.

Finish with bright paint. The young owner's name could go on the side.

PUSH/PULL TRUCK

When a child is learning to walk he can use something with a handle that he can push along while supporting himself. He will grow during this process and it helps if the handle height can be altered. Then he reaches a stage where he does not need a support for walking. He may still use a push truck for moving toys about, but interest can be increased if he is able to change to pulling it with a rope.

This truck (FIG. 5-31) is a box that will carry building blocks or other toys, mounted on four wheels and fitted with a handle that can be adjusted or removed. A projection at the front allows a rope to be attached for pulling. Make wooden wheels, but for use indoors it might be better to buy wheels 4 inches in diameter with rubber or plastic tires.

The main parts are ½-inch plywood, with softwood strips for the other parts. The suggested sizes can be altered without affecting construction (FIG. 5-32A). Three handle positions are shown, but you can arrange the angles to suit your child.

Make two sides (FIG. 5-32B). The top may be a freehand curve higher towards the back.

Make the two handle sides (FIG. 5-32C). Drill a ⅛-inch hole at each position.

Drill another ⅛-inch hole at the pivot on one box side. Pivot the handle side on a nail through this and decide on the positions you want for the handle. As drawn, (FIG. 5-32D) the angles are 30, 45, and 60 degrees, giving handle heights of about 13 inches, 16 inches, and 19 inches, respectively. Mark through where the other bolt holes are to be located. Open the holes out for ¼-inch bolts. At the top, drill for a ¾-inch dowel rod handle (FIG. 5-32E).

Complete the box. Glue and nails, or screws at the corners should be satisfactory, but you could cut other joints. Add the bottom with its projection forward (FIG. 5-32F).

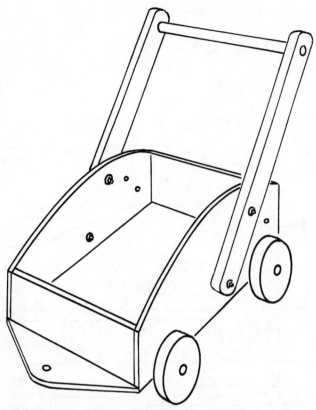

Fig. 5-31. *Alter the angle of the handle for pushing this truck, and a rope can be attached for pulling.*

Put axle strips underneath in positions that will bring the rims of the wheels a short distance in from the back and front of the box.

The wheels will probably need metal axles stronger than screws. Use steel rods of a suitable size held in holes with epoxy glue. Secure the wheels with cotter pins and washers, or by the method advised by the wheel supplier (FIG. 5-32G).

The handle bolts could have washers and wing nuts, or you might prefer nuts that require a wrench, so young hands cannot loosen them.

Paint brightly, possibly with the handles different from the box.

Materials List for Push/Pull Truck

2 sides	7 × 16 × ½ plywood	
1 back	5 × 15 × ½ plywood	
1 front	4 × 13 × ½ plywood	
1 bottom	12 × 20 × ½ plywood	
2 axles	1¼ × 1¼ × 13	
2 handle sides	¾ × 1½ × 21	
1 handle	16 × ¾ diameter	

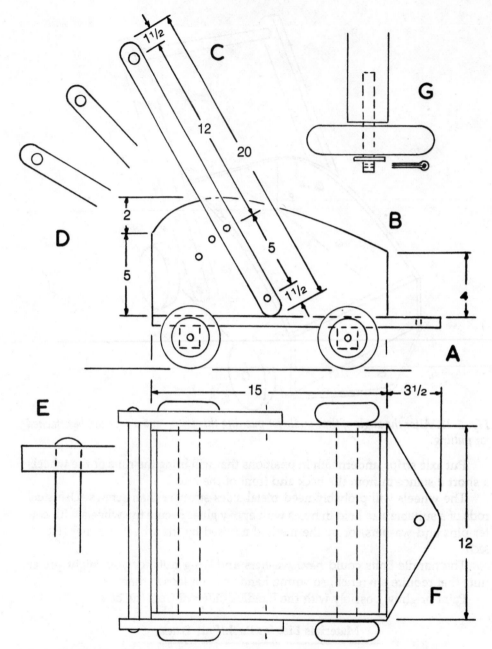

Fig. 5-32. *Sizes and construction of the push/pull truck.*

MODEL ROADS

Those popular tiny vehicles only a few inches long will be much more interesting for their young owners if they have matching model roads to drive on, instead of using the floor. This applies to all kind of cars, trucks, and other road vehicles, and there are some small train sets which are not intended for tracks that could be used on similar guided roads.

Much depends on the scale and the vehicles. If they will be moved by hand the roads can be wide enough for passing, but little powered cars are better between guides that take care of steering. Paint roads on a piece of plywood, but it is better to have definite edges, to keep cars handled by unsteady young fingers on the road.

Choose the layout. Everything could be on one piece of plywood (FIG. 5-33A). This restricts you to a size that can be stored when out of use, although if a small child is to reach over it something like 24 inches × 48 inches is an appropriate size. The alternative is an extended layout, which would have to be in linked sections (FIG. 5-33B).

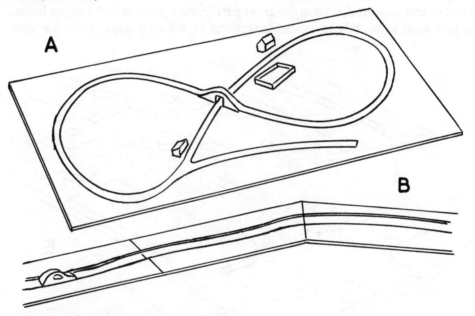

Fig. 5-33. *Suggested layout for model roads.*

Road widths are limited by plywood pieces over the base (FIG. 5-34A). For the single layout, the top piece is the same size as the bottom piece, except for the road cutouts. If you arrange any junctions or crossroads, round the corners so cars can be turned easily (FIG. 5-34B). You might have to increase the road widths toward the corners.

A child likes to take his vehicle over or under a bridge and that can be arranged for a figure-eight layout, instead of crossroads. Make a bridge from a solid block with plywood sides. The plywood stands up to make the walls (FIG. 5-34C). Curve the block ends so the wheels go up easily (FIG. 5-34D).

Any buildings or other features added to this or the longer layout should be strong and basic. If you try to make roadside signs or such things as trees and poles to scale, they will soon be broken. Shape solid blocks to look like houses or gas stations. The child is more interested in moving his vehicles than in admiring scenery.

A longer layout can be in sections of convenient length. The assembly can be arranged to go round corners and could even be made to follow the shape of a room. Parts of the road do not have to be straight, but if they wind too much, the sections have to be wide.

A standard layout, will have the same joints going together each time, but it is possible to arrange alternative assemblies. For that, jointing arrangements have to be interchangeable and the road on each part must be central at the joint and reasonably square to it.

Joints between sections can be with dowels (FIG. 5-34E). Allow about a 2-inch overlap and glue the dowels in the lower part. Have a push fit in the upper holes. If you want to be able to assemble sections in different ways, keep the joint

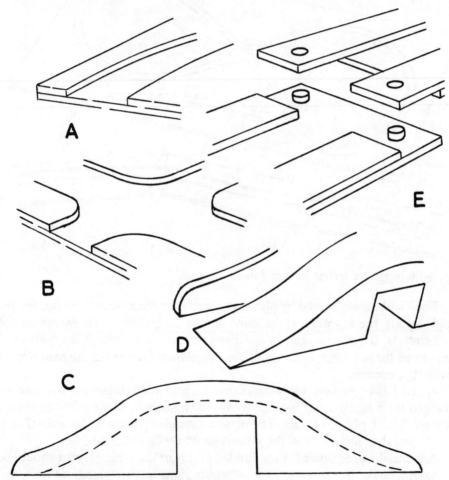

Fig. 5-34. *Construction of sections of model roads.*

details all the same. If the sections will always be assembled the same way, number the joints.

SAILING YACHT

A very small toy sailing boat may provide some interest, but it cannot sail well and its owner will get frustrated if it does not go the way intended. This sailing yacht (FIG. 5-35) at 18 inches long is about the smallest that can be put on a course and expected to keep to it. It does not have a rudder, but the mainsail can be set in relation to the wind, for controlling direction.

One problem in making a model boat hull is in dealing with the compound curves to get a good shape. This is simplified if the hull has the angular hard-chine form (FIG. 5-35A), as if it fairly easy to shape the wood symmetrically. The hull is made of two pieces of solid wood, with a waterproof plywood deck (FIG. 5-35B). The upper piece has a hold cut out; there is a plug in the deck to cover it, so the owner can load a small amount of cargo. Choose straight-grained softwood, free from knots for the hull parts.

Cut the wood for the upper part of the hull to size and mark the shape on top (FIG. 5-36A). Draw curves for the gunwales by bending a lath or strip of wood, through the center, the transom mark and the greatest width on each side. Cut out the hold.

Bevel the sides to about 10 degrees (FIG. 5-35C). So long as the two sides are the same, the exact angle is not important.

Make a piece the same width as the lower side of this block, beveled to the center (FIG. 5-35D) and glue it on.

Cut the outline. In side view cut the curve of the stem (FIG. 5-35E) and bevel the transom (FIG. 5-35F).

Leave the chine angle between the two pieces parallel for the wider part of the boat, but, with the hull inverted, plane away towards the stem and stern to get a pleasing sweep up, and blend with the chine line. Smooth the surfaces and finish by sanding.

Make and fit a plywood deck with a cutout smaller than the hold. Make a plug with a sloping top to look like a hatch or cabin top (FIG. 5-35G).

Drill a ½-inch hole for the mast.

The keel (FIG. 5-35H) is a piece of steel ¹⁄₁₆ inch thick (FIG. 5-35J) held in a slot with epoxy glue.

Make the mast from ½-inch dowel rod, tapered from above the deck to ¼ inch in diameter at the top (FIG. 5-35K). The boom and bowsprit are ¼-inch dowel rod.

Join the boom to the mast with two linked screw eyes (FIG. 5-36B).

Sew the mainsail from any light cloth with sleeves to slide over the mast and boom (FIG. 5-36C). Cut and sew the free edge to a slight curve (FIG. 5-35L). Slide the sail on and put a screw eye through the sail into the mast to take the forestay (FIG. 5-36D).

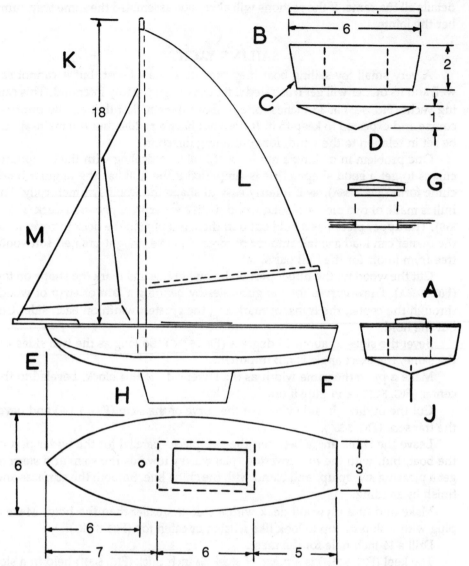

Fig. 5-35. *Sizes and sections of a sailing yacht.*

Nail or screw the bowsprit to the deck so it projects 2 inches. Drill its end for the forestay (FIG. 5-36E).

Make the foresail with clearance above the deck and forward of the mast (FIG. 5-35M). Sew a cord in a pocket to act as a forestay and turn in the other edges. Tie the cord to the end of the bowsprit and the mast screw eye.

Bend a piece of stout wire and point its ends so it can be driven into the deck forward of the mast. On this, slide a small ring and tie a cord from the foresail to it (FIG. 5-36F). On the first trial of the boat, adjust the length of this cord so the sail will fill with air to a moderate curve on either side.

Materials List for Sailing Yacht

1 hull	2	× 6	× 20	
1 hull	1	× 6	× 20	
1 deck	20	× 6	×	¼ plywood
1 hatch	¾	× 2	×	6
1 mast	22	× ½ diameter		
1 boom	12	× ¼ diameter		
1 bowsprit	5	× ¼ diameter		
1 keel	3	× 6	×	¹⁄₁₆ steel

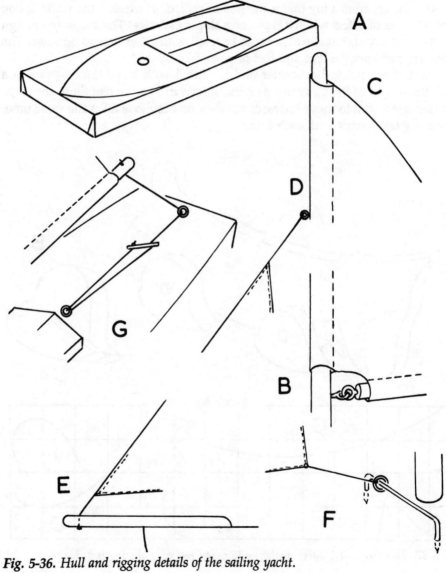

Fig. 5-36. *Hull and rigging details of the sailing yacht.*

For the main sheet you need more adjustment. A cord goes from a hole at the end of the boom, through a screw eye over the transom to another screw eye near the hatch cover. Make a little metal slide, like a tent guyline runner, to adjust the sheet length (FIG. 5-36G). When the wind is from the side, haul the sheet in. When the wind is astern, let it out.

Paint the hull inside and out to prevent water absorption. The spars could be varnished before you add the sails. If the mast is just a push fit in the hull you can lift it and lay it flat for transport.

WALKING DOG

As a change from a toy that is pushed or pulled on wheels, the walking dog "walks" on its own feet when it is put on a sloping surface. The suggested design is a dog (FIG. 5-37A), but the idea could be used with other animal outlines. The important parts are the legs and feet or paws.

The feet are pivoted off-center and are fitted with stops (FIG. 5-37B). On a slope the weight of the body makes it move forward, so the feet tilt to the stops and they are forced to move forward, but they do not move all at the same time, so the dog takes steps with each foot.

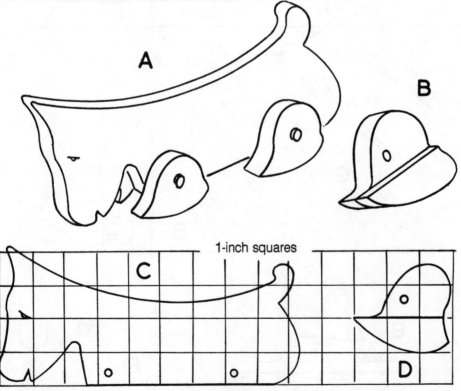

1-inch squares

Fig. 5-37. This dog will "walk" realistically when put on a sloping board.

Materials List for Walking Dog

1 body	¾ × 4½ × 10
4 feet	¾ × 3 × 4

The effect is best if you use a fairly heavy hardwood at least ¾ inch thick. The pivots are brass bolts and nuts about ⅛ inch in diameter. Sizes are based on 1-inch squares in the drawing, but you can alter sizes by assuming a different square size.

Cut the body to size (FIG. 5-37C), preferably with a scroll saw; then the edges will not need much sanding. Mark the bolt hole positions carefully.

Cut the four feet (FIG. 5-37D). The grain should be in the direction of the straight line.

Success in movement depends largely on the regular curves and smoothness of the bottoms of the feet. Check that the curves are as even as possible, and sand them smooth.

The stop pieces inside the feet need not be more than ¼ inch thick. Glue them on and check that the outlines match.

Check the bolt hole positions. There should be about ⅛-inch clearance between the body and the stops. Drill all parts for the bolts.

An overall wax finish may be worthwhile, but some initial lubrication with wax in the joints is advisable in any case. The only decoration need be drawing on eyes.

Put washers under the bolt heads and nuts. Performance will probably be better without washers between the legs and body. Adjust the nuts until you get the best performance on a slope.

BIPLANE

Biplanes may not be such a common sight in the sky today, but children are familiar with them in movies of older days and might see them doing aerobatics or crop spraying.

This model of a biplane (FIG. 5-38A), has a propeller that turns when faced into a wind or a child runs with it. There are wheels for running along the ground and a pilot that can be lifted out. Length and width are 12 inches, so the toy is easily handled and construction is robust, particularly if made of hardwood. Some parts could be plywood, although solid wood is preferable.

The fuselage is the main part and other pieces assemble to it. The tail plane or elevator and the fin or rudder fit into notches. The wheels are on a block below the bottom wing. Construction of a propeller is described, but you may be able to buy a plastic one from a model shop. It has to have light sections if it is to perform well and this means it is rather vulnerable if the child treats his biplane roughly.

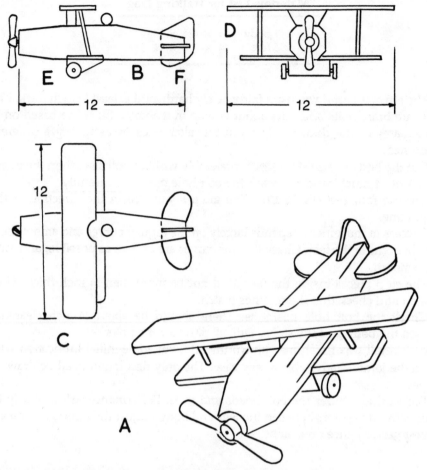

Fig. 5-38. This model biplane can withstand use by a young child.

The fuselage (FIGS. 5-38B and 5-39A) starts as a piece 2½ inches square. Plane the corners off (FIG. 5-39B). Taper the tail end in width and depth (FIG. 5-39C). Reduce the forward end to round (FIG. 5-39D). Blend the octagonal angles into the tapers and sand all over.

Make the upper and lower wings (FIGS. 5-38C and 5-39E). Round the corners and edges. Cut away the center of the trailing edge of the upper wing (FIG. 5-39F). Drill for ¼-inch dowel rods that will slope forward (FIG. 5-38D).

Cut the tail end of the fuselage through both ways for the rudder and elevator, which are ¼ inch thick (FIG. 5-39G).

Make a support block for the upper wing (FIG. 5-39H). Glue and screw it to the fuselage (FIG. 5-39J).

Notch the underside of the fuselage for the lower wing; then, attach both wings and the dowel struts.

Make and fix the undercarriage block (FIGS. 5-38E and 5-39K).

The rudder (FIG. 5-39L) incorporates the tail skid which projects below (FIG. 5-38F). This goes right through, but the elevator is in two parts (FIG. 5-39M) each side of it. Round their outer edges and glue them in.

The wheels are about 1 inch in diameter. They could be pieces of dowel rod, turned, or you could buy plastic ones. They pivot on screws.

The pilot (FIG. 5-39N) is turned and the head suitably painted. Drill a hole to suit.

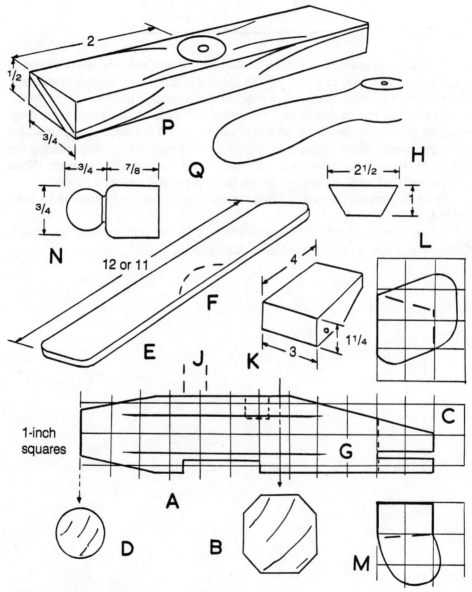

Fig. 5-39. *Details of the parts of a biplane.*

Materials List for Biplane

1 fuselage	2½	×	2½ × 13
2 wings	⅜	×	2½ × 13
1 block	1	×	1 × 4
1 block	1¼	×	3 × 5
1 rudder	¼	×	3 × 4
2 elevators	¼	×	3 × 3
1 propeller	½	×	¾ × 6
1 pilot	1	×	1 × 3
2 struts	6	×	¼ diameter

A suitable propeller is 4 inches in diameter. If you buy one do not get one much bigger than this, or it may hit the ground when the fuselage is horizontal. If you carve it yourself, start with a piece of close-grained hardwood (FIG. 5-39P). Mark the center and draw a circle there on both surfaces. At the ends, mark diagonal cuts opposite ways; these have to be cut in toward the center and should get relatively steeper. If the angles are not constant this may not matter providing the shapes are the same and opposite sides match and the propeller balances. When you are satisfied with the angles, round the ends and edges (FIG. 5-39Q).

Pivot the propeller on a roundhead screw, with a washer in front and a bead behind.

If you want a World War I appearance, paint the drab camouflage colors. Otherwise, if it is an exhibition plane, paint to suit.

6

Ride-on Toys

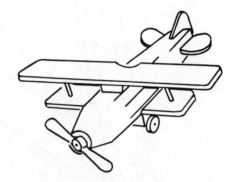

SCOOTER

A scooter to ride on by putting one foot on it and pushing against the ground with the other, may be one of the first ride-on toys that gives a child independence and a speed better than walking. This scooter is intended for a boy or girl aged 5 or 6 years (FIG. 6-1). It has 6-inch wheels, so the footboard is at a safe 4 inches above the ground. The handlebars give easy control. Check sizes against your child. The overall height is easy to alter without affecting other sizes.

The scooter should be made of a close-grained hardwood. You could use softwood for the two main parts, but the pivoting arrangements have to withstand considerable loads and the bracket and the cleats that provide the pivot should be close-grained hardwood if the scooter is to endure hard use. Failure in this linkage could be serious.

Get the wheels and steel rod for their axles first, as the wheels control some of the work you have to do on the wood. Slight variations in wheel size may not matter, but the drawings are based on 6-inch-diameter wheels, which will usually be less than 1 inch thick. Wheel axles are assumed to be ⅜-inch-diameter steel rod. The bracket pivot may be ¾-inch-diameter steel rod.

Start with the footboards (FIG. 6-2A). Cut away to give clearance for the wheel and glue and screw blocks each side. Drill across for the axle (FIG. 6-2B). You may drill after screwing, or if you drill the blocks first, make sure the holes are in line by putting the axle through them while you screw.

Mark the location of the bracket, but do not drill any holes there yet. Round all outer corners and edges.

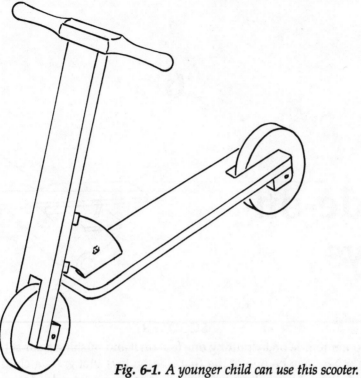

Fig. 6-1. A younger child can use this scooter.

Mark out the wood for the front (FIG. 6-2C). This is shown 3 inches wide, but if your wheel needs more than 1 inch cut away, make the front wider. It could be 4 inches without affecting the use of the scooter.

Cut away to clear the wheel and put blocks on each side for the axle (FIG. 6-2D) in the same way as on the footboard.

The bracket has to fit between two cleats fitted across (FIGS. 6-2E and 6-3A). Make them with their grain the long way and fit them with glue and screws after drilling for a ¼-inch diameter pivot rod (FIG. 6-3B). Round the outer corners.

The handlebar (FIG. 6-2F) is 1¼ inches square at the center, but the ends should be shaped to provide a grip. This is best done on a lathe, but otherwise you could reduce the ends to round by planing and sanding.

Join the handlebar to the front with a mortise-and-tenon joint, if possible (FIG. 6-2G), but you could use dowels.

The bracket (FIG. 6-2H) should be cut with its grain as shown (FIG. 6-3C) for maximum strength.

At the forward end it must be parallel and fit fairly tightly between the cleats (FIG. 6-3D). Take it in as far as possible and round its end so the front can rotate on the pivot rod. Mark through both cleat holes and make the hole in the bracket by drilling from both sides.

To take the load at the footboard, it is advisable to bolt through. Screws alone might not be strong enough and with the sloping grain, mortises-and-tenons might give way. Use a ¼-inch bolt (FIG. 6-3E). Drill the footboard and bracket; then, cut across to take the nut. Make a trial assembly.

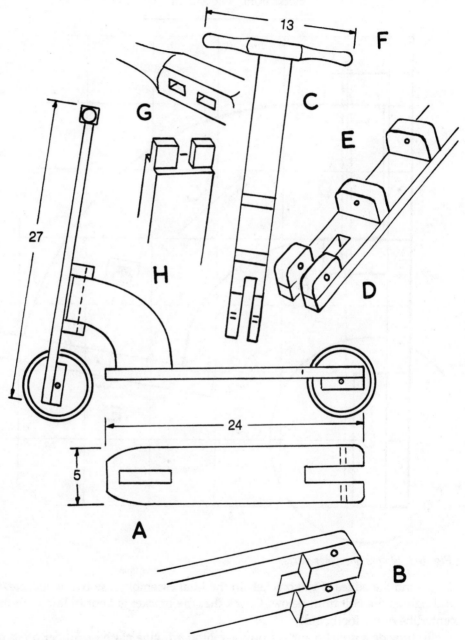

Fig. 6-2. *Size and construction of the scooter.*

1 footboard	¾ × 5 × 26
1 front	¾ × 3 or 4 × 29
1 bracket	1 × 7 × 15
blocks from	1 × 2 × 24

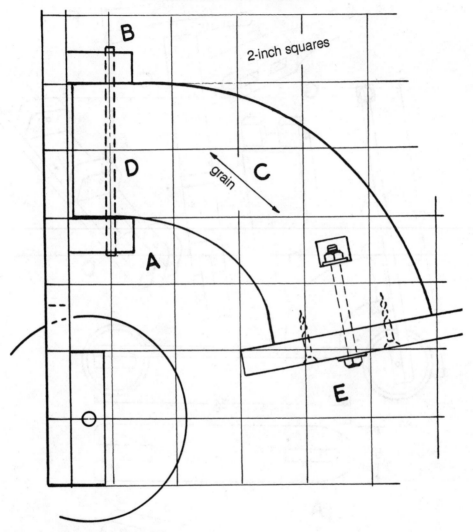

Fig. 6-3. *Shapes of scooter parts.*

Round the edges of the bracket. In the final assembly, use two woodscrews and tighten the bolt from below. Check that the bracket is kept in line with the centerline of the footboard.

To provide a nonslip surface on the footboard, glue cloth or rubber on it, or wrap it over and tack underneath.

After painting, bring the parts together and slip in the pivot rod. It could be prevented from coming out if you cut threads for nuts on the ends. Alternatively, spread the top by hammering before driving it in.

SIMPLE SLED

When the snow comes junior wants to be able to ride on a sled. If yours is an area where the period of snow is not usually long, you do not want a large sled to store for most of the year. Even if the sled could be used for long periods, it is still helpful if it is fairly light and compact, particularly if young children are involved. However, it must be able to stand up to rough use, particularly when it is overloaded or it hits obstacles.

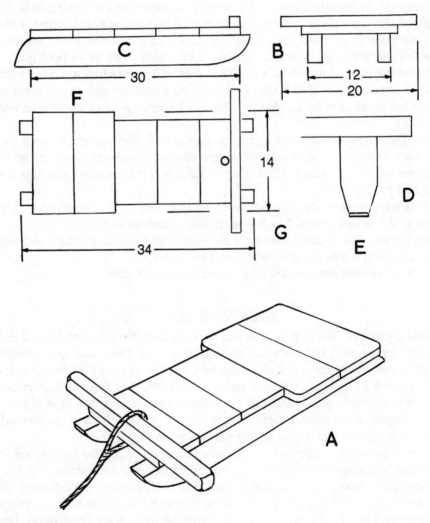

Fig. 6-4. A simple, strong, small sled.

Materials List for Simple Sled

4 runners	2 × 4 × 36
5 deck boards	1 × 6 × 15
1 crossbar	1½ × 1½ × 22

The enjoyment a child gets out of a sled is not necessarily related to the skill and time put into making it, so a sled of basic construction may satisfy your child's need (FIG. 6-4A). The size shown (FIG. 6-4B) is intended for one child, who can sit on the sled with his feet on the crossbar or lie on the sled holding the crossbar. He can tow the sled back to the start of the slope or you can give a younger child a gentler ride by towing on a level surface.

Sizes can be modified to suit the wood you might have or your needs. The length of this example is determined by five, 6-inch boards laid across. Other parts are stock sizes. Softwood should be satisfactory, but hardwood would be more durable, although heavier. Parts might be nailed, with or without glue.

Make the two runners (FIG. 6-4C). They extend 2 inches forward and behind the deck boards. If the sled is expected to only be used on soft snow, leave the bottom full width, but for a faster toy, thin the lower edges to about 1-inch wide (FIG. 6-4D).

For the fastest results, put a strip of ⅛-×-1-inch steel on the bottom edge (FIG. 6-4E). Use screws at about 4-inch intervals and countersink them, so the heads are below the surface. Then, there is no risk of them catching against anything and pulling out.

Attach the forward deck boards with the ends level with the outsides of the runners. The others extend 2 inches each side to make a seat (FIG. 6-4F).

Fit the crossbar to extend 4 inches each side, and round its edges and ends (FIG. 6-4G). Drill a hole for the towing rope behind it.

Round exposed corners and edges, and finish with paint.

ROCKING BOAT

Young children like to rock and will spend a long time just rocking if they have the opportunity, but the usual rocking horse may need adult supervision, for safety reasons. If the small child can be enclosed in a rocking boat there is much less risk of falling and it may be safe to let him play there unsupervised. Obviously, a simple box would not have much appeal and this boat (FIG. 6-5) should inspire adventurous ideas to a fertile young imagination, particularly after seeing boating pictures or seeing parents go sailing.

A boat involves compound curves and that may be a little frightening for anyone unaccustomed to boatbuilding, but this little craft does not have to float, and any minor inaccuracies do not matter. If the steps below are followed, the resulting boat will have a pleasing appearance, even if it does not finish exactly as the drawing. Most boat parts are plywood and the rockers are solid wood. Boat

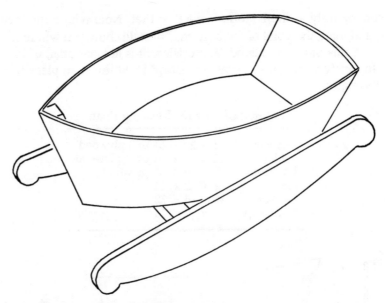

Fig. 6-5. A rocking boat will hold a small child safely.

construction is with glue, nails, and screws. The rocker parts could be tenoned or doweled.

Check the suggested sizes with your child's needs (FIG. 6-6A). He should be able to move about in the boat. Remember that you will want him to use the rocking boat when he has grown a little. Later on, you could fit a seat and a mast,—oars—when the child still wants to play with his boat after he has grown past the younger stage.

Mark out and cut the bottom to shape (FIG. 6-7A). Bevel the edge at the stern to 98 degrees (FIG. 6-7B). As a preliminary step bevel the sides the same amount. The final angle will vary with the flare of the sides, but this makes a starting angle that will be about right for much of the length.

Make the transom (FIGS. 6-6B and 6-7C). Bevel the bottom edge to 98 degrees and both sides to 105 degrees (FIG. 6-7D). This is the final bevel for the bottom edge, but the side angles may have to be modified when you bend the sides round. Curve the top edge.

Mark out and cut the two sides to match each other (FIG. 6-7E). Leave some surplus at the ends. Although you should try to fit the sides to size when you bend, it does not matter if you are not exactly on the line at bow or stern, providing that both sides match.

Cut the solid piece for the stem (FIGS. 6-6C and 6-7F) a few inches too long. Bevel the bottom to the approximate angle. This and the side angles may have to be modified when you see the actual angle the bent sides will need.

Attach one side to the transom with a few screws. Pull it round to the bow. At the same time, lift it so the hollowed bottom edge comes up to the boat bottom level, or near it. If the side falls into a neat curve and flare without the hollowed edge coming fully to the bottom, leave it at that. Note where the forward end comes, and mark the point of the bottom. This will show you where the angle of the bottom side has to be altered. A precision fit is not essential, unless it is necessary to satisfy your pride of craftsmanship! Hold the stem piece in place and check its angles.

Materials List for Rocking Boat

1 bottom	12 × 20 ×	¾ or 1 plywood
2 sides	12 × 28 ×	⅜ or ½ plywood
1 transom	9 × 10 ×	¾ plywood
1 stem	2 × 2 ×	14
2 rockers	¾ × 5 ×	32
2 crossbars	1 × 2 ×	14

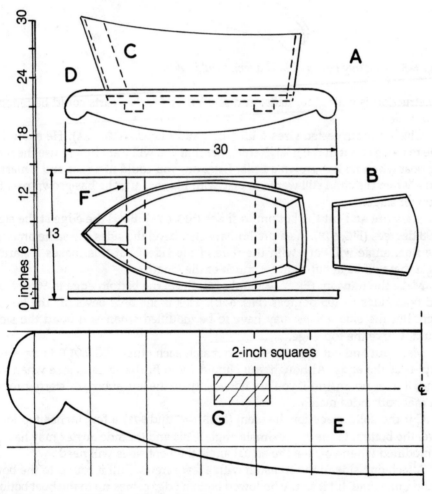

Fig. 6-6. *Sizes and shapes of the rocking boat.*

When you know what angle modifications you need, remove the side. Alter angles in the same way—both sides of the bottom and of the stem. Fasten the stem to the bottom with two screws, driven upward. If there is much surplus length of the sides left, any at the stern will not matter, it can be trimmed after screwing. However, reduce the spare wood at the stem for ease in fitting.

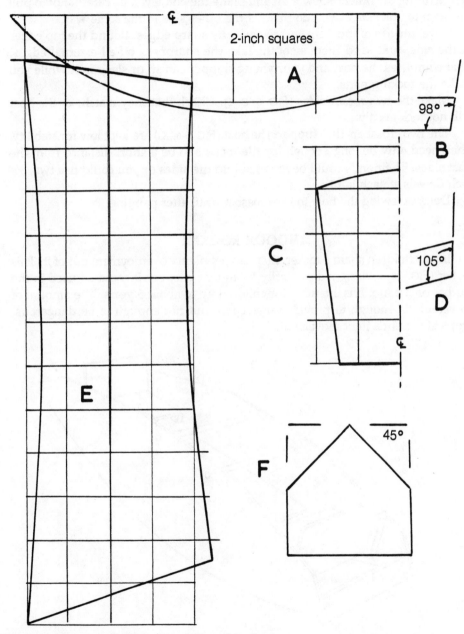

2-inch squares

98°

105°

45°

Fig. 6-7. Shapes of the boat part of the rocking boat.

Bend the two sides after attaching them firmly to the transom and a short distance along each side of the bottom. You will probably need help as you pull up the bottom edges to put flare in the sides. Screw at about 3-inches intervals. Include glue as well. Work forward a little at a time, progressing in symmetry.

At the stem you will have to complete the screwing of one side to the stem before fitting the other. Screw it on and plane the end level. Be careful not to pull the stem to one side as you do this. Fit the other side in the same way.

Level the top of the stem and remove any sharp edges. Round the top edges of the sides and sand them smooth. Take the sharpness off all external edges. That completes the boat and your young skipper can sit or sleep in it while you make the rocking parts.

Make the two rocker sides (FIG. 6-6D, E). Check that they match, or the boat will not rock evenly.

The two crossbars that support the boat (FIG. 6-6F, G) are kept low for stability. They need only be long enough for the rockers to be a short distance from the boat sides. Their ends could be tenoned into the sides or you could use two, ½-inch dowels at each joint.

Delay screwing the boat to the crossbar until after painting.

INDOOR ROCKER

If two children share a rocker, they can get plenty of enjoyment out of it. This rocker (FIG. 6-8) is designed primarily for indoor use, but it could be used in the yard or on a patio. It is intended for children up to about 5 years. The amount of movement is enough to provide satisfaction, but not enough to be dangerous. Stops at the ends limit movement.

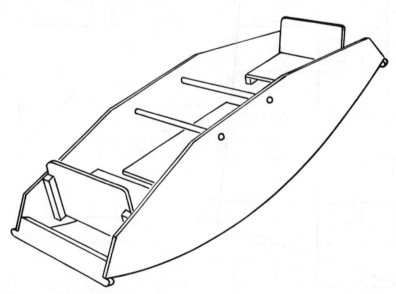

Fig. 6-8. *Two small children can use this indoor rocker.*

Most parts are made from ½-inch plywood. Other 1-inch wood could be hard or soft. Construction is with glue and nails or screws.

Start by laying out the pair of sides (FIG. 6-9A).

For the radius, make a temporary compass with an awl for center and a radius of 72 inches to the end where you use a pencil (FIG. 6-9B). Adjust the

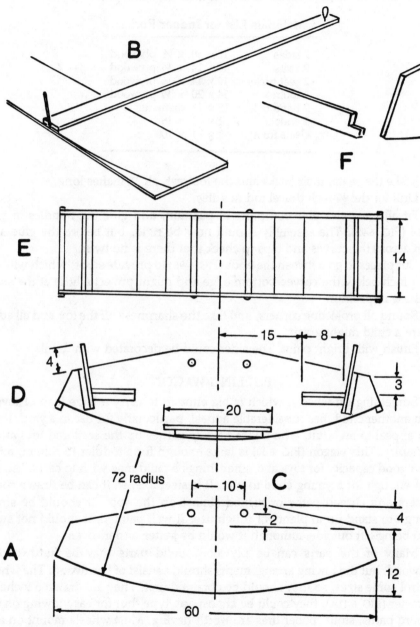

Fig. 6-9. *Marking out and laying out parts of the indoor rocker.*

board, so the compass swings to the edge and the same distance at each end, before actually marking the curve.

With the curve marked, draw the outline of the top (FIG. 6-9C). The ends slope along the line of radius, so they point to the center used to draw the curve.

On the sides, mark the positions of the seats and footrest (FIG. 6-9D). Fit 1-inch-square cleats in positions to support the plywood parts.

Materials List for Indoor Rocker

2 sides	$12 \times 60 \times \frac{1}{2}$ plywood
2 seats	$8 \times 14 \times \frac{1}{2}$ plywood
2 seat backs	$12 \times 14 \times \frac{1}{2}$ plywood
1 footrest	$14 \times 20 \times \frac{1}{2}$ plywood
2 hand rails	$16 \times \frac{3}{4}$ diameter
2 ends	$1 \times 3 \times 16$
cleats from	$1 \times 1 \times 100$

Make the seats, their backs and the footrest, all 14 inches long.

Drill for the ¾-inch dowel rod handles.

Fit all crosswise plywood parts in position, and glue the handles in their holes (FIG. 6-9E). The assembly should now be rigid, but before the glue sets, sight across the curves and tops to check that there is no twist.

Cut pieces to go between the ends (FIG. 6-9E) to provide stops, which will project 1 inch below the curved bottom edge and might project a little at the sides. Fit these in position.

Round all projecting corners, and take the sharpness off the top and all edges where a child might grasp.

Finish with bright paint. The sides could be decorated with decals.

PULLING WAGON

Something on wheels, which is big enough to carry a large load of toys or even another child, has considerable appeal, particularly for use in a yard. It will also appeal to an adult, who might have to gather up the scattered toys after a day's play. This wagon (FIG. 6-10) is large enough for a toddler to ride in, and it has a good capacity for toys and other things a child may wish to carry. Yet, it is light enough for a young child to pull. It is steerable, so it can be drawn round corners and curved paths or turned almost on the spot. It should be strong enough to stand up to plenty of rough use. If well painted, it should not suffer from being left outside, although it would be better under cover.

Many of the parts can be plywood. Solid parts may be hardwood or softwood, but the towing arrangements should consist of hardwood. The wheels control some sizes, so they should be obtained first. They are drawn 6 inches in diameter (FIG. 6-11A); they could be almost any type, but for easy towing on turf or hard paths, stout rubber tires are worth having. Most wheels mount on a ⅜-inch or ½-inch axle, and this design allows for a rod right through.

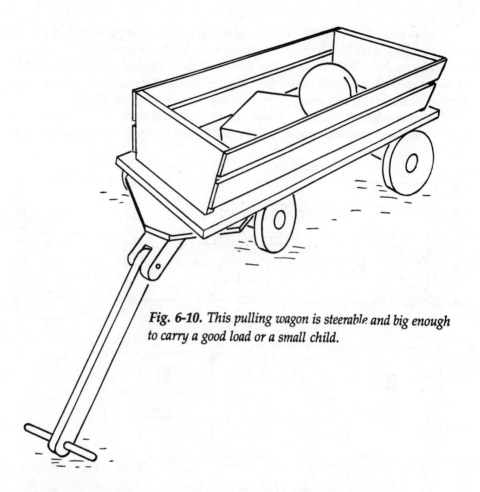

Fig. 6-10. This pulling wagon is steerable and big enough to carry a good load or a small child.

Make the base (FIG. 6-11B) and mark on it the positions of the wheel supports and the top framing.

For the ends, shape pieces to give a slight flare (FIG. 6-11C).

Make the four side strips (FIG. 6-11D) with rounded edges and outer ends and corners.

Mount these parts together on the base, with the ends 1 inch in. Use glue and screws for all assemblies.

The two wheel supports are basically the same, except that the steerable one extends to take the handle. Make the crosspieces deep enough to take the axles and allow about 1-inch wheel clearance under the wagon base.

Shape the two crosspieces (FIG. 6-11E) alike. Drill for the axle and the forward one for the pivot bolt. In both cases, you may wish to drill undersize pilot holes at this stage, to check that they are correctly in line; then, enlarge later during assembly.

Make the front arm (FIG. 6-11F, G), either tenoned or halved to its crosspiece. Put a slot in its rounded end to take the handle.

The plywood top for the rear crosspiece (FIG. 6-11H) is parallel, but the forward one (FIG. 6-11J, K) is shaped to extend over the front arm.

Make the handle (FIG. 6-11L). The grip is a piece of ¾-inch dowel rod. At both ends, keep the holes back a little from the centers of the rounded ends, to allow for the weakness of end grain. A ⅜-inch bolt will provide the pivot.

Put steel axles through the crosspieces and attach the wheels. These fit in different ways, but you will probably have to drill the axles to take retaining pins.

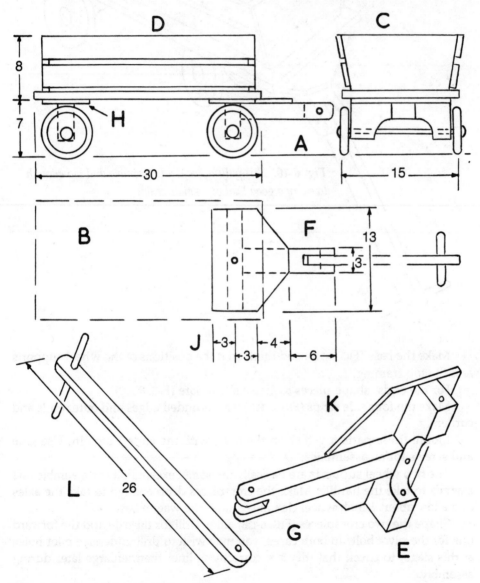

Fig. 6-11. *Sizes and parts of the pulling wagon.*

Materials List for Pulling Wagon

1 base	15 × 30 × ¾	plywood
2 ends	¾ × 7¼ × 16	
4 sides	½ × 3 × 30	
2 crosspieces	2 × 5 × 15	
1 crosspiece	6 × 15 × ½	plywood
1 crosspiece	10 × 15 × ½	plywood
1 arm	2 × 3 × 14	
1 handle	1 × 2 × 28	
1 grip	8 × ¾ diameter	

Secure the front wheel assembly with a bolt through the base. This could be a ½-inch carriage bolt with its head on top, then a washer and locking nut underneath. A child must be able to steer the wagon, but the joint need not be very slack.

Round exposed corners of the base and front wheel assembly. Paint all parts in bright colors, although varnish on the upper parts will make an attractive contrast with the lower painted parts.

PLAY BOAT

A boat to use in a swimming pool adds to the enjoyment of swimming and playing in the water. This boat does not have to be large, but one or two children should be able to use it. It opens up all sorts of imaginary themes. It would certainly become a pirate ship in the minds of most young users.

Such a boat has to float satisfactorily and still remain afloat if capsized. It has to withstand climbing on board and jumping off. If it is for use in a yard swimming pool, it is not intended to be taken to the coast or a large river. It might provide fun in a small stream, but although the boat may look large in your shop or garage, it is not big enough for use on deeper and larger waters. There will have to be parental guidance when the young enthusiasts want to take their little ship on vacation.

This boat (FIG. 6-12) is double-ended and symmetrical. The end compartments and the seat are watertight and will ensure the boat floating high, even if filled with water.

Start by making the two sides (FIG. 6-13A, B). To get the curve, mark the 9-inch height at the center and 6 inches at each end. With help, bend a strip of wood through these points and pencil the shape. Check that the two pieces make a pair. Mark where crosswise parts will come.

Put ¾-inch-square strips along both edges of each piece (FIG. 6-13C). They should be held with waterproof glue and either brass or copper nails or brass screws. If ¾-inch wood is ⅝ inch square when finished, that will be satisfactory. At the ends, leave gaps for the end boards.

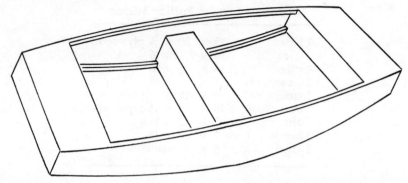

Fig. 6-12. *This play boat can be used for fun in a swimming pool.*

Make the pieces that fit across. The two ends are plain rectangular pieces (FIG. 6-13D), except you can prepare the edges which will come against the skin by beveling them slightly—80 degrees will do—but you may have to modify the angles slightly during assembly.

The two bulkheads (FIG. 6-13E, F) are also plain rectangles with similar bevels to the ends where they contact the skin. Notch the corners to fit against the strips at the sides.

The two pieces for the seat (FIG. 6-13G, H) need notches at the bottom. The edges are left square.

Start assembly on a flat floor large enough to support the boat and allow you to walk around it.

Have the two sides facing each other and upside-down resting on their straight edges. Put the two seat pieces in their marked positions; glue and screw through from the outside. Keep the edges level with the curved edges of the sides.

With help, pull in one end and clamp it temporarily over its end piece. At the other end pull in the sides, so you can glue and screw them to the end and bulkhead. Pull in temporarily at first, to check if you need to alter the angles where the pieces meet the sides. Go back to the clamped end and do the same there. Through all this assembly, check that the straight edges of the sides remain flat on the floor. Also, check by comparing diagonal measurements that the boat is assembled squarely.

Turn the boat the right side up. Put strips between the seat pieces, (FIG. 6-13J) and fit a plywood seat top in place.

When the bottom is fitted, it has to make a close fit against all the parts you have assembled so far. Turn the boat upside-down on the flat floor or a large bench. Make the surfaces smooth and even by planing or power sanding. Use a scrap piece of plywood to bend on parts of the boat to check that it will bed down closely.

If any of the joints are not as close as you wish, do not just fill with glue, as that will crack and leak if it is very thick. Use glue mixed with sawdust to fill gaps

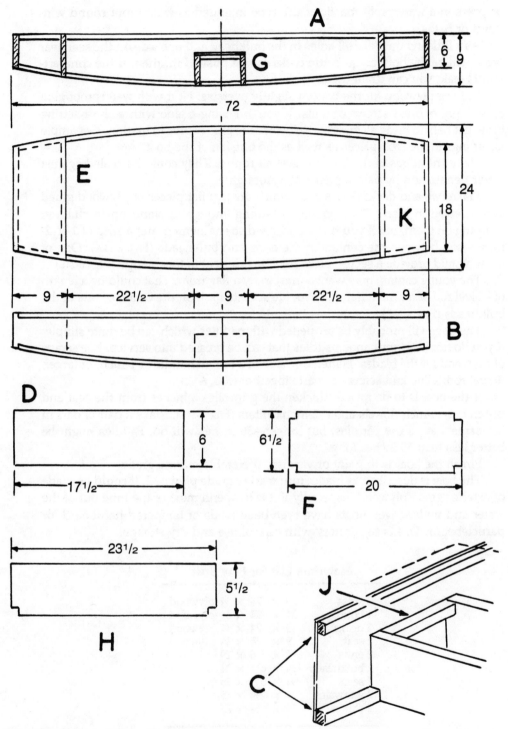

Fig. 6-13. *Sizes and the main parts of the play boat.*

or press in a waterproof mastic of the type intended to waterproof round windows or baths.

As a little insurance, drill holes in the bulkhead and one side on the seat near what will be the bottom, so bottle corks can be pushed in; then, if the compartments leak, you can drain them.

Cut the plywood for the bottom slightly oversize. Fit it with waterproof glue and plenty of brass screws or nails. If you are using a glue with a short setting time, get help to bring all joints close before the glue begins to harden. Get ample fastenings to the crosspieces as well as the outside of the boat.

Plane the edges of the bottom level all round. They could be sealed against water penetration by painting on waterproof glue.

Make two end decks (FIG. 6-13K), which are just flat pieces of plywood glued and screwed in place. They should be strong enough to stand up to children jumping on them, but if you think they need strengthening, put a strip of 1-×-2-inch wood between the centers of the ends and bulkheads (FIG. 6-14A). One of these would provide a secure place for fitting a cleat to take a rope (FIG. 6-14B).

The young captain may want a mast to fly a flag from. That could be a length of dowel rod or a broom handle. Provide sockets for it on the center of one of the bulkheads (FIG. 6-14C).

The boat will probably be propelled with paddles which can be quite simple, if you do not have any canoe paddles that can be pressed into service. Use scraps of plywood for the blades. Flatten one side of a broom handle or 1-inch, or larger, dowel rod. Glue and screw the parts together (FIG. 6-14D).

If the boat is to be rowed, thicken the gunwales 6 inches from the seat and put in two ½-inch dowels about 2-inch centers (FIG. 6-14E). Make a pair of oars in the same way as the paddles, but longer—36 inches will do. Paddles might be better less than 30 inches long.

Finish the boat with paint or varnish, preferably marine grade.

The boat is described as made from marine grade plywood. It could be made of exterior grade plywood, especially if it is to spend most of the time out of the water and under cover. Boats have even been made of tempered hardboard, or particleboard. This is satisfactory with careful use and dry storage.

Materials List for Play Boat

2 sides	9	×	74	×	¼	plywood
1 bottom	24	×	74	×	¼	plywood
2 decks	9	×	24	×	¼	plywood
1 seat	9	×	25	×	¼	plywood
2 ends	¾	×	6	×	19	
2 bulkheads	¾	×	6½	×	21	
2 seats	¾	×	5½	×	25	
2 gunwales	¾	×	¾	×	75	
2 chines	¾	×	¾	×	75	

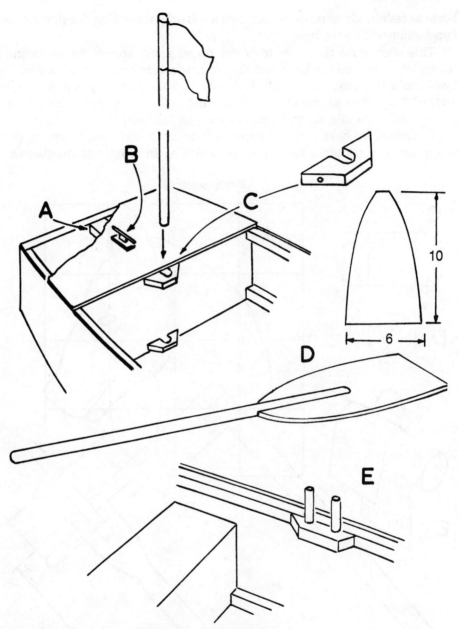

Fig. 6-14. *Decking, mast, and oars for the play boat.*

STICK HORSE

A stick with a horse's head on the end is all that the younger child needs to imagine all sorts of activities where he gallops around performing various deeds. If there are riding horses in the vicinity he will certainly emulate them with this ever-popular and simple toy. It helps if you can paint the head to simulate a horse as realistically as possible, but even if it is only something like it, the young imagination will do the rest.

This stick horse (FIG. 6-15) improves on so many specimens by having a secure joint between the head and the stick, which is locked by a handle. The head could be ½-inch plywood. The stick is made from a piece of straight-grained 1-×-2-inch softwood. The whole thing should be light enough for a young child to handle, as he holds near the point of balance.

Of course, the head could be anything you like to draw, but a horse or pony is popular. If you do not fancy your own skill as an artist, use the pattern of

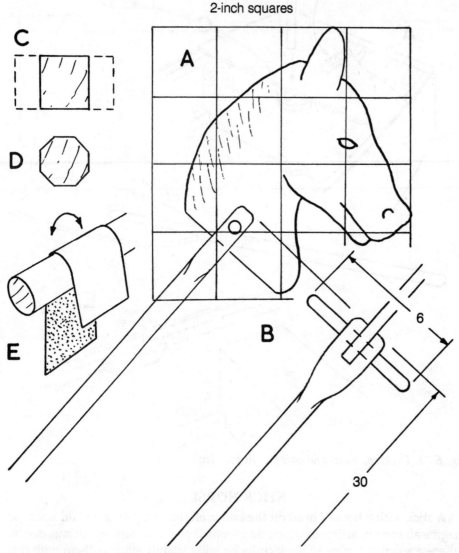

2-inch squares

Fig. 6-15. A simple stick horse for a child to pretend to ride.

squares to draw a suitable outline (FIG. 6-15A). Cut this out and well round all edges, then sand them and the surface.

You will have to relate the length of the stick to the size of the child—30 inches may be enough. Start with it longer and cut it down after the child has tried it.

Cut a slot in the end of the strip to overlap the head plywood by 2½ inches. Round the opposite sides, so the ends blend into the head, but leave the main area of the overlap with square edges (FIG. 6-15B).

About 4 inches below the joint with the head, reduce the stick to square (FIG. 6-15C), then take the corners off to make it octagonal (FIG. 6-15D). Finally, reduce it to round by planing off these angles and working sandpaper around the wood (FIG. 6-15E).

Blend the joint into the curved part, so the area behind the head is easy to grasp, without rough edges.

Glue the head into the slot. Drill across to take a length of ½-inch dowel rod to form the handle. Round the end of the stick which will rub on the ground.

Put the young rider astride his horse and let him try it out. If necessary, adjust the length of the stick; then, reclaim the toy for painting.

Unless the horse has to look realistic, paint the head brown or grey, with a black mane and white or black eyes. The stick can be the same or any color you wish.

TODDLER ROCKING HORSE

A horse is the favorite rocking toy and the youngest child may want his or her own rocking horse. This design (FIG. 6-16) is intended to provide a safe rocking for a toddler. Its size allows seating only 5 inches from the floor; the handle gives safety and control. The head is the same shape as that on the stick horse, so you can mark one from the other.

The head is best cut from ½-inch plywood. The other parts could also be plywood, or they could be made of solid wood ⅝-inch thick, to provide some weight

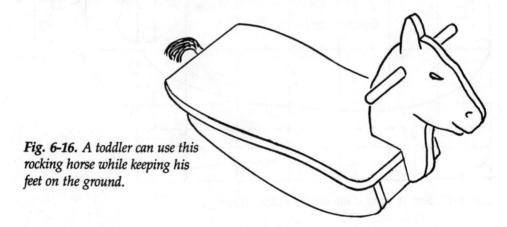

Fig. 6-16. A toddler can use this rocking horse while keeping his feet on the ground.

and reduce any tendency of the horse to slide about. You can get smoother rounded edges with solid wood than you can with plywood.

Make the two rockers, using the squared drawing as a guide to shape (FIG. 6-17A).

Cut the outline of the top (FIG. 6-17B). Keep the ends square across and mark on the positions of the rockers.

Cut pieces to fit between the ends of the rockers (FIG. 6-17C, D). Notch the front piece and the top to take the head (FIG. 6-17E).

Saw the head to shape and notch it to fit the other parts (FIG. 6-17F). Round all parts of the head that will be exposed. Drill for the handle and glue in a length of dowel rod.

Screw the crosspieces between the rockers and the top downwards into them. Glue in the head.

Materials List for Toddler Rocking Horse

1 head	8 ×	8 × ½ plywood
2 rockers	⅝ ×	4½ × 15
1 top	⅝ ×	9 × 15
2 strips	⅝ ×	2 × 9

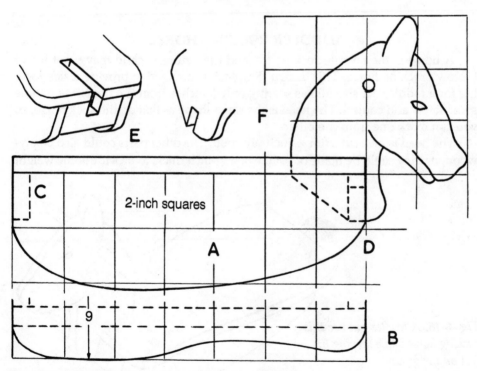

Fig. 6-17. Sizes of parts of the toddler rocking horse.

At the other end, drill a hole so a piece of rope can be glued in; then, fluff out the rope to form a tail.

Paint the eyes and mane lines on the head, and any other details you wish, such as a harness. Paint the rest of the toy in any typical horse color.

ROCKER/SLIDE

The rocker/slide toy is a combined rocker for two toddlers and a slide for first experiments in climbing and sliding. When resting on the rocking edges (FIG. 6-18A), the two children can sit facing each other and holding the crossbar. Then, they can rock to a satisfying extent, because the rocking motion will be limited by the projections on the ends. When the toy is turned over (FIG. 6-18B) there are two slopes and a flat top. One side has a piece across to aid climbing, and the other allows a gentle slide.

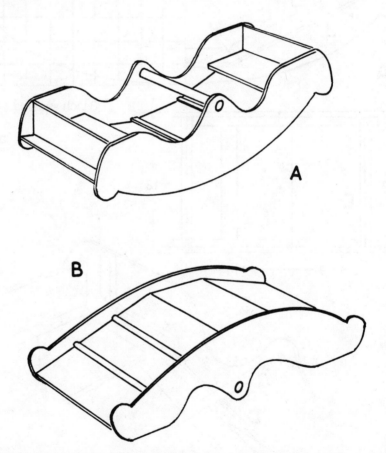

Fig. 6-18. *This toy can be used one way as a rocker for two small children (A), or turned over and used for climbing and sliding (B).*

The toy is drawn (FIG. 6-19A) 60 inches long, 18 inches wide, and 18 inches high. It is more suitable for use outdoors, but it could be used in the garage or indoors. Sizes could be altered, but anything much smaller would be difficult to arrange without excessive curve and with very short slides. Lengthening without altering width and depth would give longer slides, but the seats should still be about the same distance from the crossbar, or a toddler would not be able to grip it.

Construction is with ½ inch or thicker exterior plywood and strips of 1-×-2-inch solid wood. Join all parts with waterproof glue and nails or screws.

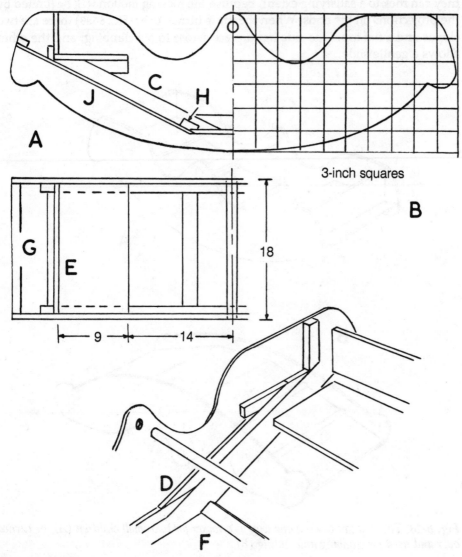

Fig. 6-19. Sizes and construction of the rocker/slide.

Materials List for Rocker/Slide

2 sides	18 × 62 × ½ plywood
2 seat parts	8 × 18 × ½ plywood
2 seat parts	10 × 18 × ½ plywood
1 bottom	12 × 18 × ½ plywood
2 slides	18 × 28 × ½ plywood
10 strips	1 × 2 × 12
4 support strips	1 × 2 × 22
1 crossbar	20 × 1 diameter
2 climbing strips	½ × 1 × 18

With the aid of the squared drawing, mark out and cut the two sides (FIG. 6-19B). On them mark the positions of the seats and slides.

Attach support strips (FIG. 6-19C, D). Check that they are symmetrical about the centerline and the opposite sides match.

Make the seat parts (FIG. 6-19E) and the bottom (FIG. 6-19F). Put a strip to cover the seat joint (FIG. 6-19G) and a beveled piece to make the joint at the bottom (FIG. 6-19H), at each side. The bottom pieces also act as footrests, so round the edge that will be towards the young feet.

Have a piece of 1-inch or 1⅛-inch dowel rod ready for the crossbar. Anything thicker would be difficult for young hands to grip.

Join the seat, bottom, and crossbar to the sides.

Have the assembly upside-down and make the slide parts (FIG. 6-19J). Bevel against the bottom panel. Round the outer ends. Join the slides to the other parts. Put two or more strips across one slope to aid climbing.

Take the sharpness off all exposed edges and corners and finish by painting brightly. Decorate with decals, but for outdoor use protect the decals with exterior varnish.

PUSH TRICYCLE

The push tricycle could be the first ride-on, self-propelling toy for a toddler. He sits astride the tricycle and moves it with his feet on the ground while he steers the front wheel. The sizes suggested (FIGS. 6-20 and 6-21) should be easy for a young toddler to manage. If he falls, it will not be very far.

Parts could be softwood, but the tricycle will be stronger if it is made of hardwood. The front steering assembly should be hardwood, even if other parts are softwood. The wheels govern other sizes and they are assumed to be 5 inches in diameter in these instructions. Buy metal or plastic ones, possibly with rubber tires, or make them on your lathe. Keep the wheel thickness to no more than 1 inch. Axles will have to suit the holes in bought wheels, but ⅜-inch steel rod should be suitable.

Lay out the seat first, and mark on it where the other parts come (FIG. 6-21A). Cut its outline and well round all edges.

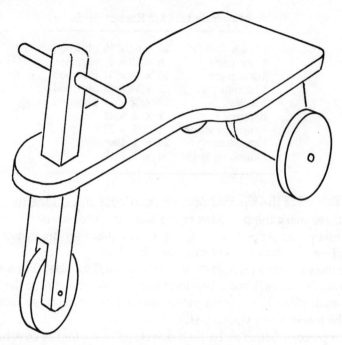

Fig. 6-20. This push tricycle is intended for a small child, who can use his feet to push on the ground.

The rear wheel supports are set in 1 inch from the seat edges and are cut to a large radius round the axle holes, for strength (FIG. 6-21B). Glue and screw a piece between them (FIG. 6-21C) and join the assembly to the seat.

The steering assembly is in two parts. Make the top part (FIG. 6-21D) with the handle through a hole (FIG. 6-21E). Round the ends of the handle and the top of the column, as the child may hit these if he falls.

Cut a slot in the bottom part to clear the wheel (FIG. 6-21F). Stiffen the outside with cheeks which go to the top (FIG. 6-21G); they provide an extra bearing surface under the seat. Round the bottom and all edges. Drill for the axle.

The steering pivot is a piece of 1-inch hardwood dowel rod (FIG. 6-21H). Take it 2 inches into the lower part and glue it there. When you assemble, take it to the same amount into the top part. Secure it with a screw.

Materials List for Push Tricycle

1 seat	¾ × 8 × 20
2 steering columns	2 × 2 × 9
2 cheeks	½ × 2 × 9
1 pivot	6 × 1 diameter
2 wheel supports	1 × 6 × 9
1 wheel support	1 × 4 × 8
1 handle	9 × ¾ diameter

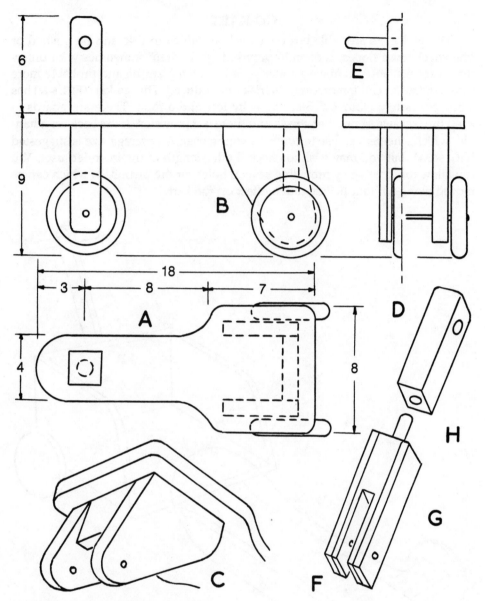

Fig. 6-21. Details of the push tricycle.

Make a trial assembly, then, paint all over. The broad part of the seat could be padded. Secure the rear wheels with cotter pins through holes in the axle. The front axle should stay in position if it is a tight fit in its holes.

GO-KART

The go-kart, a steerable box on wheels in which to ride and be pushed or freewheel down slopes, is often improvised by children, sometimes with unfortunate results. You can make a better go-kart which is strong and probably more satisfying to the child; moreover, the risks are reduced. This go-kart (FIG. 6-22) has a box seat safely mounted. Steering is by feet and a rope. There are guards to keep the feet away from the wheels and there is a provision at the back for a handle, which a helper can use to control a young user. An average size is suggested (FIG. 6-23A), but you may wish to check the leg length of the intended user. You can allow for growing by providing several holes for the pivot bolt, which can be moved along without having much effect on the kart.

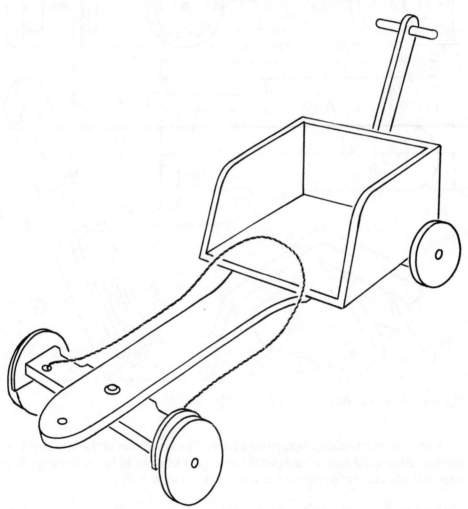

Fig. 6-22. Steer this go-kart by the feet, or a push with a handle and steer with a bridle.

Softwood should be satisfactory. Parts of the box seat could be plywood. Choose a reasonably straight-grained board, free from knots or other flaws, for the lengthwise piece. Sizes are based on 6-inch wheels with ⅜-inch holes. Other sizes can be adapted easily, but much smaller wheels are not advised.

Make the length piece (FIG. 6-23B). Reduce its forward part to 5 inches wide. This can be carried forward to take a hole for a towing rope. If you want to rear handle, allow enough length for that. Round the reduced part, which may come into contact with bare legs.

There could be steel rod axles right across, but the use of carriage bolts is shown (FIG. 6-23C). This gives a smoother and safer outside projection than if an axle goes through and is drilled for cotter pins. Choose carriage bolts long enough to go through a wheel and a block about 3 inches long (FIG. 6-23D).

Make the steering axle support (FIG. 6-23E) notched for the feet and with holes for the steering rope. At the ends, put plywood guards (FIG. 6-23F, G) to stand 1 inch outside the wheel circumference.

Drill the two parts for a ½-inch pivot bolt. The wood parts can bear against each other, but when you assemble, put large washers under the nut and bolt head. Use a locking nut.

The rear axle support is made in the same way, but there are no wheel guards. Screw it to the lengthwise piece and put packings each side under the box seat (FIG. 6-23H).

Have the box bottom with its grain across, probably making up the wood width with several pieces. The grain of the box back and sides should be horizontal. You can make up the box (FIG. 6-23J) with a variety of joints. The rear corners may receive considerable strain sometimes, so they should be strong. Dovetails would be ideal, but screwing should be satisfactory. Put sheet metal straps round near the top corners. Screw the bottom up into the other parts. Round all exposed edges. Screw through the bottom securely into the lower parts.

The rear handle could be a strip 36 inches long with a dowel across the top (FIG. 6-23K). The ¼-inch pivot bolt could have a wing nut so the handle may be removed easily when not required.

Materials List for Go-Kart

1 lengthwise piece	1 ×	7 × 40
2 axles	1 ×	4 × 17
4 axle blocks	1½ × 1½ ×	6
2 wheel guards	6 ×	9 × ½ plywood
1 handle	¾ × 1½ ×	38
1 handle	9 ×	¾ diameter
1 seat bottom	¾ ×	12 × 16
2 seat sides	¾ ×	9 × 14
1 seat back	¾ ×	9 × 16

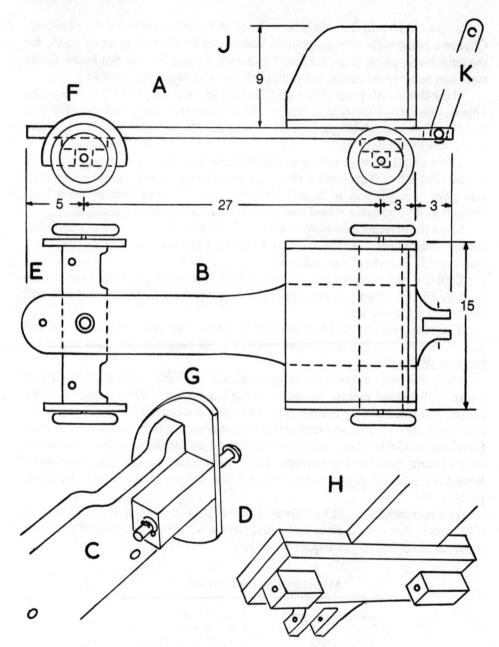

Fig. 6-23. *Sizes of the parts of a go kart.*

ROCKING DUCK

The various rocking toys that a child can ride on are divided broadly into those where he sits astride, and those where he has a chairlike seat. For a first rocking toy the child will probably prefer a seat and a handle to steady himself.

Fig. 6-24. *On this rocking duck the child sits on a seat and uses a handle, instead of sitting astride, as on a horse.*

Many of these toys are based on a horse, but this rocker with a seat is based on a duck (FIG. 6-24). It is difficult to tip, and the rocking motion is fairly mild, to suit the younger user.

Some parts are made of ¾-inch plywood. Other parts may be plywood or solid wood. The seat could be upholstered, but it is shown plain. The main duck outline is the basic part; this is fitted between two footboards, which are mounted on the rockers. Projections below the central part act as stops to prevent the toy turning over endways.

Cut the central part (FIGS. 6-25A and 6-26A). Besides the duck outline, the lower part has level ends and projections below the footboard line (FIG. 6-25B).

At each side of the duck's head are extra pieces to form its crest (FIGS. 6-25C and 6-26B). These add to appearance, but they also give extra thickness for strength in the handle joint. Glue them on. Round all edges about the head and drill for the handle.

The two footboards (FIGS. 6-25D and 6-26C) are straight pieces. Join them to the centerpiece with square strips underneath (FIGS. 6-25E and 6-26D).

Cut the two rockers (FIGS. 6-25F and 6-26E). Screw them under the footboards, with strips across all parts at the ends (FIG. 6-26F). Check that the rockers and the duck parts are upright.

Make two supports for the seat (FIGS. 6-25G and 6-26G). Glue and screw them in place.

Materials List for Rocking Duck

1 main part	18 × 34 × ¾	plywood
2 crests	8 × 12 × ⅜	plywood
1 handle	12 × ¾	diameter
2 footboards	¾ × 7½ × 34	
2 rockers	1 × 4 × 34	
2 strips	1 × 1 × 34	
2 ends	1 × 2 × 18	
2 seat supports	¾ × 10 × 10	
1 seat	10 × 10 × ¾	
1 seat back	10 × 10 × ¾	

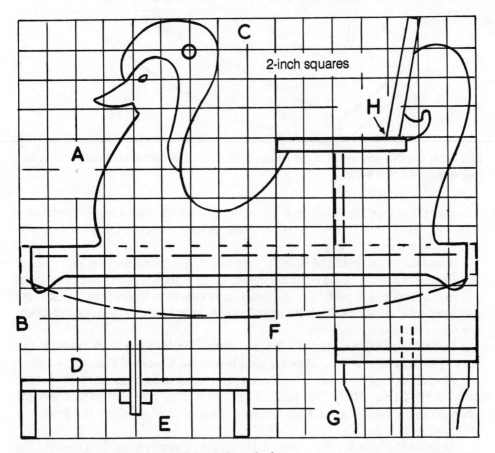

Fig. 6-25. Shapes of the parts of the rocking duck.

The seat parts (FIG. 6-26H) should be round on all exposed edges. The back fits on top of the seat (FIG. 6-25H). Glue and screw them to the supports and the center part.

The handle (FIG. 6-26J) is dowel rod with rounded ends, glued in place.

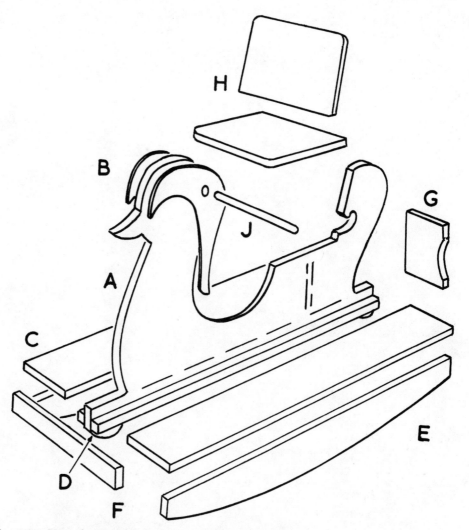

Fig. 6-26. *How the parts of the rocking duck are arranged.*

The young user will probably be glad to get on the rocking duck as it is; however, it should be painted. The duck itself might be white, with a darker color crest and eyes painted on. The other parts could be brighter, such as red or green. Nonslip plastic pieces could be glued to the footboards. The seat could be padded.

7

Ball
Games

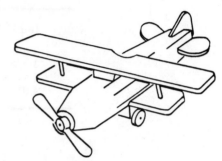

BALL BOARD

A board with holes into which balls can be thrown will provide plenty of amusement and skill testing for children of all ages. This ball board (FIG. 7-1A) is made as a box with divisions into which any scoring balls will fall, so there cannot be a dispute about which hole a ball entered. The size allows for use indoors or in the yard. Balls about 2 inches across are suitable. Hard balls will be easier to use than soft ones which bounce a lot. However, conditions are the same for all players if they use the same balls.

The size allows for making all parts from ½-inch plywood, which can be cut economically from a sheet 48 inches wide. Top and bottom should be plywood, but use solid wood for the other parts, if you wish. Construction can be with glue and nails.

Cut the matching squares for the top and bottom. Mark the centers of the holes on the top (FIG. 7-2A).

Draw the circles and cut them out. If you use a fine blade in a portable jigsaw and cut carefully, the edges should not need much further treatment. Take the sharpness off the rims and sand them.

Cut pieces for the outside of the box (FIG. 7-1B). Nail lapped corners, but you could glue small pieces inside as well.

Divide the box into nine compartments (FIGS. 7-1C and 7-2B). Cut halving joints where they cross (FIG. 7-2C).

Assemble the box framework with the divisions nailed through the sides. Level the top and bottom edges.

Nail on the bottom. If you wish to paint the inside, do it now.

Nail on the top and level all edges. Round the edges and corners.

Paint all over and add the numbers. The board is shown as if it is diagonal to the thrower, but it could be arranged squarely.

Materials List for Ball Board

(all ½ inch plywood)

1 top	24 × 24
1 bottom	24 × 24
4 sides	4 × 24
4 divisions	4 × 24

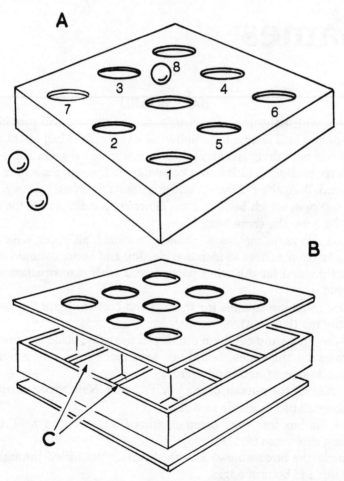

Fig. 7-1. *This ball board is in the form of a box, with holes for aiming balls at.*

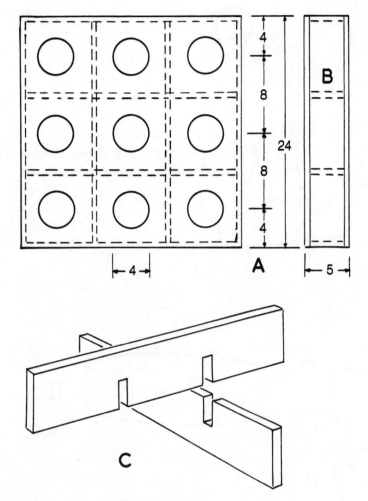

Fig. 7-2. Size and construction of the ball board.

SKITTLES

Rolling or throwing a ball at an object is an instinctive action from an early age. This urge can be directed into a game with a set of skittles, or pins. What skittles you make depends to a certain extent on the age of the child. If all he wants to do is throw or roll a ball, a few skittles that look something like people may be all that is needed. If older children want to make a competition of it, they need a set of identical skittles. The usual set for a game of nine-pins is nine arranged in a diamond pattern. With a lathe you can turn skittles (FIG. 7-3), but it is possible to make acceptable skittles without a lathe.

Even if a child uses a soft ball, the wear on a skittle can be heavy as it gets knocked along the ground. For a serious game with a hard ball, the skittles have

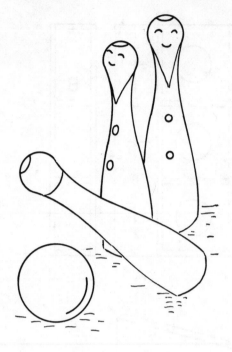

Fig. 7-3. Skittles to throw balls at will appeal to all children.

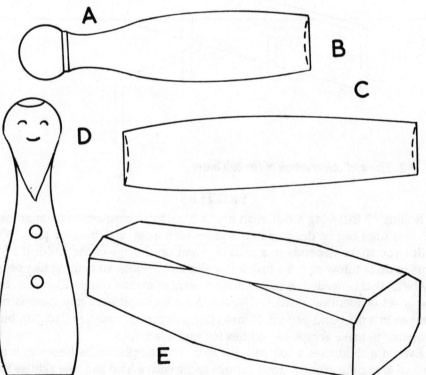

Fig. 7-4. Skittles may be turned or whittled.

to be tough. Make them from sound hardwood. Any flaws will soon result in breaks or cracks.

The size of a skittle depends on how big a game you contemplate. A young child throwing from a few feet can have skittles 6 inches high. Typically, they could be 9 inches and made from 2-inch-diameter wood. The traditional child's skittle has a ball top (FIG. 7-4A). Turn it with plenty of bulk lower down, for stability. Hollow the bottom so it will stand firmly on slightly uneven ground (FIG. 7-4B).

For more serious games, the skittles could be barrel-shaped (FIG. 7-4C). If you make the greatest diameter away from the center, so one end is heavier than the other, you can put the skittles with their heavy ends up so they tip easier, for less skillful players, or have the weight downwards to make it more difficult. Whether you make this pattern or the first one, remember you probably have to make nine. Therefore, keep the design simple; it is easier to repeat.

A simplified version of the first pattern lends itself to decoration (FIG. 7-4D), if knocking over figures is what your child prefers.

If you do not have the use of a lathe, a squared version of the barrel shape is easy to make by tapering the corners of a square piece (FIG. 7-4E). You could paint numbers on the flat sides of these skittles, so you score to which one is bowled over.

JUNIOR CROQUET

Hitting balls through hoops where there is little clearance may be too much for most children, but their own obstacles with good clearance and scaled-down balls and mallets should appeal to them. This game (FIG. 7-5A) can have as many obstacles as you wish, arranged in a series on the lawn or a hard surface; then, the balls can be hit through them in turn. Hard rubber balls are suitable.

The obstacles are made of plywood, and there are pieces to fit across them to hold them upright. Each piece has a peg (FIG. 7-6C) to push into the ground, but for use on a hard surface, the piece may be turned over and put in the slot the other way. There is still stability, but the peg points upwards out of the way.

Check the size of ball you intend using and make the obstacles with holes about twice that size (FIG. 7-6A). Cut the slots to half the depth of the wings and wide enough to make a push fit on the support piece. Make all the parts you want at one time, so they match and the supports will be interchangeable.

The support pieces (FIG. 7-5C) are rectangular as they must fit both ways (FIG. 7-6B). Make enough of these and check that they will fit the slots either way.

Make ½-inch-square pegs (FIG. 7-5D and 6C), preferably of hardwood. Taper slightly. Glue and screw to the supports.

Paint these parts and put numbers on them to show the sequence they are to be used.

The mallet could have a round head, but it is shown with a square one (FIGS. 7-5E and 7-6D). Drill through so a piece of ½-inch dowel rod can be glued in as a

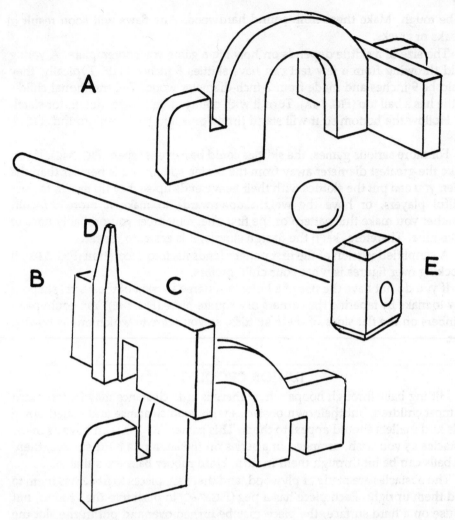

Fig. 7-5. *This junior croquet game has obstacles suitable for pegging into the ground or for use on a hard floor.*

handle. Adjust the handle length to suit the child. It should be used while standing, using both hands and with the head swung between the legs.

CLOCK GOLF

If you have a reasonably flat piece of lawn, youngsters can play golf in a rather similar way to their parents. A clock golf course will give them plenty of amusement and adults may wish to join in. There are twelve numbered positions arranged as in a clock face (FIG. 7-7A), although it does not matter if you do not have them in an exact circle. There is a hole off-center (FIG. 7-7B), and the game is

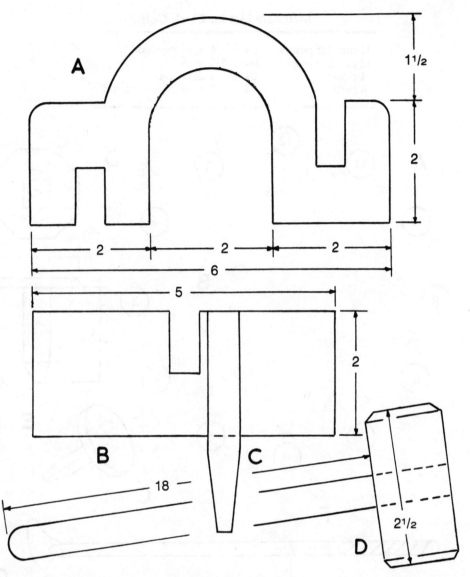

Fig. 7-6. Details of the parts for the junior croquet game.

for each child to play from each number in turn. The one who succeeds in holing his ball from each position in the least total number of shots, is the winner.

The hole can be a can, sunk in the ground. You can arrange the size of the play area to suit the children and you may have a larger hole for younger children. The ball could be a proper golf ball, or children may prefer a wooden or hard rubber ball. The making of a junior club is described.

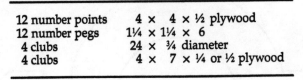

Materials List for Clock Golf

12 number points	4 × 4 × ½ plywood
12 number pegs	1¼ × 1¼ × 6
4 clubs	24 × ¾ diameter
4 clubs	4 × 7 × ¼ or ½ plywood

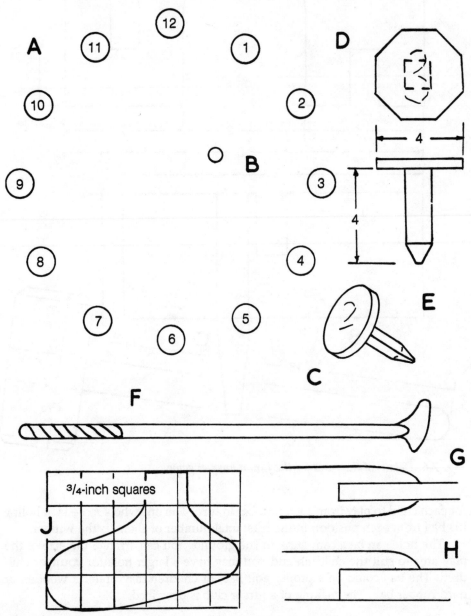

Fig. 7-7. *The layout for clock golf and the construction of parts.*

The number points may be round (FIG. 7-7C), square or octagonal (FIG. 7-7D), cut from ½-inch exterior plywood. Nail or screw them to pointed pieces (FIG. 7-7E) to push into the ground.

Paint prominent numbers in contrast to a backing color.

The suggested putter has a plywood head on a dowel rod handle (FIG. 7-7F). A length of 24 inches should suit young children.

If you can get strong hardwood plywood for the putter blade, it need only be ¼ inch thick, and it can be slotted into ¾-inch dowel rod (FIG. 7-7G). If you have to use thicker softwood plywood, it will be stronger notched into one side (FIG. 7-7H).

Cut the head to shape (FIG. 7-7J) and round all edges, except those that fit into the handle.

Make enough putters. Children may not want to share their own. Paint all over. A grip can be made by binding with electrician's or other colored tapes.

CRAZY GOLF

Something more than straightforward golf is needed if the game is to appeal to younger children. If there are hazards to be dealt with and the distances are fairly short, interest in the game is sustained much longer. Obstacles can be arranged before each hole is reached. Distance and numbers will depend on the space you have available, but by doubling back between holes, you can get quite a lot of activity into a comparatively small space.

Crazy or hazard golf can be played with fullsize clubs and balls or you can use the equipment described in the last project. If you make the croquet equipment, some of the arches can be brought into use as hazards, or obstacles.

Some hazards you can make are shown (FIG. 7-8). These obstacles are intended to be taken up when not in use. They should have enough weight to stay in place on a lawn or patio without being pegged down. Most are based on a piece of ½-inch plywood, which could be 12 × 18 inches, being satisfactory for an approach shot from about 10 feet. If your course is longer, the obstacles could be bigger. In most cases, the holes should be not more than 6 feet past the obstacle.

The basic obstacle is a tunnel (FIG. 7-8A). Bevel the base on the approach side. The size of the hole depends on the probable skill of the players, but it should be at least 1 inch bigger than the ball. Use two blocks with a plywood roof and a shaped plywood front.

A wavy slot (FIG. 7-8B) could be any length. Widening the end makes entry easier. Height should be at least 1½ times the ball diameter, or it may ride over if hit hard. There could be a plywood top.

Getting a ball over a hump is more difficult than it looks. This obstacle (FIG. 7-8C) has a gap to be aimed at. Notch plywood into the solid block.

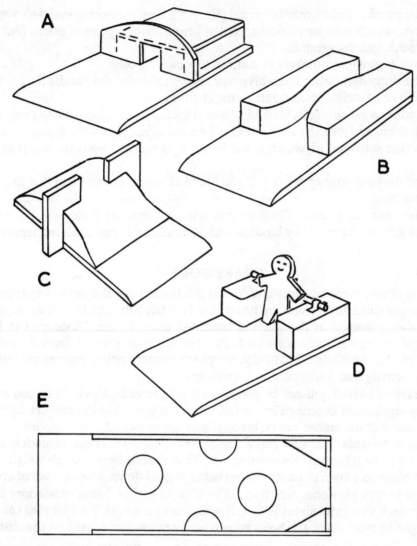

Fig. 7-8. *For crazy golf, make a variety of obstacles for use indoors or outdoors.*

A moving figure to be hit with a ball appeals to younger children. Make the man of plywood with more wood below the pivot dowel rod than above (FIG. 7-8D). To keep him upright, add more weight to his feet. You could thicken to make boots or nail on pieces of lead. Arrange a gap between the blocks to give enough clearance. The dowel could go through wood blocks with large holes, but it is shown through bent pieces of metal.

Several longer flat obstacles can be made, with islands for the ball to be hit around, usually by caroming against the sides. This one (FIG. 7-8E) is an open-ended box with sides and islands at least 3 inches high. Allow an exit gap of reasonable size, or getting a ball through may prove too frustrating.

Bases of the obstacles could be green, but use bright colors for the other parts. A prominent number painted on the approach sides will show the order of play.

POLE TENNIS

Pole tennis is a game with a satisfying demand on children's energy. Two players can compete, or one can get fun out of hitting the ball both ways. A ball is tethered by a cord to the top of a pole (FIG. 7-9A) and can be hit around it. Two players hit opposite ways and each scores a point when his opponent misses. Ordinary tennis racquets can be used, but for children it may be better to use table tennis paddles.

There can be a considerable load on the pole, so it has to be driven firmly into the ground. A pole in a single length could be used, but if it is in two parts it is more compact for storage or transport. A way is shown for driving the lower part into the ground, without damage to it, before adding the top piece.

The wood for the pole should be straight-grained and stiff. The pivot piece for the top should be close-grained hardwood. A tube, preferably brass, is needed for the joint. This has to slide closely on the poles, so getting matching sizes is a first priority. The best poles are between 1 inch and 1¼ inches in diameter.

Prepare the pivot piece (FIG. 7-9B), with a stout long screw (#12 gauge would be suitable) and a piece of brass tube to fit fairly closely over it. Drill the ⅞-inch-square wood for the tube and for the cord (about ¼-inch diameter). Round the extending ends.

Cut the two poles to length (FIG. 7-9C) and point the bottom one. Fit a ½-inch dowel with a tapered end into the top part and make a hole to take it in the lower part (FIG. 7-9D). This registers the parts, but a 9-inch tube slides from the top part over the joint and rests against a screw (FIG. 7-9E, F).

If the joint is not a very close fit and there might be a risk of it separating, drill both ends of the tube for a screw into each part of the pole. Of course, then you need a screwdriver when you wish to take the pole apart.

For hammering the bottom part into the ground without damaging its top, make a pad with a dowel to fit the hole (FIG. 7-9G). Use this to take the blows of the hammer. It may be bigger and need not be round.

Use a hard rubber ball. A large needle or bodkin will be needed to get the rope through it. Knot securely there and through the pivot piece. Have the rope long enough for the ball to be a few inches above the ground when at rest.

Grease round the screw when you first assemble it through the tube into the top of the pole.

A bat has a plywood blade let into a solid wood handle (FIG. 7-9H). Use hardwood ¼-inch plywood, as this is stronger and directs a better blow to the ball

Materials List for Pole Tennis

2 poles	38 × 1¼ diameter	
1 pivot piece	⅞ × ⅞ × 5	
2 bats	8 × 11 × ¼ plywood	
4 bat handles	1 × 1 × 12	
1 brass tube	9 to fit poles	
1 brass tube	1 to fit screw	

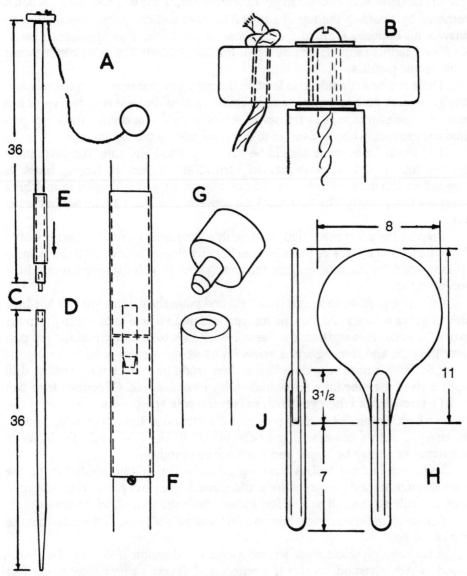

Fig. 7-9. *In pole tennis, two players hit the ball on a rope opposite ways round the pole.*

than thicker softwood plywood. Cut, so a broad part extends into the handle for strength in the joint.

For comfort and a good grip, the handle should be as thick as a child can hold. A hexagonal section is better than round and this should be at least 1 inch across the flats.

Round the ends of the handles. Cut a close-fitting slot on a blade (FIG. 7-9J). Taper over this and glue the joint. If you have to use screws as well, keep them thin.

Paint the pole parts. Leave the bats untreated, but sand them well.

8

Educational Toys

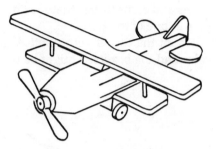

BLOCK POSTING BOX

Building blocks are traditional toys which still appeal to younger children. These toys tend to get lost and thrown all over the place and a container is essential. If a box can *also* provide some educational play, that is a bonus. The block posting box (FIG. 8-1) has a sliding lid with holes in to match the shapes of the blocks, so the child can drop blocks through, by lining up the shapes. There can be several blocks of each shape, and you will have to adjust the size of the box to suit the number of blocks you make.

Avoid any wood that may tend to splinter. A close-grained hardwood, such as beech or sycamore, with all edges and corners rounded, should be quite durable. The box should be of a similar hardwood and its lid plywood—preferably hardwood, as most softwood plywood is splintery.

The sizes suggested (FIG. 8-2A) are developed from a building block that is a 1⅜-inch cube, passing through a 1½-inch-square hole. Other shapes are proportional to this size, and all blocks could be 1⅜ inches thick. Then cut most of them sawn and planed to this thickness.

Make all the blocks. Six shapes are suggested; start with at least three of each shape. Round the edges and corners, so you finish with a smooth, sanded surface all over.

Mark out the sliding lid. The holes should allow ample clearance for tiny hands to be able to manipulate the blocks through—⅛-inch clearance should be enough. Take the sharpness off the top and bottom edges of the holes.

The box is shown with the bottom inside (FIG. 8-2B). For the simplest construction you could nail or screw it on. The lid slides over the box front and into grooves in the sides and back (FIG. 8-2C). Prepare the wood and plow grooves to allow the lid to fit easily.

You could make the box in several ways. Corners could be nailed or screwed. Dovetails would be good, but the drawing shows finger or tongue joints (FIG. 8-2D). They need not be narrow tongues, unless you have a jig that cuts them that way.

Assemble the box with the bottom glued and pinned inside. Round all the edges and corners. See that the lid will slide easily. It can be pulled out with fingers in one of the holes.

Paint the blocks with nontoxic paint. The box top could be in a contrasting color and the box itself might be painted or varnished.

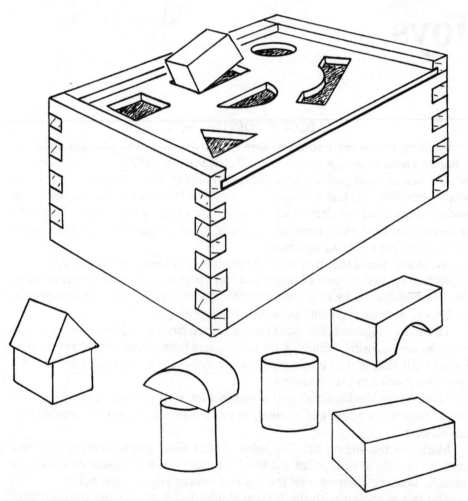

Fig. 8-1. *This block posting box takes building blocks through holes of different shapes, and the lid can be opened to retrieve them.*

Materials List for Block Posting Box	
Blocks from	1⅜ × 1¾ strip
2 box sides	¾ × 6 × 9
1 box back	¾ × 6 × 14
1 box front	¾ × 5 × 14
1 box bottom	½ × 6 × 13

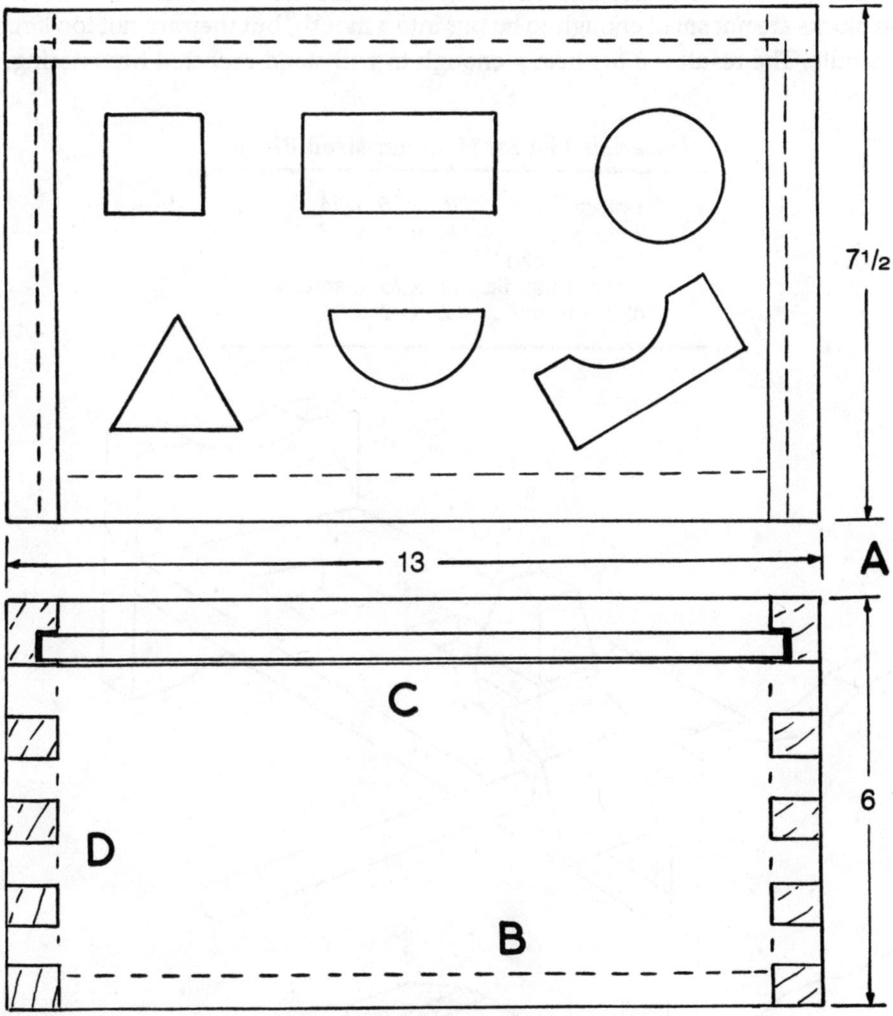

Fig. 8-2. Size and layout of the block posting box.

HAMMER-SIZED BLOCKS

A toy where pegs have to be hammered through holes is a traditional means of working off a young child's frustration. If he has to select pegs of different sizes, he will learn something about choice. This toy follows traditional form, except that the four holes are of slightly different sizes and tapered pegs have to be chosen to hammer through them. As shown, (FIG. 8-3) the holes and pegs are square, but if you have a lathe you could make similar round pegs to drive into round holes.

This toy needs to be durable, so all parts should be hardwood. It is also advisable to use mortise-and-tenon joints, so the ends do not become loose.

Sizes are not crucial, but in the suggested toy the end blocks go into 2-inch and 1¾-inch-square holes. The other two holes are 1½ inches and 1¼ inches. The blocks are not small enough to be put into a mouth, but they are not too large to handle. The result is a toy heavy enough to withstand repeated hammering.

Materials List for Hammer-sized Blocks

1 piece	¾ × 5 × 14
2 pieces	¾ × 5 × 7
1 mallet head	2 × 2 × 5
1 mallet handle	12 × ½ diameter
blocks from	2 × 2 × 14

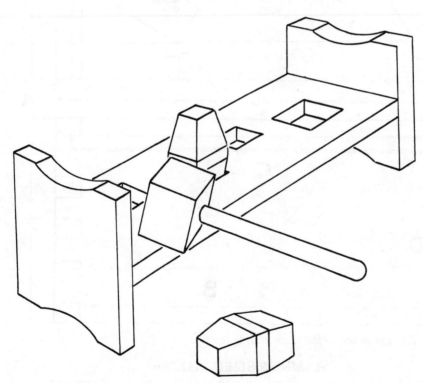

Fig. 8-3. This toy has holes of different sizes and matching blocks to be sorted and hammered through.

Mark out the large piece (FIG. 8-4A). The holes are staggered and overlap the centerline by ¼ inch. Cut the squares as accurately as possible.

At the ends divide the width into seven, and mark the three tenons (FIG. 8-4B).

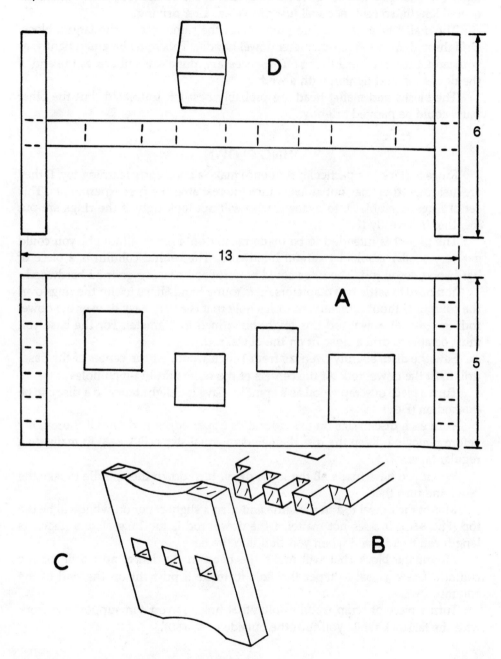

Fig. 8-4. Details of the hammer-sized block toy.

Make the uprights (FIG. 8-4C), with hollows to provide corner feet.

Mark and cut mortises. Glue the joints tightly and check for squareness.

Cut square pieces. Get each to a size that will just push into its holes; then, taper the ends to leave about ½ inch parallel at the center (FIG. 8-4D). Make the overall length, so each peg will just drop clear after driving.

The mallet head is a square piece about the same size as the largest block. Drill through for a ½-inch-diameter dowel handle. This must be glued tightly, as you cannot risk the head flying off. If necessary, put a saw cut across the end of the dowel rod and tighten with a wedge.

The blocks and mallet head are probably best left untreated, but the other parts could be painted brightly.

RING CLOWN

Rings to stack in a particular sequence make a good early learning toy. If they are just rings, they may not arouse much interest after the first experiments. This set of rings assembles into a clown who will not look right if the rings are put together incorrectly (FIG. 8-5).

The project is intended to be made mostly on a lathe; although, you could get very similar results by careful handwork. The central column is a piece of hardwood dowel rod. The rings could be softwood or close-grained hardwood.

You need to settle two diameters first. Young hands have to slip the rings over the column without difficulty, so drill a hole that is a very easy fit over the dowel rod. For ¾-inch dowel rod this might be ⅞ inch in diameter. For the base you must be able to drill a close fit on the dowel rod.

Saw the discs slightly oversize from 1-inch wood. At the center of the base, drill to fit the dowel rod. At the centers of the others drill ⅞-inch holes.

Turn a piece of scrap wood as a spindle. Give it a slight taper so a disc can be pushed on (FIG. 8-5A).

Turn each disc to size on this, round its upper edges and sand it thoroughly before removing. Keep the disc diameters in equal steps (FIG. 8-5B) to maintain a regular taper.

When you have made all the loose discs, turn down the spindle to take the base, and turn that.

Mount the dowel rod in the lathe and turn a slight taper on what will be the top (FIG. 8-5C). It does not matter if the dowel rod is too long at this stage. Its length can be adjusted when you fit it into the base.

Mount the block that will make the head in the lathe, and drill for the column. Use a chisel to taper the hole to make a push fit on the end of the column.

Turn a piece of scrap wood to plug that hole, so you can support the work with the tailstock while you turn the outside (FIG. 8-5D).

Materials List for Ring Clown

Discs from	1 × 5 × 20	
1 head	2 × 2 × 4	
1 column	8 × ¾ diameter	

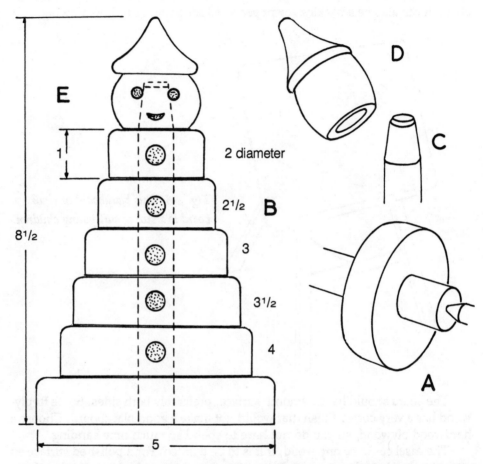

Fig. 8-5. *The parts of this clown are in the form of rings to be sorted and fitted on a rod.*

Try the parts together. Push the dowel rod through the base until there is the right degree of fit on the discs. There should be some "play" between the discs when the head is pushed tight on the top of the column (FIG. 8-5E).

Paint the wood in bright colors. A dot on each disc can represent a button. Put eyes and mouth on the head. The child can then arrange the buttons and face in line, as well as put the rings in the correct order. With the head being a push fit, it will be possible for the toy to be carried about without it falling apart.

BLACKBOARD AND EASEL

A board and chalk will keep a child happy for a long time. If the board is supported on an easel, he can draw while standing or sitting on a stool. This blackboard and easel (FIG. 8-6) is based on a traditional school design, but at a size to suit children aged 5 to 8 years. Sizes are easily modified to suit your needs, without affecting the method of construction. Besides using the board for chalk, it can also be a backing for paper, used for painting or line drawing.

Fig. 8-6. This blackboard or chalk board is a size to suit young children.

The board should have a smooth surface, preferably both sides. Some fir plywood has a very coarse finish that would not make a good blackboard. Choose a hardwood plywood, so you do not have to spend so much time sanding.

The easel could be any wood, if it is to be painted. For a polished surface an attractive hardwood would be better. Construction could be with dowels or tenons. Both methods are described.

Set out the front view of the easel (FIG. 8-7A) fullsize, either complete or one side of the centerline; this will give you the actual lengths and the angles to cut.

Mark and cut the pair of sides (FIG. 8-7B), with the positions of the cross members shown.

Decide on dowels or mortise-and-tenon joints; either would be satisfactory. If you choose dowels, they could be ¼-inch diameter, but you have to be able to drill accurately at the angle of the structure (FIG. 8-7C). Mortises need only be ¾-inch deep for stub tenons (FIG. 8-7D).

Cut the upper (FIG. 8-7E) and lower (FIG. 8-7F) crosspiece, allowing for tenons, if that will be the jointing you choose.

Assemble the frame. Compare diagonal measurements to see that it is symmetrical. Lay it on a flat surface to see that there is no twist in it.

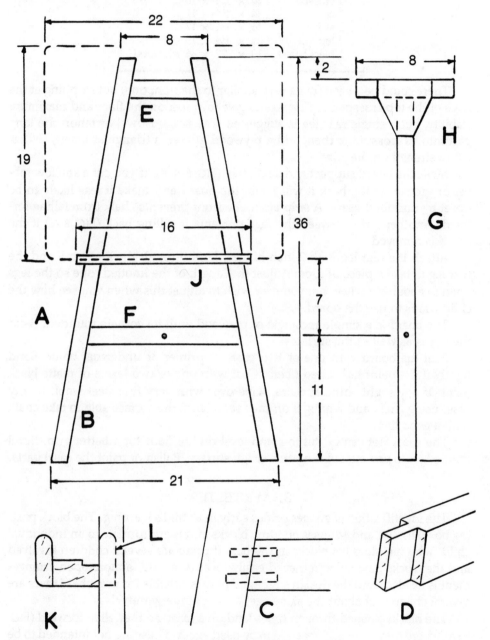

Fig. 8-7. Sizes and details of the blackboard and easel.

Materials List for Blackboard and Easel

3 legs	¾ × 1½ × 38
1 crossbar	¾ × 1½ × 20
1 crossbar	¾ × 1½ × 10
1 crossbar	¾ × 1½ × 17
2 strips	½ × 1½ × 17
1 leg top	¾ × 1½ × 10
1 blackboard	19 × 22 × ½ plywood

There could be a back frame very similar to the front one, but stopping at the edge of the top crosspiece. That would give four feet on the floor and maximum stability, but a single rear leg is suggested (FIG. 8-7G). Dowel or tenon the long part into its crosspiece; then, add a plywood gusset, a triangular insert, (FIG. 8-7H) to strengthen the joint.

Make the board support and chalk tray (FIG. 8-7J, K). If you cut a shallow rabbet or groove, at the back it will retain the board and make it less likely to be upset by unskilled users. A strip along the front prevents chalk from falling forward. Another strip between the legs prevents it rolling back (FIG. 8-7L) if the board is removed.

Attach the rear leg with 2-inch hinges. Drill through the lower rail and the rear leg to take a piece of rope. Adjust the length of the knotted rope so the legs open to about 24 inches, but you may wish to adjust this when you see how the child wants to use the board.

The board is a simple rectangle of plywood with its corners rounded. Sand the edges as well as the surfaces.

Seal the board with one or two coats of primer or undercoat paint. Sand lightly if the paint has raised fibers. Coat with one or two layers of matte black paint. If any slight shine appears, wipe over with very fine steel wool. In any case, using chalk and wiping if off may soon leave the surface able to take chalk with a good line.

The easel feet can be cut to stand level on the floor for a better grip. Bevel their edges to prevent splitting on a rough surface. Polish or paint the easel parts.

SHAPE TESTER

The identification of shapes comes early in a child's learning. The block posting box (FIGS. 8-1 and 8-2) uses building blocks and is appropriate to an individual child, who can store his blocks in the box. If there are several children involved and the blocks have to be retrieved easily for further use, a more open arrangement is needed, and the design suggested here is suitable for use where there are several children of about the same age, as in a kindergarten class.

The blocks pushed through holes land on a ramp so they slide forward (FIG. 8-8A) where they are easily reached to be used again. These are not intended to be building blocks, but are designed to aid selection. They are long enough not to go into a wrong slot on edge.

Materials List for Shape Tester

1 top	½ ×		7	×	12
2 ends	½ ×		6	×	10
1 ramp	½ ×		9	×	11
1 back	½ ×	3½	×	11
1 ledge	½ ×		1	×	11
blocks from	2 ×		2	×	18

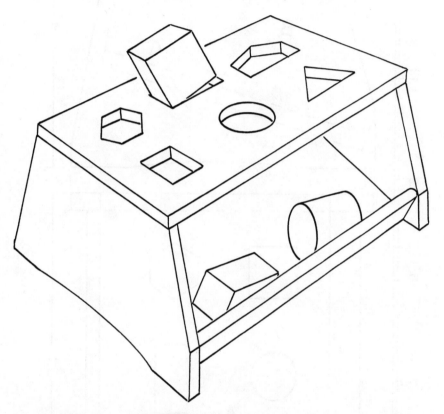

Fig. 8-8. This shape tester can be used by several children. When a block has been passed through its correct hole it slides down, ready to be used again.

All the wood for the stand could be ½ inch thick, either solid wood or plywood. Cut tenons or use thin dowels, but it will probably be satisfactory to use glue and screws. The blocks should be close-grained hardwood, as they are liable to rough treatment.

Lay out the top with the shapes for the holes (FIG. 8-9A). Allow sufficient wood between the holes for strength. The holes need not be the shapes shown, although those give a good variety. You may have to relate hole sizes to the wood you intend using for the blocks. Cut the holes, keeping the edges as square as possible, but they could be rounded or beveled top and bottom to reduce splintering, and allow easy access of the blocks.

Make the pair of ends (FIG. 8-9B). Mark on the positions of the ramp, the back and the ledge. Hollow the bottom edges so the ends will stand firmly.

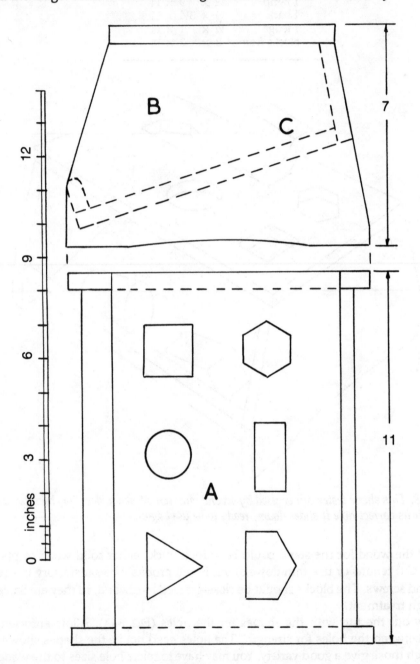

Fig. 8-9. *Suggested sizes for the shape tester.*

Make the three pieces that go between the ends (FIG. 8-9C). Round the edge of the ledge. Glue and screw them to the ends and add the top. Check that the assembly stands firm and without wobble.

Make the blocks loose fits in their holes. Make lengths 2 inches or a little more, but the pieces have to drop through onto the ramp. It will be as easy to make double length blocks and cut them in half, so you have spares. Round all edges and corners.

Paint all parts. The blocks could be all one color or they could be different, but then a child might go for a color rather than a shape after a little practice.

JIGSAW CLOCK

A clock dial is a mystery to a child, but as he learns numbers it begins to make sense. To help in learning the first numbers and the layout of a clock dial, it is useful to make a jigsaw puzzle of it (FIG. 8-10). For a young child the parts should not be too small. This puzzle has a framed base 11 inches across, with a central part carrying the hands, so the twelve pieces with the numbers are about 2½ inches × 4 inches (FIG. 8-10A).

All of the jigsaw clock could be made in ⅜-inch or ½-inch plywood, preferably hardwood. In any case, take off sharp edges and corners and sand thoroughly, so there is no risk of splintering.

Laying out starts with drawing a hexagon around a circle (FIG. 8-10B). Divide it across into 6 and divide those sectors again to make 12, so they are 30 degrees apart. The numbers will come on these lines. Further lines are needed midway between these sector lines (FIG. 8-10C) for the cuts, so they are at 15 degrees. You will find it best to do the setting out full size on paper or scrap plywood. For the central block, draw a circle and mark 12 edges on it (FIG. 8-10D).

Cut the base to shape and mount the rim on it (FIG. 8-10E). The rim may be one piece with the inside cut away, or you could miter strips. Mount the block at the center (FIG. 8-10F).

Cut twelve loose pieces. Although you have the setting out as a guide, there may be minor variations, so trim and fit as you go.

The two hands need metal washers below and above. Make the hands with inner ends to match the washers. Mount them on a round head screw (FIG. 8-10G); then, take apart for painting.

Materials List for Jigsaw Clock

2 bases	11 × 13 × ½
other parts from	11 × 22 × ½

The sectors that make the dial could be a lighter color than the other parts. The hands should be a contrasting color. Mark the numbers prominently. Adjust the hands so they will stay where put, but are not too difficult to move.

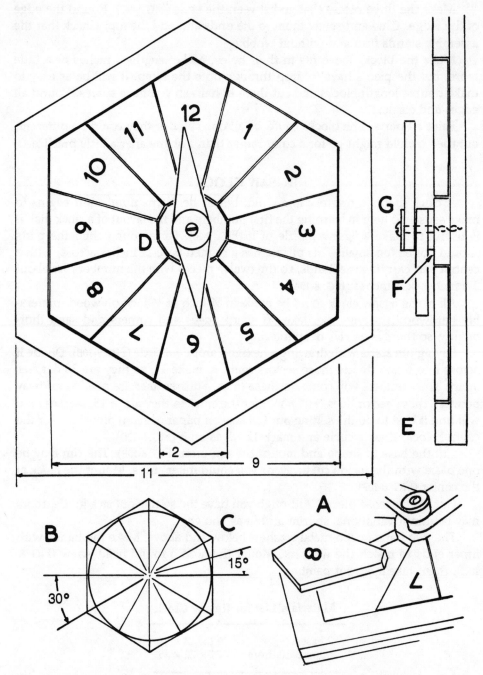

Fig. 8-10. *The numbered sections of this clock face have to be put together correctly as a jigsaw puzzle.*

PERISCOPE

A means of looking over a wall or over the heads of a crowd will appeal to any child. He can see as high as an adult can. He can see around obstructions without being seen. The answer is a periscope, which could be any size, but if a child is to handle it, it must not be too big. This periscope (FIG. 8-11A) allows for a

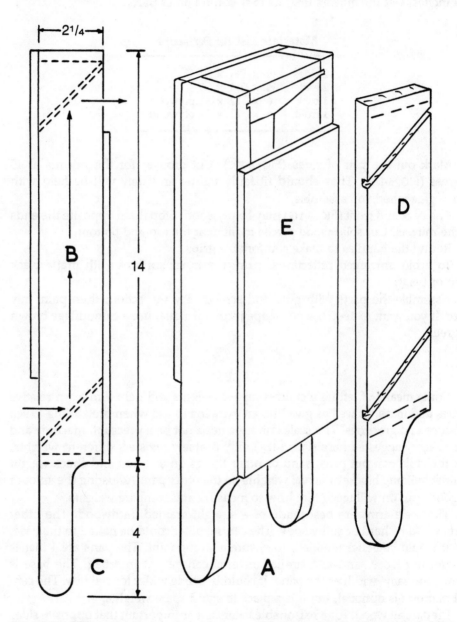

Fig. 8-11. *This periscope uses two mirrors, and has two handles for steady holding by a child.*

sight line about 12 inches above his eyes. There are two handles, so it can be held steady.

Size depends on the mirrors involved. When you look into one you get a reflection of what appears in the other (FIG. 8-11B). If a child is to use both eyes, the mirrors should be at least 4 inches wide. The suggested mirrors are 3 inches × 4 inches. Get the mirrors first, as they control other parts.

Materials List for Periscope

2 sides	½ × 2¼ × 20	
2 ends	½ × 2¼ × 6	
1 back	6 × 12 × ¼ plywood	
1 front	6 × 12 × ¼ plywood	

Mark out the pair of sides (FIG. 8-11C). Cut grooves for the mirrors at 45 degrees (FIG. 8-11D). They should fit fairly tightly and they will be held with epoxy glue when you assemble.

The back and front (FIG. 8-11E) may be plywood. Stop them opposite the ends of the mirrors. Cut solid wood pieces to fill in at the top and bottom.

Round the handles to make comfortable grips.

To avoid unwanted reflections, paint the inner surfaces with matte black stain or paint.

Assemble the parts with glue and screws. Try the action; then paint any color. If you want to keep the periscope inconspicuous, use a camouflage brown or green.

SCALES

Some means of letting a child compare weights will help him learn relative values and mass, as well as give him an extra toy to use when pretending to sell produce and groceries. The scales he uses need not be a precision machine and the design suggested here (FIG. 8-12A) only coarsely registers different weights, but the child can put peas, sand or other things on one pan and check weight against building blocks or actual weights on the other pan. Adjusting the amount of goods put on will teach him how to measure and compare weights.

The scale arms are best made of a straight-grained hardwood. The other parts could be hard or soft woods. The central pillar could be nailed to the base, but it would be better tenoned, to ensure a strong joint. The pans are 4 inches square, but loose sand and similar material can be put in a bag. The base is shown the same width as the pans. It could be made wider for stability. The central platform is optional, but it is a place to stand spare weights.

Prepare all wood. For a reasonable balance, it is important that opposite sides match, so use similar woods for opposite parts.

Make the four balance arms (FIG. 8-12B), marking them out together, symmetrical about the center hole. Drill for #8 gauge screws.

Cut the piece for the central pillar (FIG. 8-12C), with a tenon marked to go into the base. Mark the pivot points exactly level on opposite sides.

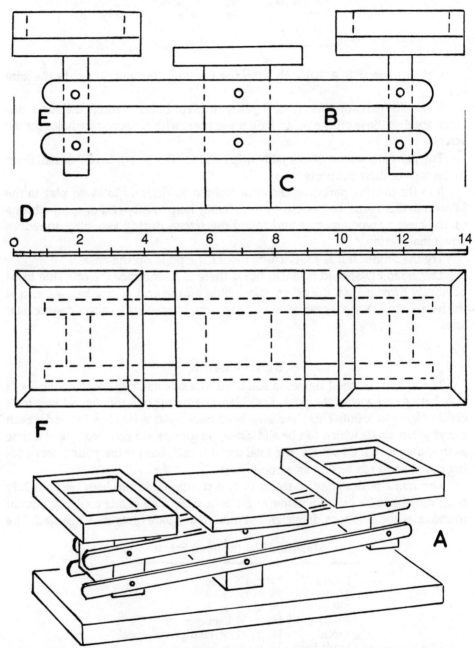

Fig. 8-12. *Wooden scales allow a child to compare weights and measure all sorts of things.*

4 balance arms	⅜ ×	¾ ×	13	
1 base	¾ ×	4 ×	13	
1 pillar	1½ ×	2 ×	6	
2 supports	¾ ×	1½ ×	5	
3 pans	½ ×	4 ×	4	
8 pan rims	⅜ ×	¾ ×	5	

Cut the base (FIG. 8-12D) with a mortise for the pillar, but do not fit the joint yet.

Make the pan supports (FIG. 8-12E) with pivot holes marked the same distance apart as those on the pillar. Drill these parts with tapping size holes for the screws.

The pans are square pieces with strips on top (FIG. 8-12F). Screw or nail them to the tops of their supports.

Join the moving parts with screws. Tighten sufficiently to avoid play in the joints, but there must be free movement. It may help to rub wax, or spray silicone on the meeting wood surface and round the screws during assembly, to reduce any initial friction.

Try the action. If it is satisfactory, mount the pillar on the base.

The assembly should balance, but if there is a tendency for one side to be obviously heavier than the other, take a little off the end of one balance arm at the heavier end. You may not achieve perfection, but the scales should settle near level.

BEAD FRAME

The abacus, or bead frame, is still used as a calculator in some countries. It may have given way to the pocket calculator here, but it is still a good way for a child to learn to count. This simplified bead frame (FIG. 8-13A) has five rods, each carrying ten beads which can be slid along, so groups are counted one at a time as they are moved. Of course, the total count is fifty, but for the young user adding beads up to ten will be an achievement.

The frame is designed to stand in two positions. It can lean back slightly from upright or be put at a flatter angle on a table. The beads could be bought round ones about ¾-inch diameter, but modified square ones are suggested. The

Materials List for Bead Frame

2 sides	¾ ×	1½ ×	14		
2 legs	¾ ×	1½ ×	9		
2 blocks	¾ ×	2 ×	5		
3 rods	14 ×	½ diameter			
5 rods	14 ×	⅛ or 5/32 diameter metal			
beads from	¾ ×	¾ ×	36		

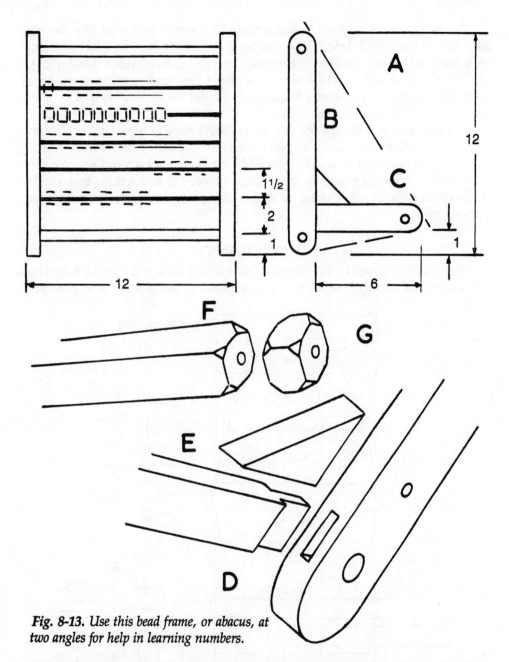

Fig. 8-13. Use this bead frame, or abacus, at two angles for help in learning numbers.

rods are metal, preferably brass or other noncorrosive material. The frame is made from ¾-inch × 1½-inch strip and ½-inch dowel rods.

Mark out the pair of sides together (FIG. 8-13B). Holes should be ½ inch deep to suit the dowels and the rods (⅛ inch or 5/32 inch, depending on their stiffness).

Make the legs (FIG. 8-13C), and cut the mortise and tenon joints (FIG. 8-13D). Round all ends. Join these parts and glue in a reinforcing block (FIG. 8-13E).

The beads can be cut from ¾-inch-square hardwood—you need fifty. Set the table saw to cut ½-inch lengths. So you have something to hold while working on at least half a bead, drill into the strip and cut the corners with a chisel (FIG. 8-13F). Then, cut off and chisel the other side (FIG. 8-13G), and so on until you have made the set. It does not matter if the beads do not finish absolutely the same, but check that there is no roughness.

Paint the beads in groups of five. You probably have to repeat colors, but on each rod have five of one color together, then five of a contrasting color.

Cut the dowels and rods to length. Slide ten beads on each rod and join the parts. With the dowels glued, there should be no need to do anything to the ends of the metal rods, but they could be dipped in epoxy glue before assembly, for extra strength.

HUMPTY DUMPTY

This toy (FIG. 8-14A) is a simple assembly exercise for a young child; when he has assembled Humpty Dumpty, he can press or hit a lever and Humpty

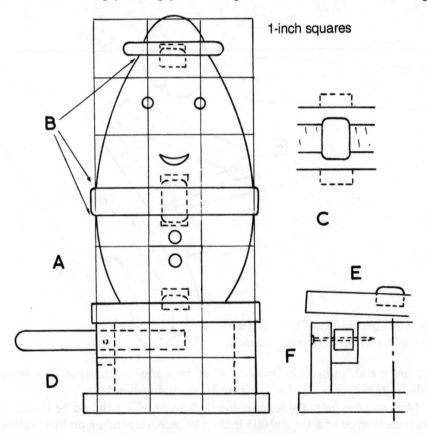

Fig. 8-14. Humpty Dumpty is in parts to be assembled; then, when a lever is moved, he falls into pieces.

Materials List for Humpty Dumpty

1 block	3½ × 3½ × 7
4 box sides	⅜ × 1¼ × 4
1 box bottom	⅜ × 4 × 4
1 box top	⅜ × 4 × 4

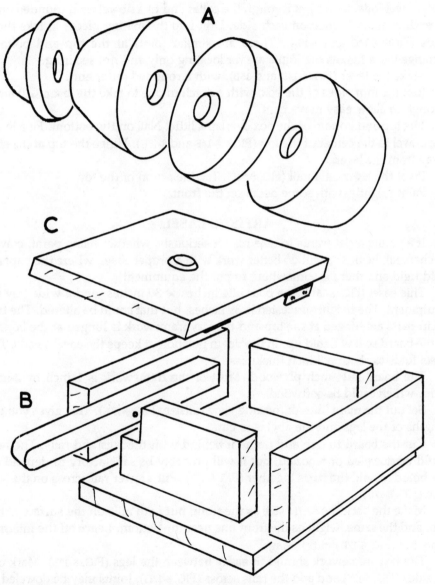

Fig. 8-15. The parts of Humpty Dumpty and his stand.

Dumpty has a great fall. The pieces are then ready to be reassembled. The four parts of the figure stand on a box containing the lever.

The egg-shaped figure may be turned in one piece on a lathe, then the parts separated with a saw. Other parts are flat pieces of wood nailed together. FIGURE 8-15 shows the separated pieces.

Turn the figure; then, use a fine saw to separate the pieces on the hat and collar lines (FIG. 8-14B). Mark the centers of the ends of the pieces.

There are small locating pieces at each center, which can be made from ½-inch dowel rods. Drill right through the collar and fit a dowel with rounded ends extending about ⅛ inch on each side. Drill into the mating pieces to take these ends (FIGS. 8-14C and 8-15A). There are similar joints at the top and bottom. Arrange loose fits, as the joints are for locating only and not securing.

Make the lever (FIG. 8-14D and 15B), with a rounded outer end.

Join the four sides of the box, with a notch in one to take the lever. Cut away enough to allow easy movement.

The top and bottom of the box overlap a little. Nail on the bottom. Fit a locating dowel to the center of the top (FIGS. 8-14E and 8-15C). Hinge the top at the side away from the lever.

Pivot the lever on a nail (FIG. 8-14F). Try the action of the toy.

Paint brightly, with some detail on the front.

ARTIST'S EASEL

If a young artist wants to take his art seriously, whether using paint, crayon or charcoal, he or she will do better work with a proper easel, where the paper is held rigid and there is somewhere to put the equipment.

This easel (FIG. 8-16) has a board 24 inches × 30 inches, and a wide tray for equipment. The height suggested is 39 inches, but that could be altered. The two main parts are hinged at the top and the tray framework is hinged at the bottom of the board so it will fold up. In the down position, it keeps the easel steady. The easel folds to about a 3-inch thickness.

The board is ½-inch plywood. Most of the framework is 1 inch by 2-inch strip, which could be softwood.

Set out the main lines of the side view fullsize (FIG. 8-17A). This gives you the lengths of the legs and the angles to cut.

Cut the board to size and frame it behind with the legs and rails. The rails could be doweled or tenoned, but it will probably be satisfactory to depend on the board to hold the parts together (FIG. 8-17B). Put a lower rail across on the surface (FIG. 8-17C).

Make the back the same size as the front, but with rails on the surface at the top, and the same height as the front one near the bottom. Leave off the intermediate rail (FIG. 8-17D) at this stage.

The tray framework should fit easily between the legs (FIG. 8-17E). Mark out its sides (FIG. 8-17F) and add the rails across (FIG. 8-17G). Joints may be doweled or tenoned. Put plywood under the tray part of the framing.

Fig. 8-16. This folding artist's easel keeps all the drawing and painting equipment together.

Use two, 2-inch hinges to join the tops of the frame together.

Hinge the tray framing to the strip under the board (FIG. 8-17H) with two, 2-inch hinges.

Adjust the easel to the angle shown. Raise the tray framing until it is parallel with the floor; mark its position on the rear legs.

Put the rail across the rear legs to support the tray framing (FIG. 8-17D). Check that the tray framing will hinge up, and the two sets of legs close together.

To secure the easel in the assembled position, put a strip under the tray framing rail (FIG. 8-17J) and use two hooks and screw eyes on the other side to hold the rails together.

Materials List for Artist's Easel

1 board	24 × 36 × ½ plywood
4 legs	1 × 2 × 44
6 rails	1 × 2 × 30
2 tray frame sides	1 × 2 × 32
2 tray frame rails	1 × 2 × 26
1 tray frame rail	1 × 1 × 26
1 tray bottom	10 × 27 × ½ plywood
1 stop	½ × ½ × 27

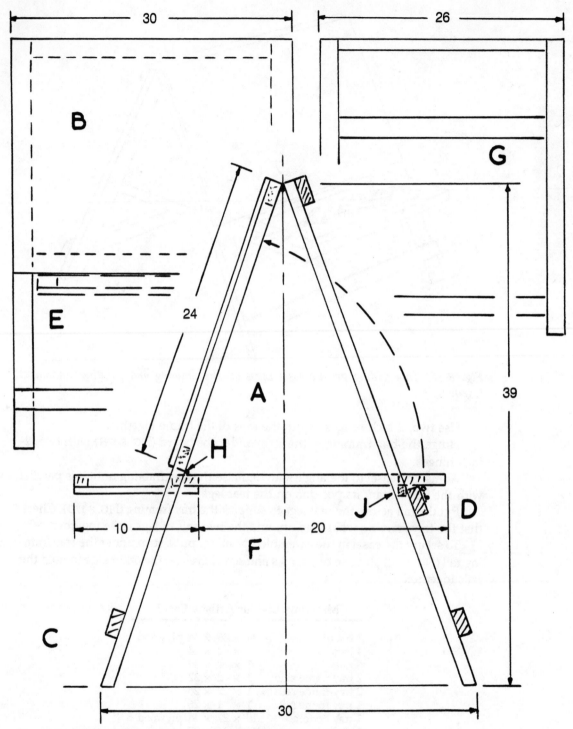

Fig. 8-17. *Sizes of parts and the method of folding the artist's easel.*

Leave the face of the board untreated. Paint or varnish the other woodwork. The tray could be lined with imitation leather or a plastic sheet.

FOUR MEN IN A BOAT AND A CAR

This is more of a test than it looks. The toy is intended for early learning. Each figure has a different size plug and the child has to find the hole to fit it in as he transfers men from the boat to the car or returns them (FIG. 8-18). For the woodworker, it is a test of turning skills.

A mild hardwood will be best for the men. The boat and car could be softwood. The car wheels are turned and glued to dowel axles that pass through the car body (FIG. 8-19A). They should be hardwood.

Check the size holes you can drill. For fairly easy sorting they could be ⅞, ¾, ⅝, and ½ inch. For more of a test they could be in closer sizes, such as ¹³⁄₁₆, ¾, ¹¹⁄₁₆, and ⅝ inch.

Drill holes of the sizes you choose in a piece of scrap wood, so you can use it to test the plugs of the men as you turn them.

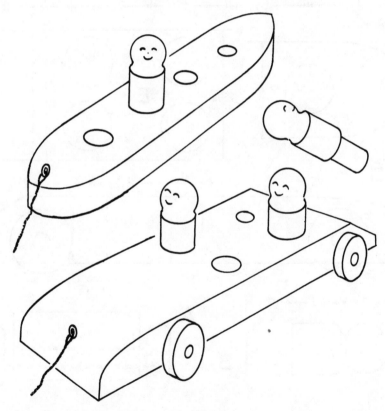

Fig. 8-18. The turned men in this toy have different sizes of plugs which have to be matched to holes when transferred from boat to car.

Materials List for Four Men in a Boat and a Car

1 boat	$1 \times 2 \times 11$
1 car	$1\frac{1}{2} \times 2\frac{3}{4} \times 11$
4 men from	$1\frac{1}{4} \times 1\frac{1}{4} \times 15$
4 wheels from	$1\frac{1}{2} \times 1\frac{1}{2} \times 6$
2 axles	$5 \times \frac{1}{4}$ diameter

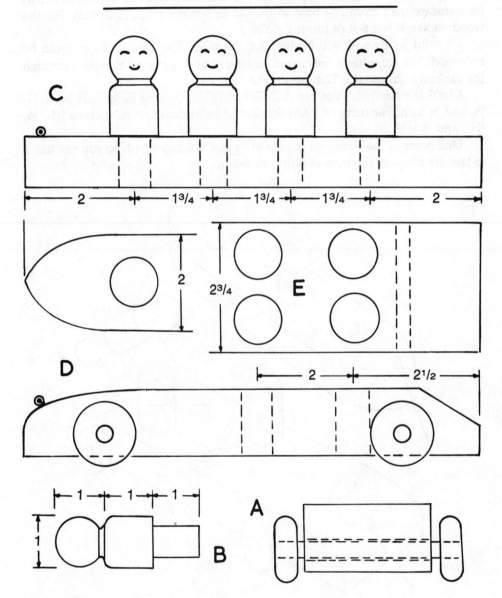

Fig. 8-19. Sizes of the men and boat and car.

Turn the four men (FIG. 8-19B). Keep the upper parts the same, but turn the plugs to slip easily into the appropriate hole.

The boat is a piece of wood pointed at both ends and with a set of holes along the center (FIG. 8-19C). Sand it well and fit a small screw eye to take a cord for dragging along the ground.

Give the car a token appearance with shaping at front and back (FIG. 8-19D). Drill four holes of appropriate sizes for the passengers (FIG. 8-19E).

The wheels could be simple discs or you could give them something of a car wheel appearance on the outside. The axle may be ¼-inch dowel rod. Drill a ⁵⁄₁₆-inch hole so it will turn easily. Wax the axle or spray with silicone, for lubrication, as you fit it in, but be careful of getting wax where the second wheel has to be glued, as wax interferes with adhesion. Fit a screw eye for towing.

Paint the men to an identical design, but use bright colors on the boat and car. Paint details on the car, if you wish.

TOOLS AND BOX

A child will be glad to have a kit of tools something like an adult uses, even if the proportions are different and there are no cutting tools. It should be possible to do something with the tools, such as assemble and take pieces apart. This tool box (FIG. 8-20A) contains three tools and an assortment of pieces of wood that can be put together with wooden "bolts," using the tools provided.

The important things are the "bolts," which are not screwed, but they can be driven into holes with the mallet, turned like real bolts and removed with the screwdriver or wrench. The strips of wood with holes in can be assembled into many forms, depending on how many you make. Everything packs into the tool box, which has a carrying handle. Close-grained hardwood is advised for all parts. It is easy to turn accurately in a lathe and it will wear better. It is also less likely to splinter dangerously.

Drill a few ¾-inch holes in scrap wood for testing the "bolts" when you turn them.

Make plenty of "bolts" from 1-inch square wood. Turn down to fit into the test holes. They should be a press fit for about 1 inch, then tapered to the end for easy entry (FIG. 8-21A). Cut a screwdriver slot across each head, ⅛ inch wide and ¼ inch deep (FIG. 8-21B).

Make a supply of washers (FIG. 8-21C) from ¼-inch plywood. Their holes should be easily fit over the "bolts."

From ⅜-×-2½-inch strip make any number of pieces with ¾-inch holes, in lengths from two holes upward (FIG. 8-21D). These are the constructional items. The more you have, the greater the possibilities for the young mechanic.

Make the screwdriver from 1½-inch-square stock (FIG. 8-21E). Take off the corners and turn down the end to about 1¼ inches diameter. Trim that to fit the screwdriver slots.

Materials List for Tools and Box

2 box ends	¾ × 7½ × 12
2 box sides	½ × 3½ × 14
1 box bottom	½ × 8 × 14
1 box handle	14 × ¾ diameter
1 screwdriver	1½ × 1½ × 10
1 hammer head	1½ × 1½ × 5
1 hammer handle	9 × ½ diameter
1 wrench	½ × 3 × 11
bolts from	1½ × 1½
strips from	⅜ × 2½
washers from	¼ plywood

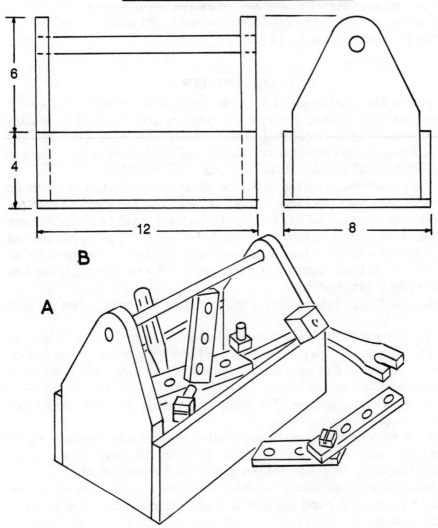

Fig. 8-20. This box carries a child's tools; use to assemble wood strips.

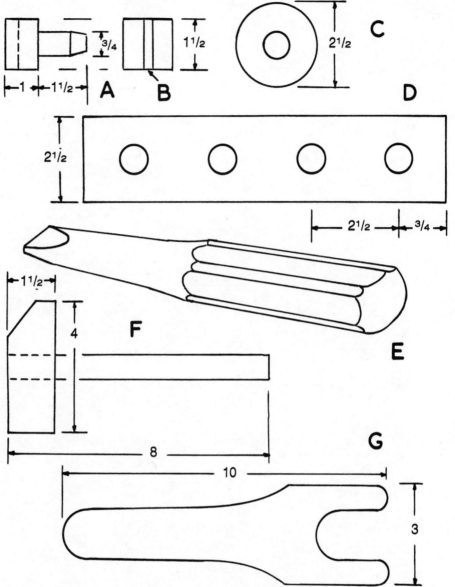

Fig. 8-21. *Sizes of the assembly parts and tools in the child's tool kit.*

The hammer or mallet is a block with a dowel handle through it (FIG. 8-21F). Whatever length you make the handle, it will be held close to the head!

Make the wrench slot an easy fit on the "bolt" heads. Round all the parts that will be handled (FIG. 8-21G).

Suggested sizes are shown for the box (FIG. 8-20B), but if you make a large number of constructional parts, you may want to make it bigger. It should be satisfactory to nail the parts together.

9

Doll Furniture and Houses

DOLL CRADLE

A young girl will welcome a cradle for her doll, but she will not be concerned whether it is an elaborately decorated one or not much more than a box. The important thing is to be able to put her doll to bed. If she can rock it, that is a bonus.

This cradle (FIG. 9-1) does everything its young owner will expect. It looks right, but it is simple and quick to make. Construction is almost completely of ½-inch plywood. It is assembled with glue and fine nails or screws. The size should suit any doll of moderate size, but measurements can be modified if your child has a doll of an unusual size.

Use the pattern of the ends (FIG. 9-2A) to mark out the head and foot ends on plywood. They are the same, except for the higher head end, which may be given a heart cutout.

Fit ½-inch-square strips inside. The cradle sides will overlap the strips (FIG. 9-2B) and the ends. The bottom fits under the strips and sides (FIG. 9-2C) and against the cradle ends. Glue and pin the strips in place. Round the tops of the side strips.

The two sides (FIG. 9-2D, E) are shown straight, but the top edges could be hollowed.

Make the bottom to extend past the sides and round the outer edges (FIG. 9-2F).

Leave edges square where they will meet, but thoroughly round all other edges. Sand well and make sure there are no splintery edges, if you are using open-grained plywood.

Join the parts with glue and plenty of fine nails, except a fine screw at the top at each corner will add strength.

Finish the cradle with paint, which may be the same all over, or you could mix colors and add decals or paint on patterns.

Materials List for Doll Cradle

1 head end	12 × 16 × ½	plywood
1 foot end	12 × 14 × ½	plywood
1 bottom	8 × 17 × ½	plywood
2 sides	6 × 17 × ½	plywood
6 strips	½ × ½ × 6	

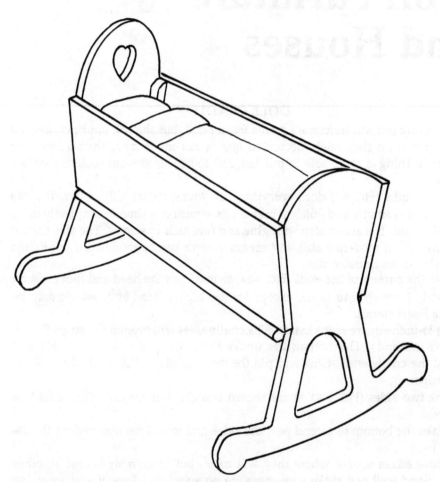

Fig. 9-1. A simple rocking cradle for a doll of moderate size.

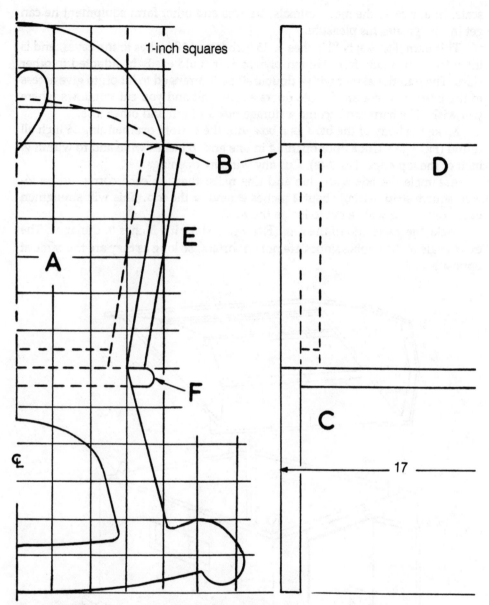

B

D

E

A

F

C

Ç

17

Fig. 9-2. The shapes of parts for the doll cradle.

BARN

Where a girl plays with dolls and a dollhouse, a boy may play with model farm animals, and he needs at least one building to use with them. The size of the building has to be related to the size of the animals, but it is better to be too large than too small. A child is less likely than his parents to notice differences in scale. In any case, the more animals, tractors and other farm equipment he can get in, the greater his pleasure.

This barn (FIG. 9-3) is 12 inches × 15 inches and 10 inches to the eaves, and is intended to be made from ½-inch plywood. It could easily be adapted to other sizes. The traditional roof with a double slope is arranged to lift off to give access to the interior. There are double doors at one end and you cut windows where you wish. The barn can become a storage box for farm and other toys.

Make the body of the barn as a box with the bottom overhanging ½ inch all round (FIG. 9-4A). Cut a door opening in one end, 6 inches wide and to within ½ inch of the top edge (FIG. 9-4B). Cut any window openings.

Assemble the box with glue and fine nails; then, in each corner add a ½-inch-square strip, letting about 2 inches extend at the top. This will strengthen each corner and will be cut to locate the roof.

Make the gable end of the roof (FIG. 9-4C). Make it 5 inches to the apex. The exact angle of the double slopes are not important, so long as they are the same at opposite sides.

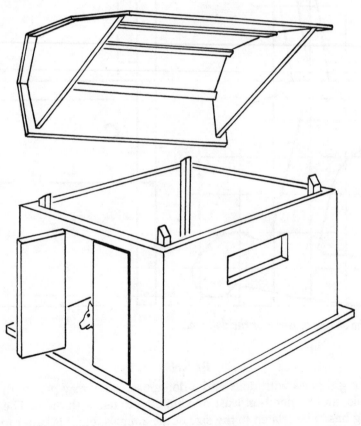

Fig. 9-3. A barn for toy farm animals. Its roof lifts off for easy access to the interior.

Materials List for Barn

1 bottom	13 × 16 × ½ plywood
2 sides	10 × 15 × ½ plywood
2 ends	10 × 12 × ½ plywood
2 gables	5 × 12 × ½ plywood
4 roof panels	5 × 16 × ½ plywood
2 doors	3 × 10 × ½ plywood
4 corner posts	½ × ½ × 12
3 joint covers	½ × 1 × 16

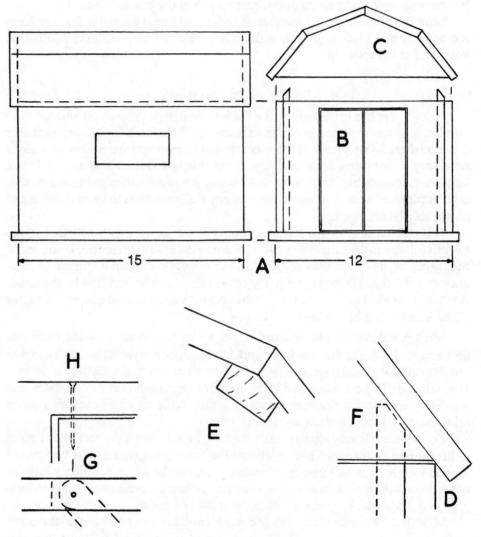

Fig. 9-4. Sizes and details of construction of the barn.

Cut plywood pieces for the roof. They should be long enough to overhang ½ inch each end when the gables are standing on the end walls. At the eaves, the roof should overhang the wall by ½ inch (FIG. 9-4D). Fit the roof plywood edges together and make strips to fit inside (FIG. 9-4E).

Assemble the roof parts so they will fit over the walls. Trim the tops of the corner posts so they fit inside and locate the roof (FIG. 9-4F). They need not fit closely against the roof; then, the contact should be where the gables rest on the end walls.

The doors are hinged on nails. Make the pair of doors to fit easily in the opening. Round their outer edges (FIG. 9-4G). Drive nails upward through the bottom and downward through the narrow top of the box end (FIG. 9-4H).

Paint the barn a light color inside, but the traditional finish for the outside is red walls with a black roof, unless there is a different color scheme adopted in your part of the country.

SIMPLE DOLLHOUSE

A dollhouse has to be fairly bulky if it is to be in true proportion and have the number of rooms expected in a fullsize home, so there has to be a compromise or the model made simpler and more compact. A close approximation to scale is necessary if furniture, dolls, and the many things a child wants to put in the house will look right. This means that unless you have unlimited space to allocate for play and storage when out of use, any dollhouse has to be as small as can reasonably be arranged.

This dollhouse (FIG. 9-5) has four rooms at a scale of 1 inch to 1 foot. One-twelfth fullsize is the proportion used for some dollhouse furniture. If you make the furniture, its size allows you to build in strength without a clumsy appearance and the chairs, tables, and many other things can be handled by the child. A tabletop would be 2½ inches to 3 inches high. A chair seat would be 1½ inches high. A bed could be 4 inches × 7 inches.

Too much detail should be avoided. For a first dollhouse, a young child will be happy with holes for windows and internal doorways, although swinging outside doors will add interest. There could be some internal papering or decorative painting. The outside could be plain paint, although outlines of doors and windows will improve the appearance. You may settle for an all-over plain paint on the roof or you may draw in tiles.

Construction is very similar to the barn. You could make the roof in one piece to lift off in a similar way, but an alternative type is suggested. The two pieces hinged together can be lifted clear, or one piece can be left in position while the other piece swings back over it. Use ½-inch plywood for most parts and join with glue and fine nails. The ends overlap the front and back.

Make the two ends (FIG. 9-6A) and mark on them the positions of the inner walls.

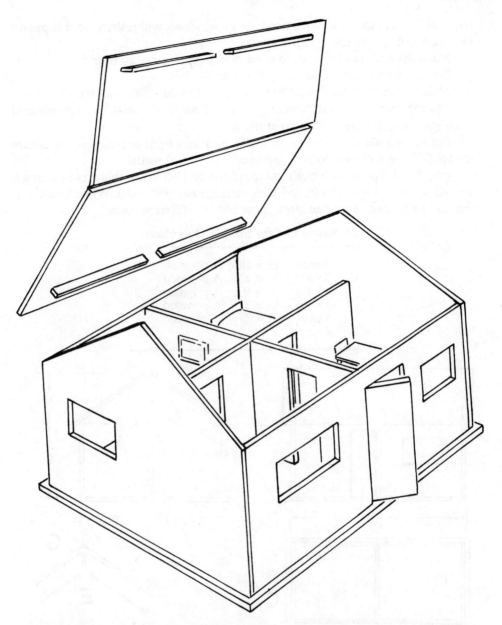

Fig. 9-5. In this simple dollhouse, there are four rooms and the roof can be lifted off.

Make the back, front, and the inner wall the same size (FIG. 9-6B). Make the two pieces that form the wall the other way.

Cut the openings for windows and doors. The inner doorways may be 3 inches wide and 7 inches high. If you want to hinge the outside doors with nails, as in the barn, take them higher so they are ¾ inch below the top edge. Window sizes can be anything you wish. A child will like to look through a window at the scene inside, but too much area used up for windows will restrict what is put on the walls and the positions of furniture.

Make the bottom (FIG. 9-6C) to overlap ½ inch or more all round.

Put the parts together, squaring them on the base.

Make the outside doors and hinge them with nails (FIG. 9-4G, H).

The roof panels should overhang 1 inch all round (FIG. 9-6D) and be mitered to fit against each other (FIG. 9-6E) at the apex.

Put strips inside (FIG. 9-6F) to fit inside back and front to position and secure the roof. There will have to be a gap over the internal walls.

Join the roof parts with cloth or tape glued on (FIG. 9-6G); this acts as a hinge, and allows one panel to be folded back on the other (FIG. 9-6H). When you paint, this can be treated as a ridge piece, possibly of a different color.

Materials List for Simple Doll House

2 ends	15 × 18 × ½	plywood
3 walls	9 × 22 × ½	plywood
2 walls	9 × 9 × ½	plywood
2 roofs	13 × 25 × ½	plywood
1 base	19 × 23 × ½	plywood
4 strips	½ × 1 × 11	

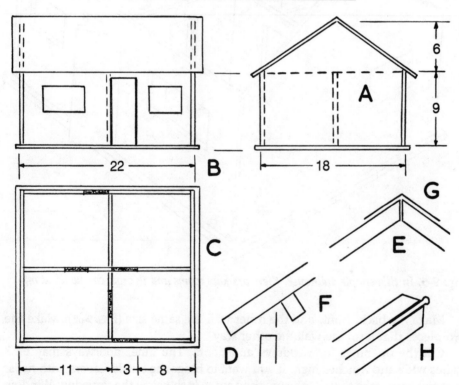

Fig. 9-6. Sizes of the simple dollhouse and its roof details.

Make sure the whole house is free of sharp or rough edges. Paint everything, but you could put paper on some walls and glue down cloth to represent carpet. You may be able to obtain paper to represent cladding or bricks for the walls and tiles for the roof, but be careful that it is reasonably within scale.

SIMPLE DOLL FURNITURE

A very young girl does not have a delicate touch and any furniture made for her dollhouse has to be durable. You may be capable of making things fairly closely to scale, but in her hands, a table leg ¼ inch square will not last long and proportionate chair parts will be even more fragile. If you are to make furniture for the dollhouse just described, or something comparable, you will need to keep overall sizes proportional, but most detail will have to be omitted or indicated by paint. The young homeowner will get her enjoyment out of what appears to be just blocks.

If the furniture is to be 1/12 scale, every 1 foot on the real thing will be 1 inch in your model, so anything less than 3 or 4 inches fullsize will be finer than it is advisable to make in this rather basic doll furniture, for young hands to use. Your basic heights will be 1½ inches for chair seats, 2½ inches for the table, and 3 inches for the kitchen cabinets and side tables. Chair seats will be about 1 inch square. A tabletop could be 3 inches × 4 inches. A bed would be 3 inches to 5 inches wide and 7 inches long. Built-in furniture might have a finer construction as it will not be handled as much. However, something like 10-inch shelves would be ⅞ inch wide, and the scale thickness would have to be increased to ⅛ inch for strength.

Many things might be just solid blocks of wood. Thin plywood is worth having. You may be able to find aircraft plywood down to ⅟₁₆ inch thick, but ⅛-inch plywood is worth having for its strength, even if it is overscale for what it represents. Veneer ⅟₁₆ inch thick also has uses; at true scale, that represents ¾ inch. Sheet metal can be used, as it is stronger than wood in thicknesses nearer scale size for some parts. Aluminum joined to wood with epoxy and painted, can simulate such things as sofa backs in a realistic way.

How you make the furniture and what shaping you give it depends, to an extent, on your equipment. A scroll saw allows quite fine detail in thick pieces of wood. A bandsaw with a fine blade can also follow tight curves. You can do similar work in less thick wood with a hand coping saw or fretsaw. Most shapes are possible with whatever tools you have, providing you are ingenious and patient.

Chairs

The young homeowner might want four or six side chairs for use at a table and more for bedrooms. Simplest is a block with a piece of thin plywood as a back (FIG. 9-7A). You can get a very similar effect by sawing from a solid block (FIG. 9-7B). If you want to do it with straight cuts, drill across at the angle and cut into the hole (FIG. 9-7C).

To get the effect of legs, without cutting away enough to weaken the wood, drill across both ways so there are feet left (FIG. 9-7D). A series of chairs can be made from a strip of wood (FIG. 9-7E).

An arm chair is best made with a sloping block, a thin plywood back and two sides (FIG. 9-7F). Leave the chair solid, or make feet by drilling across, as in the earlier chairs.

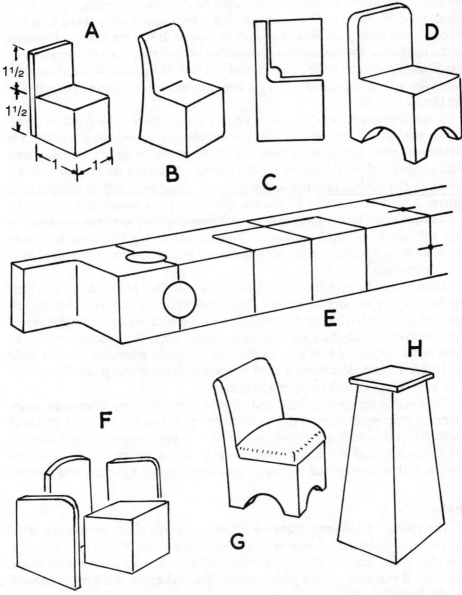

Fig. 9-7. Some simple furniture for a dollhouse, cut from solid wood and built up.

You can improve the appearance of this and other chairs by providing upholstery. This does not include padding, but cloth stuck over shaped wood can have the appearance of upholstery. You might upholster chairs for the best room and leave the others plain. Curve the top of the wood slightly for the right appearance (FIG. 9-7G).

For a love seat or divan, use similar methods with a long block instead of a square one. Using cloth to cover the arms and back as well as the seat will give it an air of luxury, even if it is nonresilient wood underneath.

A form or stool is best treated as a block, perhaps with a thin overhanging top. A tall stool for use at a breakfast bar or in the kitchen could be a tapered block with a thin top (FIG. 9-7H).

Tables

The simplest table in the size we want is just a block of wood, possibly 3 inches × 5 inches and 2½ inches high. It could be made a little more authentic by tapering underneath (FIG. 9-8A). Another way of using a block is to put a piece of ⅛-inch plywood on top. If you have to use thicker plywood, taper underneath to give thin edges (FIG. 9-8B).

It would be unwise to make a table with legs, unless they were very thick, but you could make something like a trestle or refectory table. Shape two ends ⅜ inch thick and nail a piece between them. Then nail on the top (FIG. 9-8C). Fine panel or veneer pins are useful for such small assemblies. Round all edges.

Beds

The simplest bed is a block of wood of the right size. A bed head can be a piece of plywood (FIG. 9-8D). The block should be 7 inches long for correct scale and width could be from 2½ inches, up to as much as 6 inches for a king size bed. The surface should be 1½ inches from the floor. Provide head and foot boards, with a lighter piece between (FIG. 9-8E); this allows you to simulate legs.

If the younger housewife insists on something more comfortable for her dolls, there could be two side pieces with cloth stretched across and tacked underneath (FIG. 9-8F).

Side Pieces

Side tables, sideboards, chests of drawers, dressers, and similar things which fit against the walls are best made as blocks. Drawers and doors should be painted on. Any opening pieces would be too fragile for the young owner to handle. A simple block can have lines on (FIG. 9-9A). It would look better with a thin veneer or plywood overlapping top (FIG. 9-9B). You could cut back a toe board (FIG. 9-9C). A shaped back will make a plain block more lifelike (FIG. 9-9D). Handles could be little pieces glued on (FIG. 9-9E).

To make a Welsh dresser, or something similar, take sides up each edge of a block and fit a top and shelves (FIG. 9-9F). A piece of veneer, or even cardboard,

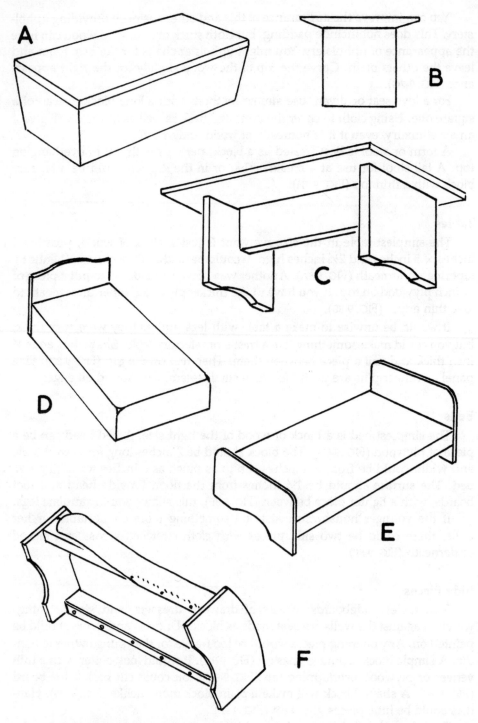

Fig. 9-8. Tables and beds for a dollhouse.

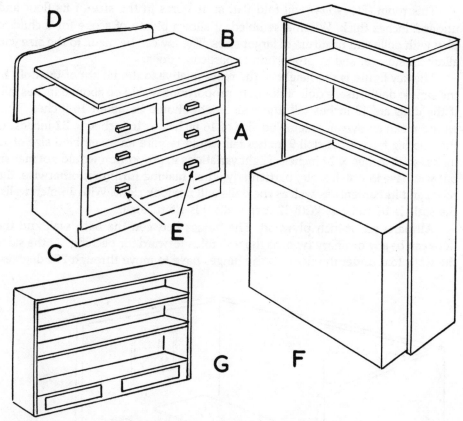

Fig. 9-9. More basic furniture for use in a dollhouse.

on the back will provide stiffness. If the shelves are ⅛-inch solid wood or ply-wood you should be able to glue and use the finest pins.

A bookcase can be made in a similar way, but for the sake of stiffness include one or more blocks, which could be painted to look like drawers (FIG. 9-9G). Without this stiffening, the shelves might soon fold.

DOLL'S ROOM

A problem for you, the builder, is the size of a dollhouse. If it is to be reasonably compact for storage reasons, its scale will be less than most of the dolls the child wants to use with it. For the simple dollhouse and the furniture to go with it, as just described, a correctly proportioned doll would be about 6 inches tall. You may provide dolls of that size, but several other of the child's favorites are likely to be larger. There is obviously an upper limit and you cannot provide homes for large dolls. However, there is a way of allowing the child to play with rather bigger dolls than would match a complete dollhouse, and that is by providing a room. It can be furnished in many ways and used with larger dolls, while the stored size is within the limits you stipulate.

This room (FIG. 9-10A) will fold flat, so it stores in the size of its floor and under 2 inches thick. When assembled, it allows plenty of scope for a child to play with dolls and furniture of larger sizes. The toy can be made to the size you allow for storage, and in proportion to particular dolls.

The key figure is the height of the room relative to the height of the doll. In the simple dollhouse, a doll of the right proportions would be about 6 inches tall. If the dolls are 12 inches tall, the wall height should be about 16 inches. That would mean an overall assembled size of 16 inches × 16 inches × 32 inches. Is that too big for you? A doll 9 inches tall would require an assembled size of 12 inches × 12 inches × 24 inches. Slight variations in proportion would not matter, but you have to watch scale, particularly when making furniture; otherwise, the room and its contents as well as the dolls will not look right. With 16-inch walls, the scale is 1/6 fullsize. With 12-inch walls it is 1/8 fullsize.

All parts are ½-inch plywood. The hinges between the back wall and the floor can be any ordinary type, as the wall folds forward for packing. At the sides the walls fold under the floor, so the hinges have to move through 270 degrees.

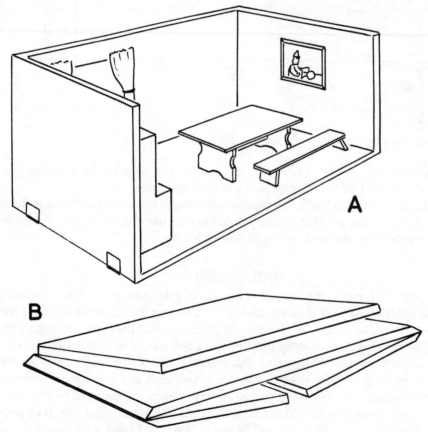

Fig. 9-10. Fold this doll's room flat when out of use.

Ordinary hinges will not move that much, and you require backflap hinges which are designed to swing at least that far.

For the purposes of these instructions it is assumed you will make a room of 1/6 scale with walls 16 inches. But if you want to come to a 1/8 scale reduction in proportion, 16 inches then becomes 12 inches.

Cut the bottom to size (FIG. 9-11A). Bevel its end to 45 degrees (FIG. 9-11B).

Make the back the same length as the edges between the bottom bevels (FIG. 9-11C). It will fit between the ends and hinges on top of the floor when assembled.

The two ends have their bottom edges beveled to fit against the ends of the bottom. When in position, they should have their tops level with the back.

Three 2-inch hinges are sufficient for the back (FIG. 9-11D).

Backflap hinges are narrower and extend further—two 1½-inch backflaps should be sufficient at each end (FIG. 9-11E).

Materials List for Doll's Room

1 bottom	16 × 33 or 12 × 25 × ½ plywood
1 back	16 × 33 or 12 × 25 × ½ plywood
2 ends	16 × 16 or 12 × 12 × ½ plywood

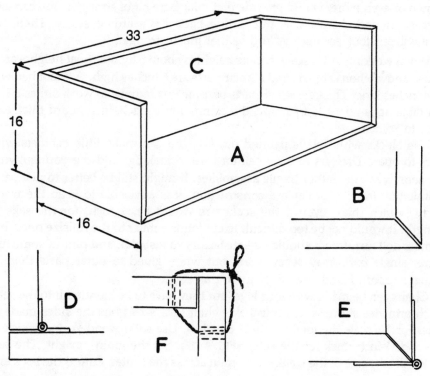

Fig. 9-11. Sizes and details of the doll's room.

Check that the parts fold (FIG. 9-10B).

To hold the walls up, you could fit small hooks and eyes at the top corners. But a simple way of holding the assembled parts together, that does not cause obstructions to interfere with folding flat, is to drill holes in the top corners and tie with string (FIG. 9-11F).

Cover the floor with cloth to represent carpet. Paper the walls, or paint them. Cut windows, if you wish. There could be a back door. Paint outside with a neutral color. If the room will sometimes be a bedroom, then change to a kitchen or living room, the room parts have to be adapted. So, they should be fairly plain.

LARGER DOLL FURNITURE

If you make the doll's room to 1/6 scale, or want to make furniture to use elsewhere with dolls about 12 inches tall, it becomes possible to use methods very much like the making of fullsize furniture, as scale details are mostly large enough to withstand reasonable handling; for instance, a 3-inch-square table leg would be ½ inch square in the model. You can always add a little without spoiling the scale effect enough to notice, so a leg might be 9/16 inch square. This applies to many parts, which would benefit by being a little oversize. Some fullsize chair legs are less than 1½-inches square, and the scale size would be ¼-inch square. This scale is beginning to get fragile for a child to handle, but adding 1/16 inch or even more, would provide that vital extra bit of strength. You can also taper, so an end is scale size, but further back it is a little oversize. Then, the piece will still look satisfactory and be that much stronger.

When working to 1/6 scale, a table height is about 5 inches. Seat heights are 3 inches, and kitchen cabinets and similar parts are 6 inches high. A 7 foot bed will be 14 inches long. Thicknesses of parts become less tedious to work on, as a 1¼-inch tabletop is about ¼ inch and the commonly used ¾-inch board thickness scales to ⅛ inch.

Use blocks with details painted on, but you can make little cabinets with doors to open. Drawers to slide call for care in making, and the young owner may soon break the rather fragile assemblies. It might still be better to just paint on imitation fronts. For carcase construction, it is advisable to keep the wood nearly ¼ inch thick, even if the scale size would be ⅛ inch, for the sake of strength. It would not be too difficult to cut joints similar to the fullsize ones, but for most doll furniture it should be satisfactory to just glue and pin. In some furniture, single parts may seem weak, but when glued to other parts there is mutual support. Handle carefully up to that stage.

Chairs can be made with four legs, but they have to be blended into the seat, which provides stiffness. A typical side chair (FIG. 9-12A) has the sides made as units. For 1/6 scale the total height is 6 inches. Use solid wood 3/16-inch thick or plywood ¼-inch thick for the sides (FIG. 9-12B). Set the grain upright. The seat block will take care of the weak short grain across the center. Round the back and

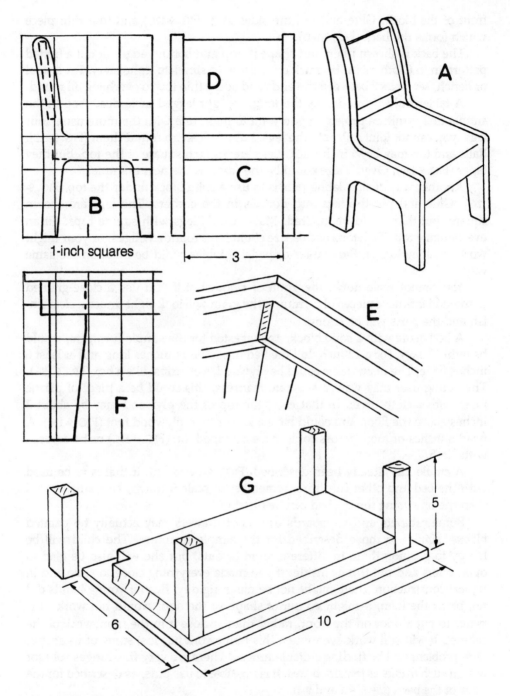

1-inch squares

Fig. 9-12. *Chair and table for use with dolls larger than would fit into a dollhouse.*

front of the block. Glue and pin the sides to it (FIG. 9-12C) and to a thin piece which forms the back (FIG. 9-12D).

The back is shown plain, but shape its top and bottom edges or cut a fretted pattern in it. Cloth might be stuck on the seat to simulate upholstery. For a stool or bench, set a block between the ends and add a thin top to overhang all round.

A table could be made like the long, straight legged table described in the simple doll furniture project. If you want to make one with the more usual four legs, you cannot joint rails into the legs, but they can go round them (FIG. 9-12E). Rails and top may be ¼ inch thick. Legs are 9/16 inch square at the top, but they taper (FIG. 9-12F). Overall size could be the same as the next example.

Another way of simulating rails is to use a solid block under the top (FIG. 9-12G). Glue and pin the legs into notches in the corners. The legs are shown square, but they could be tapered. Make turned legs with square tops. Fit an overhanging top. Tabletops of this size could have rounded edges, or your might work small moldings. Side tables or bedside tables could be made in the same way.

You cannot scale down the grain of wood, but if you use a close-grained hardwood for these pieces of furniture, the grain will look right under a clear finish and the parts will be strong.

A bed made with a solid block, as suggested for the simple furniture, would be rather heavy. For a 12-inch doll the bed has to be 14 inches long and at least 6 inches wide. The main frame could be plywood over strips, like a box (FIG. 9-13A). The young user may want a separate mattress; this could be a piece of plastic foam with a cloth cover. In that case, the top of the plywood may be about 2 inches above the floor. You could have a low or high plywood foot (FIG. 9-13B). A head 6 inches or more across could have a shaped top (FIG. 9-13C) or be covered with cloth.

A cradle has already been described (FIGS. 9-1 and 9-2). If that is to be used with the bed and other furniture, remember to scale it down, so a smaller doll than the one using the big bed can be fitted in.

Some cabinets and cupboards or sets of drawers may actually be painted blocks, similar to those described for the simple furniture. The child will be happy to position them in different room layouts, but she will also be glad to open doors and put things inside. If you made everything close to scale and in typical construction, there might not be much rigidity. Even if young hands did not break the item, it might go out of shape so the door would not work. It is better to put a door on the front, rather than enclose it in the framework of the cabinet. It will still work even when this framework has lost some of its shape. One problem will be finding suitable hinges. There are very fine hinges sold for use on such things as jewelry boxes. It is possible to use pins, as described for the door of the barn (FIGS. 9-3 and 9-4).

There can be a block to form the bottom of a cabinet and provide stiffness (FIG. 9-13D). Other parts can be ¼ inch thick, with a double thickness for more stiffness at the top (FIG. 9-13E). Fit the back within the other parts; this also aids

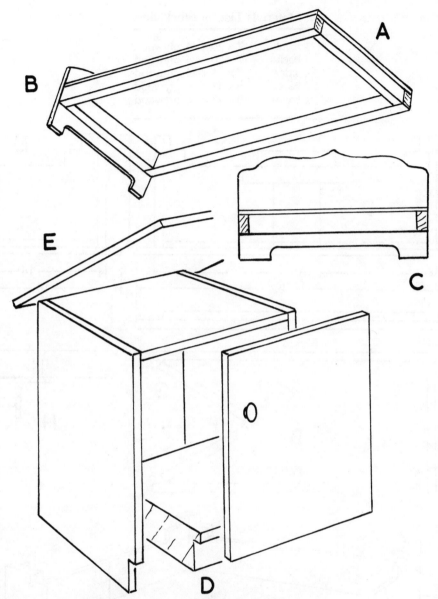

Fig. 9-13. Bed and cabinet details to accompany the table and chair.

rigidity. Put a shelf inside, if you wish, but for the sort of things a child will want to stow it may be better to leave the inside clear.

STOCKADE

Some sort of stockade, or enclosure is needed, when a child wants to play with his farm animals. On another occasion, his toy soldiers need a fort. He may want to corral his toy horses. The settlers may have to defend their stockade

1 front	$7 \times 20 \times \frac{1}{2}$ plywood
1 back	$7 \times 20 \times \frac{1}{2}$ plywood
4 sides	$7 \times 8 \times \frac{1}{2}$ plywood
2 bases	$9 \times 14 \times \frac{1}{2}$ plywood
2 bases	$10 \times 17 \times \frac{1}{2}$ plywood

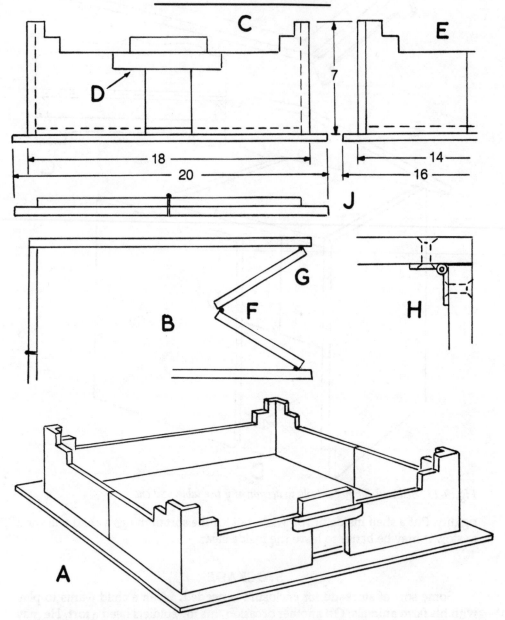

Fig. 9-14. *A fold-flat stockade may serve as a farmyard or a fort.*

against Indians. With a bit of imagination this same enclosure may serve all these purposes, as well as be a doll's playground or yard.

This stockade is intended to serve all those purposes (FIG. 9-14A). It is kept steady on a base, but the walls and base will fold flat. When closed, the package is no more than 9 inches × 16 inches and 3 inches thick. It assembles to 7½ inches high, 16 inches wide, and 20 inches long. Sizes could be varied, but the ends must fold within the length of the sides (FIG. 9-14B). All parts are ½-inch plywood. The hinges may be ordinary 1½-inch size, but if you can cut piano hinges to length, they can be almost as long as the edges they join.

The front (FIG. 9-14C) has a doorway in it. To stiffen the otherwise weak part over it, put a strip across (FIG. 9-14D). Shape the top edge by cutting down in 1-inch steps. The back can be the same or just taken straight across without the doorway.

There are four identical end pieces (FIG. 9-14E), with pairs meeting on their lower edges. Shape the top edges to match the front.

Take the sharpness off all angles and edges that young hands will touch.

Hinge the end pairs on the outside (FIG. 9-14F) and join them to the back and front with hinges inside (FIG. 9-14G). It may be satisfactory to screw the hinges, but soft metal rivets taken through will be stronger (FIG. 9-14H).

With the walls hinged to each other, measure inside them for the size of the base. Cut two pieces to fit inside and to be hinged at the middle (FIG. 9-14J). Join these to pieces that will extend 1 inch outside. The base should be tight enough to hold the walls in shape, but fold after removal.

Finish the wood with paint. The color scheme will depend on the main purpose of the stockade.

TWO-LEVEL CAR PARK

If a child has several toy cars, trucks, and vans, he will want somewhere to park them. The size of the car park will depend on the vehicles, but if there are several all about the same scale, a two-floor park can be arranged for him to push his fleet of cars into. He could also pretend he has a sales room or a garage.

This two-level car park (FIG. 9-15A) is intended for cars and other vehicles, up to about 6 inches long. It is shown on a base of the same area as the walls, but that could be extended to provide more open parking area. Sizes could be altered if the cars are a different size, but the example shown allows a young child to peer through and examine his stock of cars, pushing them up and down the ramp without undue effort.

All of the construction may be with ½-inch plywood. With careful cutting, using glue and plenty of pins, join parts without strengthening pieces. If necessary, add ½-inch-square strips around the walls under the upper floor.

Mark out and cut the internal wall (FIG. 9-15B).

Use it as a guide for size when marking the further solid wall and the one that supports the ramp.

4 walls	9½ × 18 × ½	plywood
2 floors	18 × 18 × ½	plywood
1 ramp	5 × 15 × ½	plywood

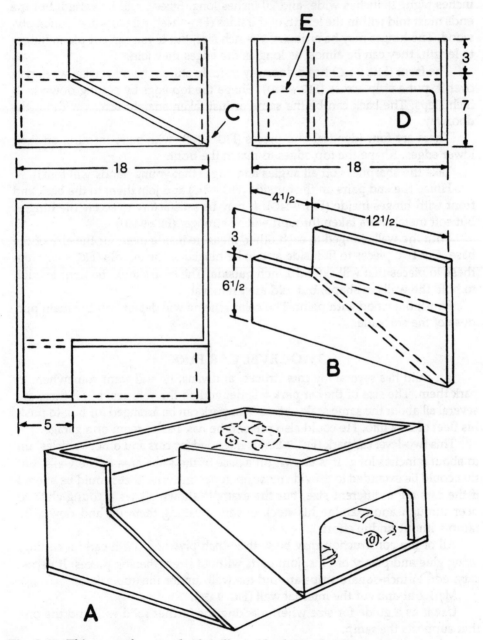

Fig. 9-15. This car park on two levels will provide plenty of activity with toy cars.

Mark out the base, with the positions of the other parts. Where the ramp comes, cut it back so the beveled end of the ramp can be cut down to floor level (FIG. 9-15C).

Make the front wall to cover the end of the ramp wall, but cut it away so cars can go in (FIG. 9-15D). Treat the back wall in the same way, but with a wider opening (FIG. 9-15E). Mark the position of the upper floor on the walls, and join the parts together. Make the ramp and fit it in position.

Paint to suit, maybe with commercial signs included. Floors should look like concrete.

DOLLS' STACKING BEDS

Putting dolls to bed is one of the pleasures of a young girl. This project is for a pair of identical beds which can be used side by side or stacked to make a bunk bed (FIG. 9-16). The suggested sizes are 8 inches wide and 18 inches long, which should suit many dolls, but you can make the beds any other size, providing they match, if you want to fit one above the other.

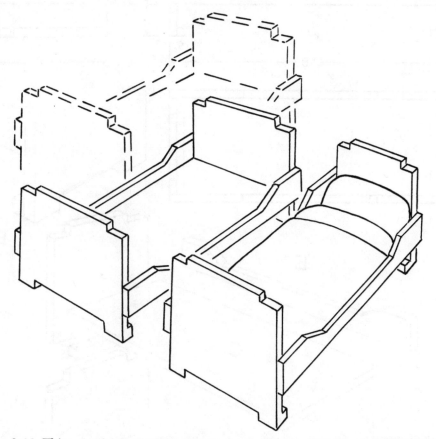

Fig. 9-16. This pair of dolls' beds may be used separately or stacked to make a bunk bed.

All parts can be ½ inch thick, of solid wood or plywood. Assembly should be satisfactory with glue and nails.

A pair of beds are best made at the same time, so parts are cut to the same size. In this way, a fit will be easier to obtain than if you make one bed and then have to fit a second one to it. The instructions are for one bed.

Materials List for Two Dolls' Stacking Beds

2 bases	½ × 8 × 18	
4 ends	½ × 8 × 9	
4 sides	½ × 2 × 18	
4 strips	½ × ½ × 9	

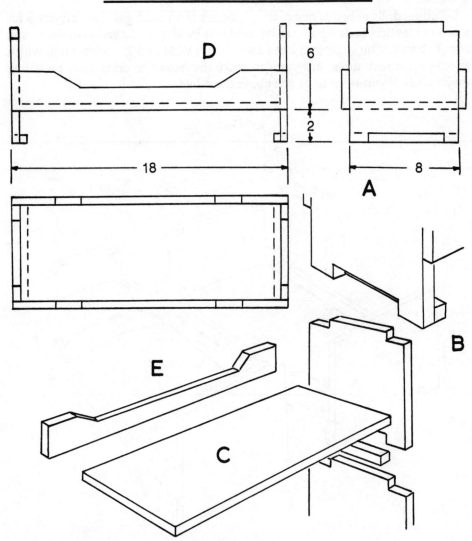

Fig. 9-17. Details of a doll's stacking bed.

The key parts are the ends (FIG. 9-17A), where the top of one has to fit into the bottom of the other. Make the ends and put a strip across the insides of the bottom edges (FIG. 9-17B).

Make the bed base to fit between the ends (FIG. 9-17C).

The two sides overlap the other parts (FIG. 9-17D, E). Round the top edges and the exposed ends.

Glue and nail the parts together. Check that the ends are parallel to each other and square to the base. This is important if two beds are to stack any way they are brought together.

Paint brightly and decorate with decals, if you wish.

DOLL'S FOLDING CHAIR

A doll's folding chair is a high chair that a girl can use to seat her doll at table height, but it can be folded so the bottom part forms a table in front of the seat when she wants to play with the doll nearer floor level (FIG. 9-18). The chair base is 15 inches square, and the chair would normally occupy that area and a height of 35 inches. But you can take the assembly apart when the child has grown out of playing with dolls and you want to keep the chair for another child. If you take off the hinges and unscrew the seat, the upper part of the cone will go inside the lower part and the seat will go inside that, reducing the package to a cube of about 15-inch sides.

Fig. 9-18. This doll's chair can be used as a high chair or folded, so the base forms a table in front of a lower chair.

Materials List for Doll's Folding Chair

4 panels	15 × 16 × ½ plywood
4 panels	11 × 12 × ½ plywood
1 tabletop	15 × 15 × ½ plywood
12 strips	¾ × ¾ × 16
12 strips	¾ × ¾ × 12
4 seat framing	¾ × ¾ × 10
seat plywood from cutout panels	

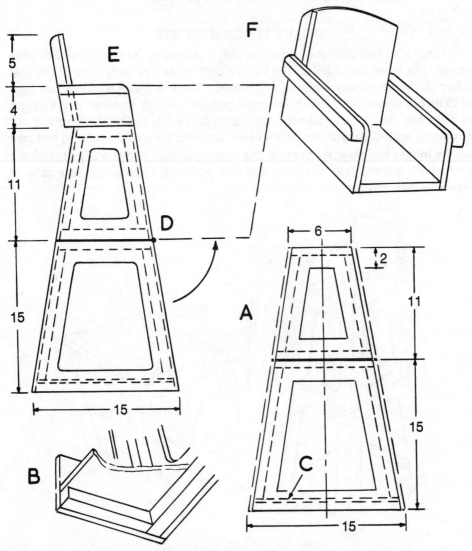

Fig. 9-19. *Sizes and details of the parts of the doll's folding chair.*

Construction is with ½ inch or thinner plywood and softwood strips ¾-inch square. Parts can be glued and held with fine nails. Although the shape is conical, and this affects angles, the amount is so slight that you can work with square sections. If you want to be precise, corner angles are under 92 degrees.

Set out a side view of the support (FIG. 9-19A), allowing for the thickness of plywood the other way. Make two sides to this pattern, with a cut across where shown. Lighten the panels by cutting the centers out 2 inches in all round.

Frame these parts all round with ¾-inch strips.

Make the panels in the other direction. Clean the internal cutout edges all round.

Join the parts to make the square shapes. As you do this, include a piece of plywood inside the bottom (FIG. 9-19B, C). This forms the tabletop when the chair is folded. Frame inside all parts.

Hinge the parts together (FIG. 9-19D). Two, 2-inch hinges should be satisfactory. Fold the bottom up against the top part; this gives you the angle for the seat.

The front and back of the seat follow the angle of the conical base/table (FIG. 9-19E).

Make the seat (FIG. 9-19F), with a base as wide as the support and extending 1½ inches at the back. Cut the sides 4 inches high to fit each side of the base. Make the back with stiffening uprights, and nail the sides to this and all parts to the base.

Join the seat to its support with a few screws, so it can be removed.

Finish with paint, although if you and the young owner want it to look more like existing furniture, you could stain and varnish the wood.

10

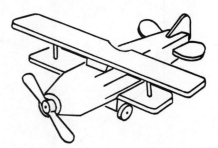

Playhouses

TAKE-DOWN PLAYHOUSE

A playhouse has to be comparatively large if it is to be a useful size; a permanent one may be too big for storage when not required. This certainly applies indoors and may be a problem outside. There is also the effect of the weather on a year-round structure, so even for outside use you may wish to bring a playhouse under shelter in bad weather. To reduce the size for storage it is helpful if the house can be taken apart or folded.

This playhouse (FIG. 10-1) has its four walls held together with pegs and the roof is held down with turnbuttons. The parts are all ½-inch plywood. When taken down, the largest piece is the roof, 48 inches × 66 inches, and the other pieces go against it to make a package less than 6 inches thick. When assembled, the playhouse is intended to stand directly on the ground, but is rigid and a child 42 inches tall can stand over all the inside area.

The sizes suggested (FIG. 10-2A) allow for cutting economically from standard 48-×-96-inch sheets, with the back, front, and ends from two sheets and the roof from another. Exterior grade plywood should be used, although other grades should stand up to occasional use outdoors if protected with paint. The design is basic and you may wish to add to it. But if you want the parts to pack into the minimum space, remember that such things as window and door framing will add to thickness. Much can be done with paint.

Mark out the front and one end of a sheet of plywood (FIG. 10-2B, C). The top slopes 6 inches. Cut out the window and door. Round these internal edges.

Make a matching end and the back from another sheet.

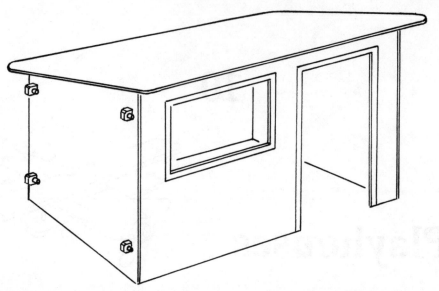

Fig. 10-1. This simple playhouse is designed to take down, so the parts may be stored flat.

Use ¾- × -1½-inch wood to make eight joint pieces (FIG. 10-2D). Drill holes for ⅝-inch dowel rods, so the inner edge of a hole will come within the thickness of the end plywood (FIG. 10-2E).

Locate the joint pieces on the inside surfaces of the front and back 6 inches from top and bottom (FIG. 10-2F). Opposite them on the ends and cut slots that allow an easy fit (FIG. 10-2G). Make dowel pegs by planing slopes to allow driving in (FIG. 10-2H). Cut these too long at first; trim to length after trial assemblies. Round the edges of all projecting joint parts.

Make the roof the full 48-inch width of a sheet and arrange it to overhang more at the front than the back. A 3-inch overhang at the ends should be enough. Round the corners.

To locate and secure the roof, put blocks inside, near the corners. It may be sufficient to do this only at the ends,or you may have to put more along back and front. Much depends on the stiffness of the plywood.

Materials List for Take-down Playhouse

1 front	48 × 60 × ½ plywood
2 ends	36 × 48 × ½ plywood
1 back	42 × 60 × ½ plywood
1 roof	48 × 66 × ½ plywood
8 joints	¾ × 1½ × 5
8 pegs	4 × ⅝ diameter
6 blocks	1 × 2 × 2
6 turnbuttons	½ × 1 × 4

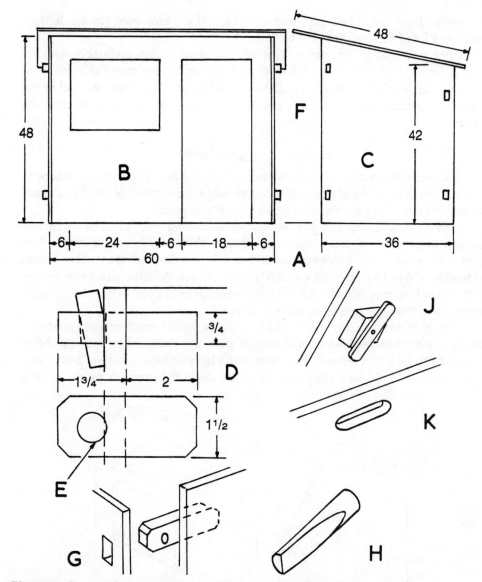

Fig. 10-2. *Suggested sizes and the method of arranging assembly of parts in the take-down playhouse.*

Make turnbuttons to fit on the blocks (FIG. 10-2J). Opposite them in the upright parts, make slots with plenty of clearance (FIG. 10-2K), so the turnbuttons can pull the roof tight.

There could be windows cut in other walls. It would be unwise to cut another doorway as that might weaken the assembly. It would be possible to put cleats for removable shelves inside. There could be a cord about a window to take a curtain. There could be a plywood door hinged on. However, young children will get a lot of fun out of a very basic house.

Paint with a light color inside. Outside can be any color, preferably with the roof different from the walls. A border of a different color round the door and window will improve appearance. Draw on siding or tiles. Make sure all of the wood is covered, particularly the bottom edges, which will come against the ground.

FOLDING PLAYHOUSE

An alternative way of dealing with a playhouse that you wish to reduce in size for storage is making it foldable; this reduces the number of loose parts and avoids the need for pegs or other small connecting pieces.

This playhouse (FIG. 10-3) has the end walls divided vertically. The division is hinged outside; then, the corners are hinged inside to the other walls. This allows the ends to fold between the front and back walls (FIG. 10-4A). That folded assembly is about 6 inches thick and 60 inches square. Additionally, there are the two parts of the roof folded together and two sections of floor. When the house is assembled, the floor keeps the walls in shape.

The main parts are plywood, which could be ½-inch-thick exterior grade, or use a ¼-inch thickness, as all of the main parts are stiffened by framing. Most framing can be 1 inch square, but some parts have to be a 1-inch-×-2-inch section. The roof could be a simple single slope, as in the previous example, or it

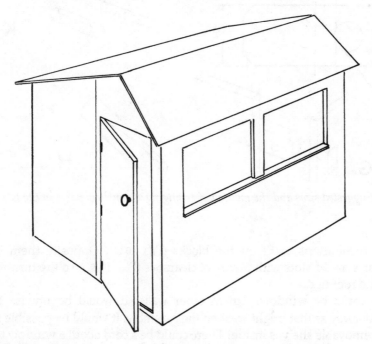

Fig. 10-3. This playhouse is arranged for the main parts to fold together.

Materials List for Folding Playhouse

2 ends	48 × 60 × ½ plywood
2 sides	48 × 60 × ½ plywood
1 roof	48 × 68 × ½ plywood
1 roof	28 × 68 × ½ plywood
2 floors	24 × 60 × ½ plywood
1 door	24 × 48 × ½ plywood
12 framing	1 × 2 × 60
16 framing	1 × 1 × 60
16 framing	1 × 1 × 30

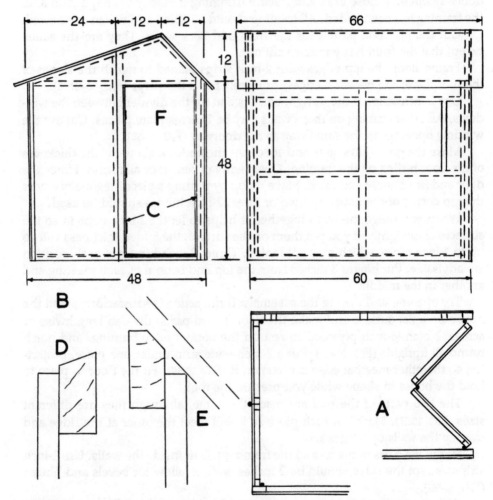

Fig. 10-4. *Sizes of the folding playhouse and the method of hinging the end walls for folding.*

could be taken to a center ridge, but it is shown assymmetrical. This gives most headroom toward the front, where it is most needed. Also, it allows a door in the end a few inches higher than at the front.

The two-part ends fit between back and front walls, so allow for this as you make parts. The main panels cut conveniently from the 48-inch width of standard plywood sheets. Roof panel sizes will have to be obtained from the other parts after they are made.

Lay out an end (FIG. 10-4B) to get the slopes of the roof, then cut the piece down the middle ready for framing (FIG. 10-5A). All of the framing may be 1-inch-square strips, except the two uprights alongside the doorway (FIG. 10-4C). Cut the doorway opening close to size, but leave trimming it exactly to shape until after the framing has been added. All framing should be glued and nailed or screwed.

Cut the plywood panels for the front and back walls. They are the same, except that the front has windows cut out.

Frame along the top edges with 2-inch strips planed to match the slopes of the roof. Bevel the plywood edges, or merely bevel the strips (FIG. 10-4D, E).

Use 2-inch strips at the upright corners and for the divider between the windows. All other framing on these walls may be 1-inch-square pieces. Cut out the window openings in the same way as the doorway (FIG. 10-5B).

Make the door (FIGS. 10-4F and 10-5C). At the bottom, allow for the thickness of the floor resting on the framing. Give plenty of clearance all round. Hinge the door and fit a handle and catch. Make a stop by putting a piece diagonally across the top corner of the doorway. Two or three, 2-inch hinges should be used.

When you hinge the walls together, it helps to let the hinge flaps in so the surfaces close tightly. If you put them on the surface, the folded thickness will go up to 1 inch more, which may not matter. Three, 2-inch hinges at each position are advisable. Put hinges 3 inches from the top and bottom of each meeting and another in the middle.

Try opening and closing the assembly. If the action is satisfactory, stand the house on a flat surface and make the floor in two parts, divided lengthwise or across. Notch ½-inch plywood to rest on the bottom edge framing, and notch round all uprights (FIG. 10-5D). Put a 2-inch-wide strip under one piece, projecting so the other meeting edge can rest on it (FIG. 10-5E). Fit the floor in place to hold the house in shape while you prepare the roof.

The two parts of the roof are made the same, although they are different sizes (FIG. 10-5F). Mark out each piece so it will meet the other at the ridge and overlap the walls by 3 inches.

Frame the parts of the roof so the framing will fit inside the walls. Use 1-inch strips; except the ridge should be 2 inches wide to allow for bevels and hinges (FIG. 10-5G).

With the roof and floor in position, the whole house should be rigid. Check the removal of these parts and of folding the walls.

The outside of the front wall is not affected by other parts when folded. Frame the window openings, or a sill might project at the bottom. The window

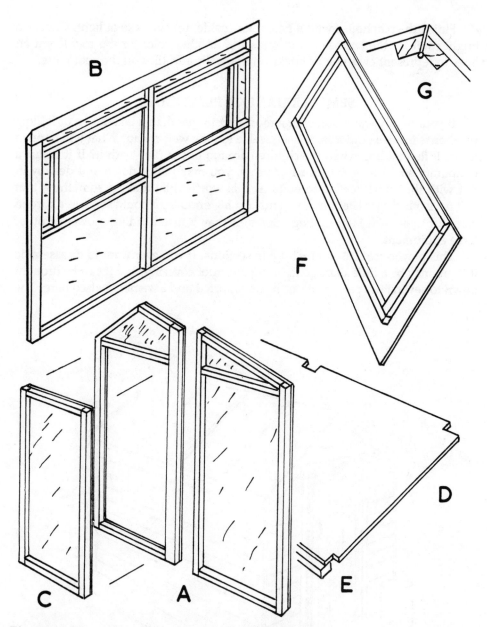

Fig. 10-5. Construction of the parts of the folding playhouse.

openings could be covered with transparent plastic, covered outside with framing strips.

Inside it would be possible to add hinged shelves or a table, providing it did not project outside the line of framing when folded. A table flap could hinge up from one side at a corner and be supported by a bracket hinging out from the other side. Add more framing strips as needed for these additions.

Finish the playhouse with a pale color inside, for the sake of light. Choose a bright color for the outside of the walls and another color for the roof. Paint on lines to represent cladding or bricks on the walls and tiles on the roof parts.

SEMI-PERMANENT PLAYHOUSE

If your family wants something more substantial than a take-down or folding playhouse for use outdoors, it is advisable to look well ahead. What will happen to the little building when the children are too old to play with it? If it is just a temporary structure good for a few years, you may pull it down and destroy it. But with the effort needed to build it, it is worthwhile making something that will have other uses later on. If you make it big enough, it could serve as a garden store for tools. If it is given large doors, it may house a riding mower or other large equipment.

This playhouse (FIG. 10-6) is built in sections. If you ever want to disassemble it there may be a little damage to lining and roof covering, but it can be brought down to several flat parts that can be transported and assembled elsewhere. The

Fig. 10-6. *This playhouse is intended for long-term use and is sectional for semi-permanent construction.*

design is for a little building that should look good in your yard, whether it is used by children or for storage. If you want to change the sizes (FIG. 10-7A), the same method of construction can be used.

The playhouse is made as separate walls, which could be produced elsewhere and assembled on the site. The roof is made in position. Walls are framed and covered with horizontal boarding. The roof can be boarded or covered with plywood. There might be a plywood lining inside, and that would be advisable for year-round use.

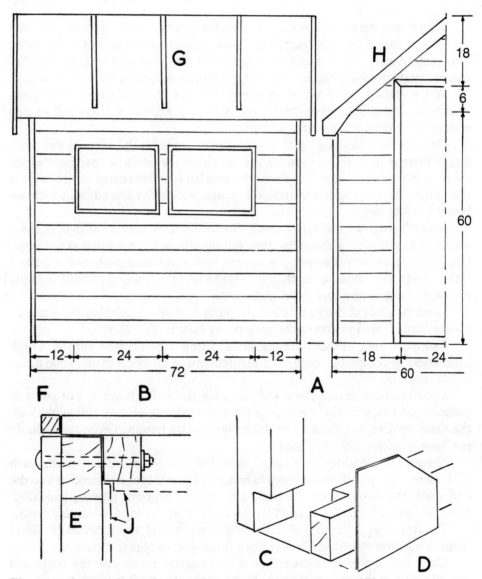

Fig. 10-7. *Suggested sizes for the semi-permanent playhouse and details at corners.*

A concrete base is advisable. There is a wood floor, which fits inside, but if this and the walls are not to suffer from rot, something better than earth underneath is advisable. The concrete might be just the area of the building, or it could extend to make a path all round. For durability, it would be even better to raise the building a few inches on bricks all round the walls.

A door in one end and windows in one side are suggested. The other two walls are solid. Fit large double doors to the opposite end and seal them at first, if you expect to store large items later. For children's use, the number of windows are best kept to the minimum needed to let in light. Then, they should be high enough for safety.

Before starting construction, consider the joints. At the corners the side uprights fit inside the end walls, but the covering boards continue (FIG. 10-7B). The framing will get considerable strength from the covering boards and the lining, but parts need to be secured during construction. Use halving joints (FIG. 10-7C). At the corners, provide further strengthening with metal covers (FIG. 10-7D). These could be aluminum or galvanized iron about #20 gauge. They will be thin enough not to matter under the lining.

Make the two side walls (FIG. 10-8A). The back wall is the same as the front, except there is no space or need for the rail above the window openings (which are only in the front). Boarding should be shiplap or other boards which overlap (FIG. 10-8B). All framing is 2 inches × 2 inches, except the top edges, which are better 3 inches deep.

Make the two end walls (FIG. 10-8C). The back wall is boarded all over so there is no need for the piece above the door, but otherwise it is the same as the front. Use 2 inch square wood, except the outer uprights and the top edges should be 3 inches deep. The corner uprights are wider to take the lining (FIG. 10-7E) and the top edges have to take roof joints (FIG. 10-8D).

Level the ends of the boards in both parts so when assembled there can be square strips fitted in to cover the ends of the boards (FIG. 10-7F).

Assemble with ½-inch carriage bolts, using four at each corner. Check squareness by comparing diagonal measurements at the base; then, fasten down to the concrete.

Make the floor in one piece and assemble the walls round it, but you will probably get a closer fit by making the floor in two parts, so they will go through the doorway. Use particleboard or thick plywood on framing (FIG. 10-8E). You do not have to fasten down the floor.

The roof is supported on a ridge piece, the side walls and one purlin each side. Bevel the top of the ridge piece to match the roof slopes and notch it into the end walls (FIG. 10-9A). Notch the purlins horizontal supports into the ends (FIG. 10-9B). If a smooth slope is needed for the roof, bevel the tops of the side walls.

The two sides of the roof are each single pieces of plywood nailed on. Bevel them to meet on the ridge. Thicken their three outer edges (FIG. 10-9C).

Cover the roof with tarred felt or other material, taken over the ridge and turned under at the ends and eaves. Nail battens over it (FIG. 10-7G).

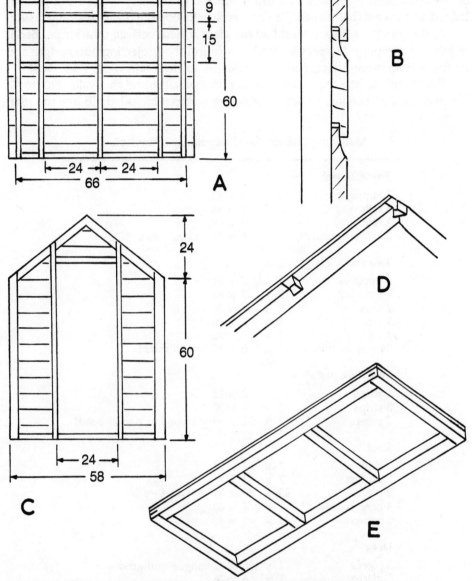

Fig. 10-8. The main sections of the semi-permanent playhouse.

At the ends appearance will be improved by fitting bargeboards (FIGS. 10-7H and 10-9D). Nail the strips on and thicken their ends with pieces underneath.

Frame round the doorway to cover the ends of the boards (FIG. 10-10A), including a strip across the front of the bottom framing to make up the thickness and strips as stops at the sides.

The door could be framed plywood, but it would be a better match to the rest of the building if it is made of vertical boards, (preferably tongue-and-groove) ledged and braced (FIG. 10-10B). The braces should slope up from the hinged side.

At the windows, frame round so the glass is held between the strips. Bed it in jointing compound to prevent leakage. Round the projecting outer edges and let the bottom piece project further and slope, to shed rain water (FIG. 10-10C).

If you wish to line the building, nail plywood all round the walls (FIG. 10-7J). There could be fiberglass or other insulating material included. To line the roof,

Materials List for Semi-permanent Playhouse

Two side walls

10 uprights	2 ×	2 × 62	
5 rails	2 ×	2 × 68	
2 rails	2 ×	3 × 68	
20 shiplap boards	1 ×	6 × 74	or equivalent

Two end walls

4 uprights	2 ×	2 × 74	
4 uprights	2 ×	3 × 62	
2 rails	2 ×	2 × 60	
1 rail	2 ×	2 × 30	
4 tops	2 ×	3 × 42	
24 shiplap boards	1 ×	6 × 60	or equivalent

Two floor parts

4 strips	2 ×	2 × 72	
8 strips	2 ×	2 × 30	
2 pieces	3 ×	72 × ¾	plywood or particleboard

Roof

1 ridge	2 ×	4 × 74	
2 purlins	2 ×	3 × 74	
2 pieces	48 ×	80 × ½	plywood
4 bargeboards	1 ×	4 × 48	
6 battens	½ ×	1 × 48	

Door

5 pieces	1 ×	6 × 62	tongue-and-groove
5 pieces	1 ×	6 × 26	
4 door frames	¾ ×	2 × 62	
2 door frames	¾ ×	2 × 26	
2 doorstops	¾ ×	1½ × 62	

Framing

4 corners	1 ×	1 × 62	
8 window frames	¾ ×	1½ × 16	
6 window frames	¾ ×	1½ × 26	
2 window frames	¾ ×	2½ × 26	

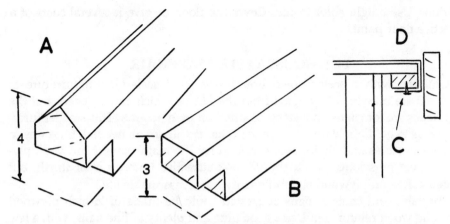

Fig. 10-9. *The ridge (A), a purlin (B), and the roof arrangement at an end (C).*

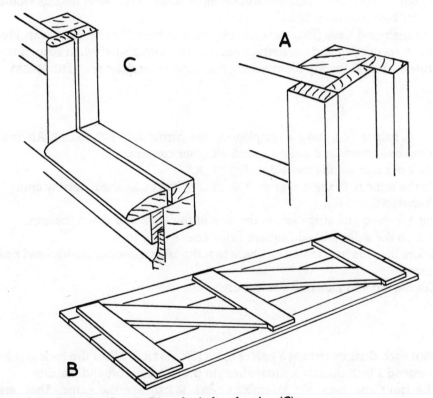

Fig. 10-10. *Door details, (A, B) and window framing (C).*

there will have to be a few strips added to come level with the undersides of the purlins, so there is sufficient framing for nailing up the plywood.

You might paint the roof black, but the walls can be a bright color, with a contrasting shade highlighting the bargeboards and the framing round the windows and door. Use a light color inside. Cover the floor, or give it several coats of a protective floor paint.

PLAYHOUSE TABLE AND CHAIR

Children with a scaled-down house will want scaled-down furniture to match. There may be a few items from the house which can be used, but the basic needs are for chairs and a table to suit their own heights. This smaller furniture needs to be durable for a few years; then, it will not be needed. One way to make small tables and chairs uses plywood for the main parts. Hardwood plywood would be strong, and it should look attractive under a clear finish, but painted softwood plywood of good quality has a reasonable life.

The table and chair designs suggested could be made of ½-inch plywood with solid wood reinforcing. Use a good glue and plenty of fine nails, with a few screws at ends of joints. Sizes given should suit children of the age to use a playhouse, but try your own children with stools or boxes to see what heights would suit them, before construction.

The chair and table (FIG. 10-11A, B) are made in basically the same way. Plywood corners overlap and are strengthened inside with a solid wood strip. Similar strips are put at the top for attaching the tabletop or chair seat (FIG. 10-12A).

Table

It will help if you make a template of one corner leg (FIG. 10-12B). Alternatively, cut one corner and use it to mark all other corners.

Mark out and cut the two sides (FIG. 10-12C).

Do the same with the two ends (FIG. 10-12D), but make them narrow enough to fit between the sides.

Put 1-inch-square strips across the tops of the ends and down the legs.

Join on the sides and add square strips across their tops.

Before the glue has hardened, check that the table assembly stands level and is square.

Cut the top and glue and screw it on.

Chair

Start each chair by cutting a pair of sides (FIG. 10-11C). Allow the back and its leg to extend 1 inch outside a square line, to provide comfort and stability.

The front and back leg assemblies (FIG. 10-11D) are the same. They are between the sides and come low enough to allow the seat to fit between the sides. The parts of the back legs are assembled upright (FIG. 10-11E), although the side parts slope.

Join the parts in the same ways as the table legs, with strips inside the leg joints and under the seat.

Make the seat to fit between the side parts and extend forward with a rounded edge.

Screw two strips between the back uprights (FIG. 10-11F), or tenon through.

Round all edges, particularly around the seat area. Paint or use a clear finish on table and chairs.

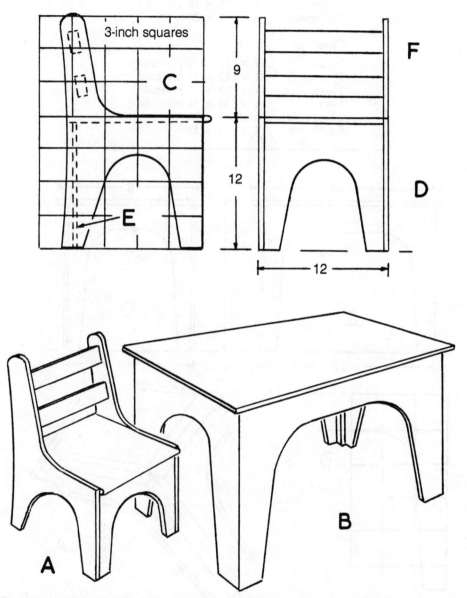

Fig. 10-11. Make furniture for a playhouse simple; this chair and table are made mostly from plywood.

Materials List for Playhouse Table and Chair

Table

2 sides	17½ ×	22 ×	½ plywood
2 ends	15 ×	17½ ×	½ plywood
1 top	18 ×	24 ×	½ plywood
6 stiffeners	1 ×	1 ×	18
2 stiffeners	1 ×	1 ×	22

Chair

2 sides	14 ×	21 ×	½ plywood
1 front	11 ×	12 ×	½ plywood
1 back	11 ×	12 ×	½ plywood
1 seat	11 ×	13 ×	½ plywood
2 back rails	1 ×	2 ×	12
8 stiffeners	1 ×	1 ×	12

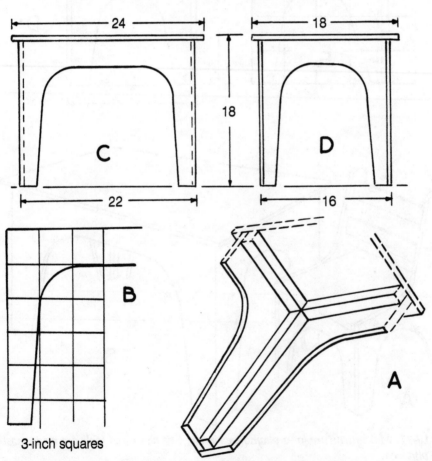

3-inch squares

Fig. 10-12. Construction of the playhouse table, showing framing inside.

CHILDREN'S STORE

Make-believe selling groceries or other goods, or even genuine cookies or drinks, will entertain and occupy children for a long time. This store folds flat and is just about small enough to set up indoors, although it would be better in the yard. When assembled, there is a large opening with a counter at the front and shelves at the back for stock. A door at one or both ends allows entry. The sides fold, so back and front come close together for storage. The roof lifts off and is hinged along the ridge. When assembled, the roof fits over the other parts and, with the shelves, will keep the store in shape.

Construction is with ¼-inch plywood on a framing of 1-inch square strips for most parts. The shelves and counter may be solid wood. The bottom is open to the ground, but you could make a plywood floor to fit inside.

The general appearance is plain (FIG. 10-13), but you can decorate the store with painted signs, ornamental figures and anything you or the children fancy. An area could be left with a matte black surface for the storekeeper to chalk on details of special offers. The sizes suggested (FIG. 10-14A) will probably be accept-able, but check your available space and the heights of the children. Construc-tion could be the same with the widely different sizes.

Mark out and cut the front (FIGS. 10-14B and 10-15A). Cut the opening. Make the back the same, but without the opening.

Stiffen all edges of both pieces with strips glued and nailed on.

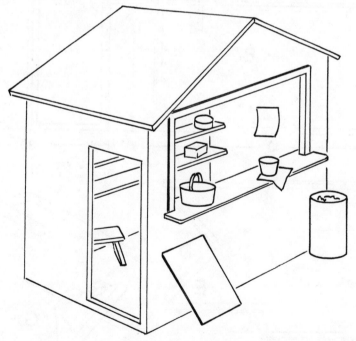

Fig. 10-13. This folding children's store allows make-believe buying and selling of various goods.

Make the four side panels (FIGS. 10-14C and 10-15B). Cut out the doorway (FIG. 10-15C) and put a strip above it when you frame the panel. Put shelf supports on the back pair of panels (FIG. 10-15D).

Hinge the side panels to each other outside (FIG. 10-14D). Three, 2-inch hinges should be sufficient.

Hinge the sides to back and front with the hinges inside (FIG. 10-14E). Check the folding action.

Make the shelves. Notch them round the corner framing and make them a tight fit against the panels, so they keep the assembly square.

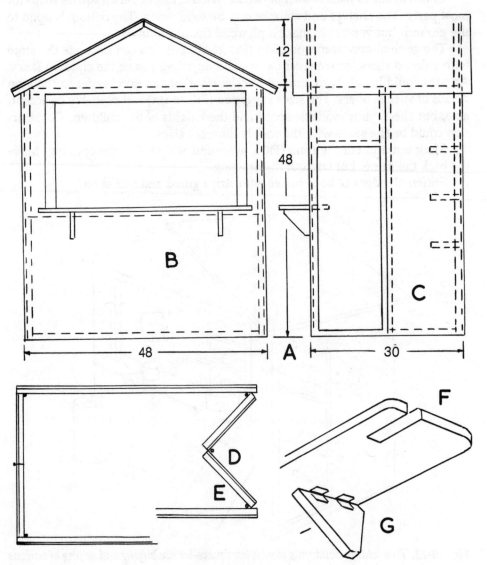

Fig. 10-14. *Suggested sizes for the store, and the method of folding.*

Materials List for Children's Store

1 front	48 × 60 × ¼ plywood
1 back	48 × 60 × ¼ plywood
4 sides	15 × 48 × ¼ plywood
2 roofs	34 × 36 × ¼ plywood
18 framing strips	1 × 1 × 50
9 framing strips	1 × 1 × 16
2 framing strips	1 × 1 × 26
8 roof strips	1 × 2 × 36
3 shelves	¾ × 6 × 48
1 counter	1 × 12 × 45
2 counter brackets	1 × 8 × 8

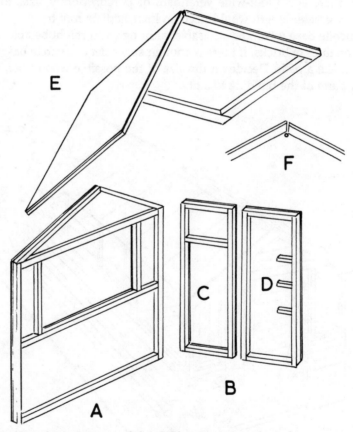

Fig. 10-15. How the main parts of the children's store are framed.

Make the counter to fit over the edge of the front opening. Notch it so it can be pressed into place (FIG. 10-14F). (It has to be taken out for storage.) Hinge two brackets underneath (FIG. 10-14G).

Cut the roof panels so they overhang all round by the width of their 1-inch-×-2-inch framing, with a reasonable clearance for easy fitting (FIG. 10-15E). Miter where they meet at the ridge for hinging inside (FIG. 10-15F). The roof will be kept in place by its own weight.

Check folding actions, then paint all over.

RUMPUS ROOM

If the numbers and ages of children warrant it and you have the space, a substantial building away from the house allows activities and noise that might not be acceptable indoors. When the children grow out of it, you could convert it to a tool store or a place to rest away from household chores. The suggested rumpus room (FIG. 10-16) has a wood floor. The walls are covered with shiplap boards. There is standing headroom for adults. The enclosed space is about 7 feet × 8 feet; then there is a 3-foot-wide verandah, or porch. Modify sizes to suit your needs. Any greater length would need an intermediate roof truss.

A concrete base would be advisable, although you might be able to support the floor on lines of bricks. If there is enough space, let a concrete base extend all round to make a path. Decide on the size of the possible wood floor, and make the other parts of the building to suit.

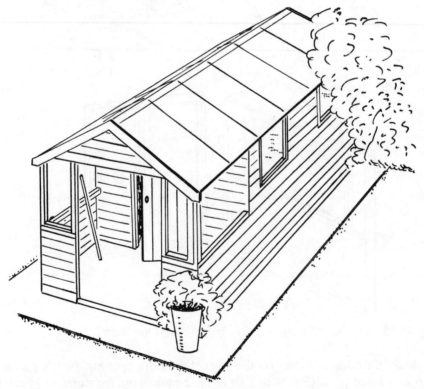

Fig. 10-16. A rumpus room might be a more substantial structure. This one has a verandah or porch, and might be insulated for year round use.

The assembled size and appearance are shown (FIG. 10-17A), but most parts can be prefabricated elsewhere, if necessary, and assembled on the site. The two side walls stand on the floor (FIG. 10-19A); then the back (FIG. 10-19B) and front (FIG. 10-19C) fit between the sides with the covering boards overlapping (FIG. 10-18A). The partition (FIG. 10-19D) also fits between the sides. The roof (FIG. 10-19E) may be plywood or boarded and made in position after the other sections have been erected. There are bargeboards providing decoration at the ends of the roof

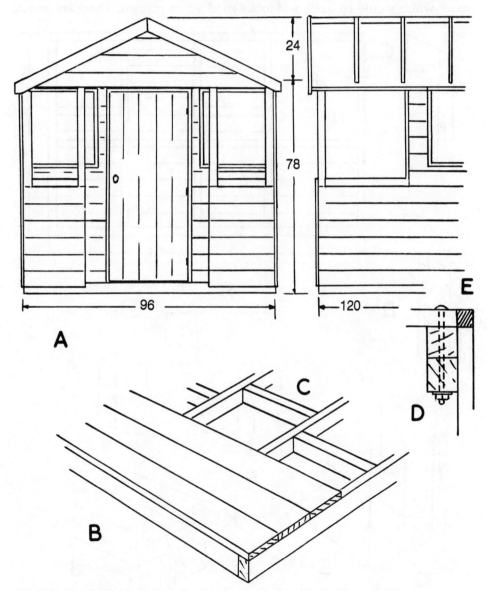

Fig. 10-17. *Suggested sizes for the rumpus room, showing details of the floor construction and wall corner joints.*

(FIG. 10-19F). A central front door is drawn, but you could have another at the back. Windows are kept fairly high, so there is less risk of breakage if there is "a rumpus in the rumpus room." One at each side of the door may give enough light, but they can go in one or both sides and in the back. Much depends on the situation of the building and the directions you wish the windows to face. Some windows could be fixed and others made to open.

There are several possible ways of cladding or covering the walls. Use plywood, which would be quick and looks good when painted. There are several

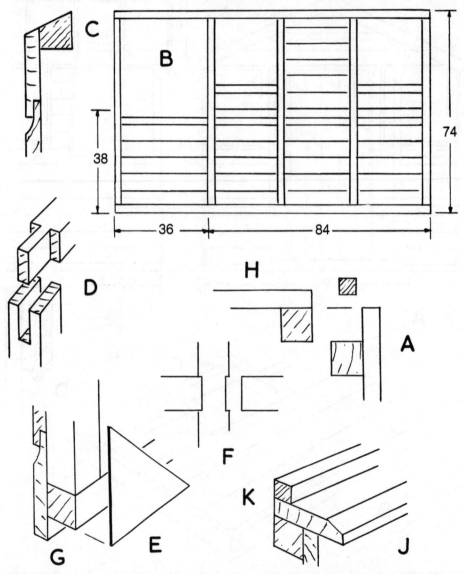

Fig. 10-18. *A wall of the rumpus room, with windows and details of the framing construction.*

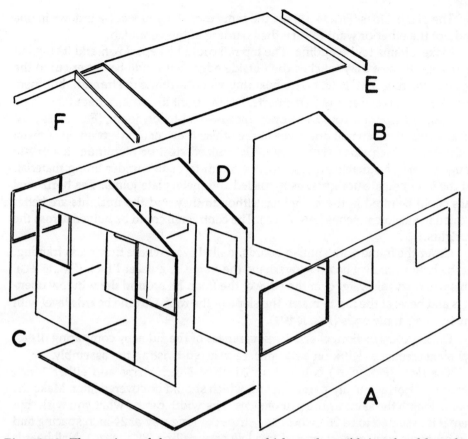

Fig. 10-19. *The sections of the rumpus room, which can be prefabricated and brought together on site.*

types of prepared board that can be used, preferably over tarred paper or other waterproof material. The drawings show shiplap boards nominally 1-inch thick and 6 inches wide. With their good overlap the building may be sufficiently weathertight without tarred paper.

You will have to decide if the building is to be lined. In some climates or for summer use only you may leave the building with only the outside boarding. The alternative is to line the walls and roof with plywood or particleboard, nailed to the framing. The air gap between that and the outer covering may provide sufficient insulation or you could fill the space with fiberglass or other insulating material. Even if you do not fully line the building, it might be advisable to line the walls up to about 36 inches, to take knocks from furniture or bodies; otherwise, a rumpus may push the covering outwards.

The verandah is shown with boarding up to 48 inches from the ground. You may wish to cover the full height in the direction of the prevailing wind or it may suit the particular situation to not have cladding in one direction. Decide on this before making the sides.

The pair of sides (FIG. 10-18B) are the same except if you want windows in one and not the other or want to vary the boarding at the verandah.

Make a frame to the outline. The top rail could be kept down and its top left square so the roof only touches the outside edge, but it will be better cut to the slope of the roof (FIG. 10-18C). The boarding will contribute to strength, but there must be joints between the frame parts. For the front to corner where there is no covering to help, you could use open mortise-and-tenon joints (FIG. 10-18D). At other joints, you can nail one piece to the other; then, nail on a triangle of metal with about 6-inch sides (FIG. 10-18E). Galvanized steel or aluminum about #18 gauge would be suitable and not thick enough to matter under lining material. Fit the intermediate uprights, using nailed and metal plate joints. The horizontal rails could be fitted in the same way, although they and the uprights are better located in shallow notches (FIG. 10-18F). The central rail could be halved across the uprights.

Cover the frame with shiplap boards, nailed everywhere they cross framing. At the bottom allow a board to overhang the frame by at least 1 inch (FIG. 10-18G). This will carry rainwater over the edge of the floor. Fit around the window openings and bevel at the top to match the slope of the roof. Cut the boards level with the framing at the ends (FIG. 10-18H).

During construction, check the squareness of the sides by comparing diagonal measurements. Work on a flat surface to avoid twisting the assembly.

The floor (FIG. 10-17B) is based on 2-inch-×-3-inch strips and either 1-inch boards or flooring quality particleboard, which should be covered later. Make the overall length the same as the pair of sides. The width can be what you wish, but here it is assumed to be 96 inches. Lay strips the long way at 24-inch spacing and put other pieces across, staggered to allow easy nailing (FIG. 10-17C). Nail boards on top. Check that the assembly is square and flat. Use it as a guide when making other parts.

The three crosswise assemblies have similar shapes, but differ in detail. Start with the partition (FIG. 10-20A). Its frame fits between the uprights of the sides. Check this width on the floor. Its height at the eaves should fit inside the top rail of the side and continue its slope (FIG. 10-18C). The apex will be 102 inches above the ground.

Make the partition framing with similar joints to those of the sides, with metal plates where necessary. Provide cutout places for lengthwise parts. A 2-inch-×-3-inch piece goes through at the ridge (FIG. 10-20B). Cut away for this, and strengthen with a strip across (FIG. 10-20C). Halfway down the slopes there are 2-inch-square supports going through (FIG. 10-20D). Cut away and strengthen under the slots (FIG. 10-20E). At the windows, double the widths of the uprights (FIG. 10-20F).

Cover with shiplap boards, extended at the sides (FIGS. 10-18A and 10-20G) to overlap the uprights of the sides. You will have to notch round the horizontal members that go through on the sides, but that can be done during assembly.

The back is almost the same as the partition, except the windows may not be needed. The shiplap boards have to overlap the corner uprights of the sides. The ridge and supporting timbers will go through to support the overhang of the roof.

The front (FIG. 10-20H) should have the frame outline as the other parts. Arrange a rail across joining the rafters just above where they meet the uprights (FIG. 10-20J), and two pillars joined into them (FIG. 10-20K). Rails at the top of the boarding should match the heights of the rails in the sides. The lower coverings should overlap the side coverings.

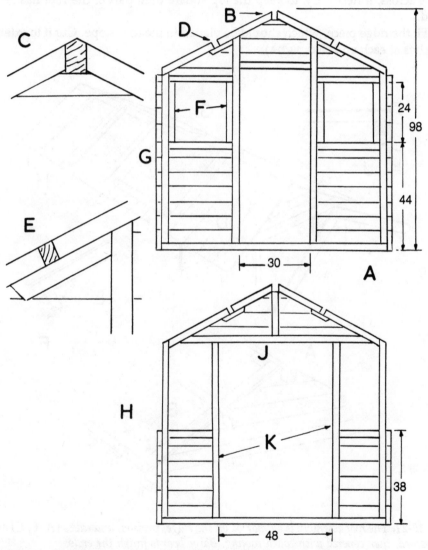

Fig. 10-20. Details of the crosswise assemblies for the rumpus room.

Line the window frames with overhanging sills (FIG. 10-18J) and sides and tops which need not project much. Strips round the inner edges (FIG. 10-18K) provide rabbets for putting in the glass as a last step during assembly. If the building will be lined, allow for the window framing material going over the lining.

Assembly is with carriage bolts. They could be ⅜ inch in diameter and arranged four in each overlap. Use large washers under the nuts inside (FIG. 10-17D). Mount the assembly on the floor with coach screws driven downwards. Fill the corners between the board ends with square strips (FIG. 10-17E).

Although the floor will keep the assembly square at the bottom, it may twist out of shape at the top. Compare diagonal measurements and put temporary strips across, if necessary, to keep the top square until part of the roof has been fitted.

Fit the ridge piece, which should be planed to the roof slope. Cut it to extend 3 inches at each end (FIG. 10-21A).

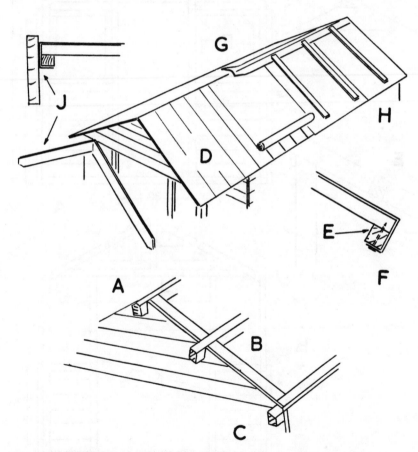

Fig. 10-21. *The roof assembly is supported on the ridge, purlins, and eaves (A, B, C) and is boarded, then covered with rolled roofing. Barge boards finish the ends.*

Fit the supports in the same way (FIG. 10-21B). At the eaves make blocks to extend the same amount and support the roof there (FIG. 10-21C).

Cover the roof with boards meeting on the ridge (FIG. 10-21D) or use plywood. A 3-inch overhang at the eaves should be enough. Thicken at the ends and eaves underneath with 1-inch square strips (FIG. 10-21E).

With the roof boarded, the whole structure should rigid and square.

Cover the roof with rolled roofing or other covering material, wrapping at the ends and under the eaves (FIG. 10-21F), using nails with large heads spaced as

Materials List for Rumpus Room

2 sides

10 uprights	2 ×	2 ×	76	
6 rails	2 ×	2 ×	122	
4 rails	2 ×	2 ×	30	
Covering from twelve	1 ×	6 ×	120	shiplap boards

1 floor

5 joists	2 ×	3 ×	122
20 joists	2 ×	3 ×	24
20 boards	1 ×	6 ×	98

Front, back, and partition

8 uprights	2 ×	2 ×	76	
2 uprights	2 ×	2 ×	90	
rails from six	2 ×	2 ×	98	
6 rafters	2 ×	2 ×	60	
covering from forty	1 ×	6 ×	98	shiplap boards

Window frames

4 sills	¾ ×	5 ×	30
12 frames	¾ ×	3½ ×	30
16 strips	¾ ×	¾ ×	30

Door

2 frames	¾ ×	3½ ×	78	
1 frame	¾ ×	3½ ×	32	
3 ledgers	1 ×	6 ×	30	
2 braces	1 ×	6 ×	40	
5 boards	1 ×	6 ×	78	tongue-and-groove

Roof

1 ridge	2 ×	3 ×	130
2 supports	2 ×	2 ×	130
18 battens	⅜ ×	1 ×	60
4 bargeboards	1 ×	4 ×	64
1 inch boards or plywood to cover two slopes		64 ×	130

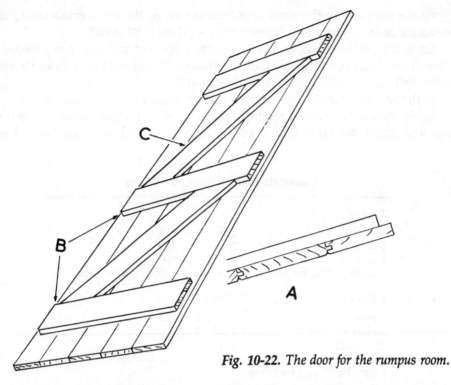

Fig. 10-22. The door for the rumpus room.

close as necessary. Appearance and strength may be improved with a strip of covering material along the ridge (FIG. 10-21G).

Use light battens at about 12-inch intervals over the roof covering (FIG. 10-21H); they improve appearance and hold the covering down firmer.

Make bargeboards for the ends. They are boards mitered at the ridge and shaped at the bottom (FIG. 10-21J). Cut out an emblem, such as a Boy Scout Badge, if appropriate, to put at the apex of the bargeboards at the front.

Cover the edges of the shiplap boards round the verandah with a handrail, similar to the window sills, only thicker.

Line round the doorway in a similar way to the window. A strip will act as a doorstop and prevent drafts.

A door could be made with stiffened plywood, but an appropriate door for this building would be ledged and braced. Use tongue-and-groove boards (FIG. 10-22A). Arrange ledgers across (FIG. 10-22B), short enough to clear the door stops in the frame. Put on diagonal struts, sloping from the hinge side upward (FIG. 10-22C) to prevent the door from sagging. With hinges and a lock or catch, the door will be complete.

Lining may be with plywood nailed to the framing all round and under the roof. Make sure all nuts are tight before covering them.

Finish with paint or preservative. Window recesses should have, at least, the first coat of paint before bedding the glass in putty. The roof covering and woodwork will probably be finished black, but the walls can be any color you wish.

Index

Other Bestsellers of Related Interest

MAKING MOVABLE WOODEN TOYS—Alan and Gill Bridgewater

This book contains 20 toy projects that will challenge and excite the creative woodworker in you. From Russian nesting dolls to an American folk art baby rattle, traditional pull-along toys to English soldiers, these are the toys adults enjoy making and children enjoy playing with! The designs employ whittling and lathe work among other techniques. Precise, over-the-shoulder instructions and numerous work-in-progress illustrations guide you through every step of construction. 240 pages, 106 illustrations. Book No. 3079, $18.95 paperback, $23.95 hardcover

CRAFTS FOR KIDS: A Month-By-Month Idea Book—Barbara L. Dondiego

Creative and educational crafts for small children designed by a professional! More than 160 craft and cooking projects that can be made easily and inexpensively, from readily available materials! Step-by-step instructions plus exceptional illustrations enhance each project which are arranged by months to take advantage of special seasonal occasions! 224 pages, 156 illustrations. Book No. 1784, $13.95 paperback, $17.95 hardcover

MAKING POTPOURRI, COLOGNES AND SOAPS—102 NATURAL RECIPES—David A. Webb

Fill your home with the scents of spring—all year long! This down-to-earth guide reintroduces the almost forgotten art of home crafts. You'll learn how to use simple ingredients (flowers, fruits, spices, and herbs) to make a variety of useful scented products, from soaps and deodorant to potpourris and colognes. Webb demystifies this age-old craft and offers step-by-step diagrams, work-in-progress photographs, and easy-to-follow recipes to give you everything you need to successfully create your own home crafts. 144 pages, 98 illustrations. Book No. 2918, $12.95 paperback, $14.95 hardcover

WOODCRAFTING HERITAGE TOYS: A Treasury of Classic Projects—H. LeRoy Marlow

This classic treasury is for the woodworker who wants projects demanding more skill and artistry than the ordinary quick-and-easy plans found in most books. It is a collection of 17 delightful and *original* keepsake-quality wooden toys. Each toy is made entirely of wood fastened by glue—no nails, screws, staples. Full-scale patterns are included. 192 pages, 167 illustrations. Book No. 2863, $19.95 paperback, $24.95 hardcover

---

Look for These and Other TAB Books at Your Local Bookstore

To Order Call Toll Free 1-800-822-8158

(in PA and AK call 717-794-2191)

or write to TAB BOOKS Inc., Blue Ridge Summit, PA 17294-0840.

Title	Product No.	Quantity	Price

	Subtotal $ _____
☐ Check or money order made payable to TAB BOOKS Inc.	Postage and Handling ($3.00 in U.S., $5.00 outside U.S.) $ _____
Charge my ☐ VISA ☐ MasterCard ☐ American Express	In PA, NY, & ME add applicable sales tax $ _____
Acct. No. _____ Exp. _____	TOTAL $ _____
Signature: _____	TAB BOOKS catalog free with purchase; otherwise send $1.00 in check or money order and receive $1.00 credit on your next purchase.
Name: _____	*Orders outside U.S. must pay with international money order in U.S. dollars.*
City: _____	**TAB Guarantee: If for any reason you are not satisfied with the book(s) you order, simply return it (them) within 15 days and receive a full**
State: _____ Zip: _____	**refund.** BC